MEXICO: the Trick is Living Here

How to Live, Work and Retire in Mexico

3rd Edition

First Published 2005
2nd Edition Published 2007
3rd Edition Published 2013
home-sweet-mexico.com
409 West 40th Street
Vancouver, WA 98660
info@home-sweet-mexico.com

ISBN 978-0-9797332-1-5
Cover design and illustrations by Julia C Taylor
Photos taken by Julia C Taylor, unless otherwise indicated.

The third edition of this book is dedicated to my entire family for whole-heartedly facing three concurrent cancer experiences. Members of all three generations have been afflicted: at ages 65, 36, and 4. One of us has passed on and the rest of us carry on, putting one foot in front of the other.

MEXICO: the Trick is Living Here

How to Live, Work and Retire in Mexico

Table of Contents

"I don't ask why,
I just ask how—
and that is hard
enough to figure
out."

1 Move to Mexico?

A Wonderfully Crazy Idea

First, let me say that if you want to move to Mexico, I think you're just a little bit crazy. But I like that in my people. I, of course, am not crazy. I didn't really have a choice about moving here. My husband, Luis, is Mexican and cannot get a visa to live in the U.S. until he has remained outside for ten years -- but that is a story for the men and women of the U.S. legislature. For you, this story is about moving to Mexico and all of its ups and downs.

Our first months in Mexico were hard. My first boss didn't pay me for a month's wages, our landlords were unfair, and neither of us knew anyone nor had family nearby. After trying a second job and quitting, I found a great school to teach in, where we both got our teacher's diplomas. We have gotten to know many people in our neighborhood and have found a colorful little cottage to live in. Our success here has come as a result of our faith, the goodness of the people of Mexico, my extreme flexibility, and Luis's understanding and guidance.

Neither of us wanted to move and we were definitely not prepared for an international adventure. We had just a few months to make a plan and save as much money as possible. I didn't want to give up the wealth and comforts of my birth country. Luis wasn't ready to come back to the country that still represented poverty and powerlessness for him. We were both afraid for our financial future (and still are, but less so). I missed my family and friends who had surrounded me all my life (I still do, but that will never end). I was overwhelmed by the noise and smells of Mexico. I was livid at the laws written by my government, which treated Luis as if he were a criminal, and completely disregarded my life as a citizen. While Luis began the process of a second "coming of age" in Mexico and I began the process of adjusting to a new culture, we both were battling anger. Through it all, Mexico came shining through. Mexico, with its people and energy, has won us over.

Though smaller than the U.S., Mexico is a relatively large country and is filled with an incredible variety of people, climates, and degrees of modernity. My signature way of judging cities is by whether or not they have soap in the bathrooms. I am glad to report that Cuernavaca, the city we now call home, usually has running water, soap, and toilet paper available in its bathrooms. Most places, on the other hand, usually don't. Before you hop on the plane down here, put a bottle of hand sanitizer and a roll of toilet paper into your handbag.

Cuernavaca has the disadvantage of being very expensive due to the rich Mexicans who move here from Mexico City and the Americans who come here to retire or to study Spanish. It has the advantage of being an open, safe[*] city where foreigners are welcomed, women have careers, and bathrooms have soap and toilet paper. I will include specific information about Cuernavaca for those who think they would like to take up residence here and as a specific example of life in Mexico. Also included is information on other places, such as Los Cabos, to try to give you a well-rounded picture of Mexico. I will also share my thoughts and experiences as an American woman living in Mexico. It is something that I have found lacking in books sold as the "real" experiences of Americans in Mexico. Somehow they don't relate the chronic culture shock, loneliness, and sometimes downright annoyance one feels when living in a culture different from one's own. It wasn't until an acquaintance asked me, "Julia, what do you *like* about Mexico?" that I realized that in my struggle to understand my own feelings about living within another culture I would describe only my frustrations.

So, moving to Mexico is hard, but it is an incredibly enriching experience. Mexicans are warm and helpful. Neighborhoods are filled with people who interact with each other on a daily basis. Your days of spotting a fleeting image of your neighbor, whose name you don't know, as he pulls his car out of his garage and speeds away down the extra-wide, smoothly paved road in front of your house are over. That's right: there's no such thing as a smoothly paved road in Mexico. Ha! No, what I mean is that here you will walk past your neighbor on the sidewalk and exchange friendly greetings. "*Buenos días, Don Lupe*," you will say. "*Buenos días*," he will say. Here you will join the parade of people carrying their household garbage bags along the sidewalk to the garbage truck and say thank you

---

[*] It was safe when I first wrote the book in 2005. Now you will need to make your own choice.

to the garbage man, who will help you to toss your bags into the truck. If you pick the right neighborhood you will buy handmade tortillas on your way to the store for milk, cheese, meat, fresh baked sweet bread—whatever you want. Here you will be awakened in the morning by parades of children dressed in costumes or school uniforms celebrating one of many holidays, or the gas truck's overly loud siren alerting potential customers of its passing. Once you figure it out, living in Mexico is a wonderfully crazy idea.

The Key to It All: Interpersonal Relationships

The key to survival in Mexico is a person's relationships with friends, neighbors, and various service personnel. Face to face interaction on a daily basis is a crucial element in getting anything to work out; therefore, in order to live here, you must know at least a little Spanish. The more you know, the more quickly and deeply you will learn about your new home. This is good news. It means you can develop a sense of community that is possibly stronger than the one you have back home. The other good news is that your Spanish doesn't have to be

Itinerant knife sharpener

very good to be acceptable. Mexicans aren't picky; they just want to be able to talk to you.

Throughout this book I often advise you to ask around for further information. If there is one thing I have learned from Luis, it is the value of talking to people for information. **There are no consistent rules in Mexico, except one: everything is different from place to place, person in charge to person in charge, and day to day.** To a foreigner from up north where things operate on predictable schedules, printed clearly

Though not exactly a typical scene in Mexico, I love the mix of modern and traditional captured in this photo.

on paper, with regular rules, it can seem like Mexico is in complete chaos. Mexicans understand the infinite variations and irregularities in their environment. Seeking their perspective is the only way you will make sense out of things. Ask questions.

It is also imperative that you learn the habits of greetings and farewells, wave, smile, and never shout nor scowl. Finally, you must be prepared to handle culture shock, which affects everyone in its own way.

You can read more about the following topics on my web site:
• The importance of learning Spanish [http://www.home-sweet-mexico.com/study-spanish-in-Mexico.html]
• Using Spanish language study as a way to prepare to live in Mexico. [http://www.home-sweet-mexico.com/study-spanish-pre-retire-in-Mexico.html]
• Choosing a Spanish Language School [http://www.home-sweet-mexico.com/language-classes.html]

At first there will be some things that seem crazy to you because they are vastly different than what you are used to. People are reasonable everywhere, it's just that sometimes different perspectives and assumptions apply. Be flexible and eventually you, too, will be able to see things through a Mexican lens. (See Chapter 14 for more cultural information.)

2 Transportation and Driving

Taxis

Taxis are a good way to get around in Mexico. They can be especially helpful when you don't know exactly how to get to a new place in the city. There are a few habits that can make your experiences with taxis as safe and efficient as possible. Normally the quickest way to get a taxi is to stand on a main street and wait. An empty taxi is sure to drive by within a couple of minutes. When it does, you raise your index finger and the driver will pull over. If you travel at night, it's safer to call a radio taxi if you have access to a phone. Ask people which are the best taxi companies in town and keep one of their business cards in your wallet.

Before getting into the taxi, it is best to ask the driver how much he (so far I haven't seen a woman taxi driver, but one driver told me he knew two women taxi drivers in all of Cuernavaca) will charge you to go to wherever you want to go. [*Cuanto cobra para ir a _____?*] They usually have the front windows rolled down, so you just have to lean over and ask them.

As I have had more and more experience riding in taxis, I've gotten increasingly tired of depending on the "prayer method" to keep me safe. Sometimes I ask the driver how much it will cost if he drives slowly and carefully. This takes away my bargaining power, but I find that all drivers say they will drive with extra caution... and some of them actually do. The other day a driver told me that he likes having passengers like me because it reminds him that we're all fathers, mothers, husbands and wives and that it's important to be careful. He didn't put on his seatbelt, though! Anyway, you lean over and ask the driver the price. If the price is reasonable, then you can climb in—but not in the front seat as I did once.

Women do *not* ride in the front seat of the taxi. I realized my mistake the instant I closed the door and saw the elated look of surprise on the driver's face. It was too late to get out again as we were in first gear and already rolling, so I stuck out the trip, which was thankfully a short one. On our way, I gracefully deflected the questions of the driver. Was I married? Wouldn't I like to go somewhere with him? Our apartment was in a busy area of our neighborhood, and as I gratefully indicated where he should let me out I was aware of the store owners and neighbors who would see me, the stupid American, getting out of the front seat of the taxi (at least I hoped they would just think me stupid and not loose). What I didn't count on was that my husband had locked himself out of our apartment and was waiting for me to get home. He was on the roof with a bunch of our landlords' sons watching the street below (that's what you do on the roof—watch the movement of the neighborhood below). Oh man, I even had an audience. I had to chalk that up as one of my most embarrassing moments. Of course, Luis wasn't at all bothered, and was even surprised to hear about the driver's line of conversation. (I had to break it to him that Mexico would be a bit nicer without all the men.)

When you get to your destination, you can climb out and pay the driver through the window or pay him from the back seat just as you are arriving at your destination. It is best to have the amount ready in your pocket before hailing the taxi and, if needed, you can discreetly prepare the payment as you are riding. Unless you've gotten really lost and the trip has been unduly long you already know how much you will owe the driver. You don't have to tip the driver, but if he helps you unload parcels or provides extra information about the city, it is a nice gesture to increase the agreed upon price by ten to twenty pesos. Drivers can make change, but it is helpful if you are prepared with bills of reasonable size. Try to avoid showing more cash than is required for a typical taxi ride. This is a little dangerous, but mostly it's just extremely tacky.

Taxi Prices

In many cities, taxis do not use meters to determine the fare, but rather an agreed upon price. With experience both drivers and passengers develop an informal fare-zone map in their heads. If you are new to a city don't stress over taxi prices. So what if you pay an extra five or 10 pesos more for a few trips while you are learning to get around. There are enough drivers who don't pad their prices for newcomers that you will eventually learn the top and bottom of the accepted range of prices. For longer trips, where the cost will be more substantial, just ask a local about how much you should expect to pay to a certain destination prior to hailing a taxi.

Even if drivers in a city do use meters, it's still reasonable to ask them about how much the trip will cost to a particular destination. If you've already asked a local how much the trip should cost, you'll know if the driver's ballpark amount matches up.

Here in Cuernavaca taxi drivers don't use meters and a normal taxi ride will cost you thirty to thirty-five pesos; going from one side of the city to the other side, sixty. Prices vary from city to city. The best way to find out the going rates in a new city is to ask the people who sell authorized taxi tickets in the airport or bus terminal. You can identify them by looking for a booth with a sign that says "*taxis autorizados*." This is the best place to get a taxi when you are first arriving at a bus station or airport. They are safe and reliable and you can take a moment to look at their fare map, which is usually posted inside the booth for their own reference. This will help with future trips. If you later choose to flag a taxi down from the street you will have an idea of the going rate for trips of different distances. Even if people only go for a block or two, taxi drivers will charge the minimum fare, which is commonly fifteen pesos. Prices increase about ten pesos per trip at night.

Busses

Bus service in Mexico is not what it is in the States—it's better. Anywhere you want to go you can get there by bus, both in the city and traveling between cities. Speaking Spanish is helpful for finding the right bus and getting off at unfamiliar stops. You can always ask the driver if he goes to your destination. If he doesn't, he will usually point you in the right direction (sometimes literally with a gesture of his hand). Once you get on the right bus, you can ask him to tell you where to get off in order to reach your destination. Usually they remember you and tell you which way to walk, although you can help yourself out by watching for street signs and other landmarks. Another way to find out about bus routes is in a travel guide such as *Let's Go*.

City Busses

City busses, which are called *rutas* in Cuernavaca and *combis*, or *camiones*, in other cities, are very different from those that we have in the States. I really like their service because busses travel their routes frequently, and, in general, you can get on and off anywhere along the route that you want to. Once you know which route you will take, it is usually best to wait for the bus at a corner, or near a speed bump where it will have to slow down anyway. Usually, the presence of other people standing near one of these places or near a blue sign with a white drawing of a bus will clue you in to where to wait.

Another thing that I like about the bus system here is that since everyone uses it, it is easy to figure out how to get places you have never been to before. You can ask pretty much anyone standing on the street which bus will take you to any given destination. I personally find this much more convenient than having to plan everything ahead with route maps on the internet – especially if my plans change at the last minute. Often if a driver sees you hurrying down the road, he will stop and wait for you. Occasionally another passenger will see you hurrying along, take pity on you, and call out to the driver, *"suban"* [they get on] and he will wait for you.

For example, once as Luis and I were heading out for an evening with a friend, he got ahead of me as I closed our gate and I ran to catch up. In a light hearted mood, Luis began to run too, drawing us into a footrace down our cobble stoned street. Just then, we saw the bus cruise past the intersection. "That's the one we wanted," I said, knowing the next one would come by in about ten minutes. "We might as well stop running now." We were laughing when we heard a bus-like gear grinding, muffler roaring noise. I assumed it was another vehicle out on the road, but somehow Luis knew it was our bus. He sped up again and I followed him around the corner. Sure enough, there was the bus, stopped about half a block down, a passenger's head sticking out the window peering back to see if we were coming.

Here in Cuernavaca, it is in the driver's interest to wait for you because he pays a daily base fee to the route owner, then keeps the fares that exceed that amount. Unfortunately, this can cause the occasional Indy-500 race up the road as two drivers try to beat each other out for the fares along the route. There is a network of assistants along the route who check the drivers' times for them in an effort to keep them spread out and avoid top-speed races through residential neighborhoods.

Since so many people use the busses here, they run frequently and all day. In town it is rare that you have to wait more than five minutes for your bus. My neighborhood is served by only one route and these come by every ten minutes. You don't have to plan around a bus schedule; pretty much you can walk out to the street whenever you are ready and go. Taking into consideration the heavy Cuernavaca traffic, there is little advantage to having a car unless you are going to an outlying area. A bus might take you a few minutes longer to travel from place to place but eliminates the effort of finding and paying for parking, as well as providing theft prevention. I find it so freeing to hop off of a bus and walk a couple blocks and be done. I don't have to worry about protecting a huge, very expensive metal object.

Busses are different from those in the States in another way. The service approximates the speed of a car as they drive just as fast—and whether or not you are seated is your problem, not theirs. Basically, it goes like this. You select your bus by reading the signs painted on or hung in the front window. When you spot your bus approaching you raise your right index finger to shoulder height. The bus pulls to the curb near you. You hop on and keep one hand on one of the hand holds mounted within. With your free hand you give the driver your fare (N$ 6.50 in Cuernavaca, N$ 7 and $ 8 pesos depending on the bus in Los Cabos.). Keep holding on tight while he makes change (that's right folks, you don't have to have exact change) because he will be accelerating at mach 10.

This bus goes to Tepoztlán via *Morelos*, passing the landmarks of *Buena Vista* and *Transito*.

Once you have your change you monkey-bar your way back to an available seat, trying not to fall into people's laps while he careens around corners. If there are no aisle seats available you can select a quiet, clean looking person who has a space between them and the window. You stop by the seat in front of them, make eye contact, and if necessary ask in a very quiet voice, "Will you let me pass?" [*Me da permiso?*] They will either swing their legs out into the aisle or stand up to let you in. You slide in without stepping on them (keep holding on) and settle into your seat. If you get to have a seat to yourself, which is often enough, you can make the logistical decision of whether or not you want to remain on the aisle or scoot over next to the window. If I'm getting off soon, I usually crowd the aisle, but if I am headed out near the end of the line, I usually scoot over by the window, gaze out and forget about who gets on or off of the bus. Occasionally, you will have to stand in the aisle. You set your back pack down by your feet – don't keep wearing it or you'll drive everyone nuts because backpacks aim right at their faces -- and hold onto the overhead bar or the handles of the seats.

Traveling on full busses is a challenge for Americans and Canadians since our personal space is about twice that of Mexicans. Most city busses are at least small; some are converted VW busses and, by necessity, people pack themselves into the seats. It is inconceivable to wait for the next bus rather than just packing yourself onto the first bus that comes by. You will ride with your leg touching your neighbor's, you will occasionally rub bums with other passengers as you work your way down the center aisle of a standing-room-only bus and you will brush hands with others who are holding onto the various bars and hand holds. It is OK to touch other people's hands while holding on, but it is best to just scoot your hand away slowly if this happens. Mexicans are so gentle and impersonal about it, though, that I don't feel uncomfortable. In general, people avoid eye contact on busses unless asking for or offering seat space. It is best to avoid swiveling your head around to look at other passengers. I don't even do this when Luis and I are separated on a full bus. I just go into my own world and don't worry about where he is seated or standing. It is also important to keep a stone face. Don't smile more than a little and definitely don't grimace, roll your eyes or frown. Even if you are just pondering what to make for dinner at night, others will think that your facial expressions relate to the situation at hand. Many times Luis has commented to me that my *gestos* [faces] make it look like I am mad.

If you are tall you may not be as happy with the busses as I am. I'm only 5-foot-4 and fit well into the little seats. Taller people often have to cram their legs in at an angle or stand with their heads bent under the low ceilings.

It is easy to take the bus drivers' tendency to accelerate and throw you into people as a lack of attention to their passengers, but they do actually avoid accelerating for people who really need the extra time. A friend of mine told me that while she was pregnant, even very pregnant, the busses still accelerated while she was in the aisle, but now that she is boarding with her infant in her arms and doesn't have two hands free, the drivers wait until she is seated before taking off. I have also seen that they give the extremely elderly extra time. Those of us who are between the ages of 1 and 85, will have to brace ourselves, though.

So when your ride comes to an end, how do you get off? Look ahead out the window for landmarks. When you know your stop is coming up, you politely weave your way through the crowd to either of the doors. If you go to the front door, near the driver, it is best to tell him where you would like to get off, but if your Spanish isn't up to it, you can just look at him and he will pull over so you can pop out of the door. If you go to the back door you have to look around for the bell. It can be anywhere in the ceiling over the door or on either of the vertical hand holds. Sometimes it is spray painted with fluorescent paint to help you spot it, but don't count on this being the case. You push the button and a buzzer near the driver will sound. The bus will slow; the door swing open, and out you go. Bus drivers tend to open the door first then do rolling stops. Stepping off a rolling bus can give you a knee injury, so it is your prerogative to stand on the stairs and wait for the bus to come to a complete stop. It is also important to be sure that no vital body parts will be sheared off as the bus passes a foot away from a telephone pole. Always look before you exit.

If you are ever jammed onto a really full bus and can't quite get to the door on time, or the back door buzzer doesn't sound, you can say *"bajan,"* which means someone is getting down, and the driver will stop. You may feel that you have to raise your voice in order to be heard over the roaring of the engine, but it is surprising how low you should keep your voice. One time I called out from the back of the bus and nearly scared everyone out of their skins. I looked up to see a bus load of startled faces looking back at me, including the driver's. I chalked that one up to another embarrassing lesson in bus etiquette and hopped off.

Inter-city Busses

If you are traveling between cities, the bus service is unequivocally better than in the countries to the north. For example, the 50-minute trip from Cuernavaca to Mexico City's southern bus station, *Taxqueña,* costs 90 pesos. The busses are spotlessly clean and leave on time every ten minutes. During the trip a movie is shown, of which you will have time to see about half. The highways in central Mexico are excellent and the ride is smooth and quiet. You can sleep, read, or watch the movie. There is a slightly sticky bathroom in the back of the bus for your convenience.

If you are using the excellent nationwide network of busses, the advice of a travel guide such as *Let's Go* will be very helpful in figuring out from where you can board a bus in order to get to your destination. Some routes are less frequent and it is important to know if only one bus per day departs to your destination, if the trip is overnight, or any other details which are also found in good travel guides. Don't just whip out your map and assume that the bus will take the road on the map that cuts the shortest path from point "A" to point "B." Bus routes are planned based on quality and safety of the road, not the length of the trip. Some "direct" trips are more circuitous than a northerner would expect.

Whenever possible we travel first class on direct busses. The expense isn't much higher and the cleanliness, bathrooms, and assigned seating make the trip relaxing. Second class busses aren't bad either, but sometimes you have to jockey for a seat, and on rare occasions stand in the aisle. Additionally, no bathrooms are provided. Other levels of service besides first and second class are sometimes advertised and offered, but frankly they don't really make sense to either of us. I think they are other names for first class invented by individual bus companies. If there is no clear demarcation between first and second class you take what is available, and don't worry about what the service is called. In most cities or towns there are only one or two bus lines that service a particular destination and their levels of service are similar. People generally know which companies serve which places and will tell you their name. This way you can go directly to the correct bus line's counter.

Purchasing your tickets isn't very hard if you know to look at the destination listings behind the counters. Cruise the bus terminal looking at the names of the cities and towns posted on the signs above and behind the counters. Basically, finding the right bus is a matter of names. With just the name of your destination, you can find the most obscure little ticket counters. If at first you don't see the name of your destination posted and don't know the name of the bus company, just go up to any ticket sales person and say the name of your destination, raising your voice toward the end of the name, so that they know it is a question. They know which booth sells tickets to every destination and will point you in the right direction. When you see your destination, approach the counter and read the departure times listed next to the name. (Departure times in the afternoon are usually listed in military time, for example, 5:00 p.m. is 17:00.) Often the price is also listed. When you are ready, you approach the counter and state your destination name to the attendant. If you are lucky and the service is first class, they will ask you which seats you would like. You can request a low seat number, which will be near the front of the bus (this is important when riding in the mountains where the roads are curvy) or adjoining seats when traveling with others, and can also choose between aisle and window seats. The best seats to avoid getting motion sick are the two front seats near the door (not on the left behind the driver) because you can see the road.

Ask what time the bus leaves. Often you will have only five minutes to get out to the *Anden* [boarding area] and board the bus. Other times you will have to find someplace to sit and rest, though I rarely have had to wait more than thirty minutes. When traveling to a destination which is served only once or twice a day, or when you require seats at the front of the bus, you can go to the station to purchase tickets a day (or even a few hours) in advance. Occasionally, the departure time instructions are more complex and this may be because your bus is only stopping at the terminal *de paso*. This means that the bus pulls into the terminal, opens the doors long enough to board one or two people, who don't have assigned seats, and immediately pulls out. In these situations the bus won't necessarily arrive at a particular time. The people in the terminal know more or less at what time to expect the bus and will have you be ready. As buses come in, watch the signs on the window for your destination (or one at the terminus of the route, if you are getting off along the way). Keep an eye on the right people, because they'll help you to get ready on time, but won't bend over backwards to find you if you aren't paying attention.

If you are on a second class bus, you can get off the bus pretty much anywhere along the route that you want. Even busses that say *directo* on the front will sometimes stop at major intersections for people to de-board. Generally, the word *directo* just means that the bus goes from point "A" to point "B" without collecting more passengers at a third location. Often as a bus enters a city people get up with their things and walk up to the door and ask the driver to let them out. You can do this, too. Be polite to the driver and give him enough warning to get into the correct lane so that he can stop safely. If you have luggage in the compartment below you should probably ride to the actual terminal so the driver won't have to stop the bus long enough to open the luggage compartment below. In our case, we can get off on a main street as the bus is entering Cuernavaca and wait at a bus stop for our neighborhood route, rather than going all of the way to the terminal, which is farther from our house.

When traveling in the country, you can wait on the shoulder of the highway and hail a second class bus as it goes by. Don't worry about distinguishing second from first class busses. Hail any bus that has your destination posted on the front. If it doesn't stop, it was probably first class. If it is second class and can stop, it will pull onto the shoulder long enough for you to run and hop on. The driver will sell you your ticket. You can also request to be let out in the country, but you will be charged to whatever city is a little further down the highway.

Going to the Bathroom

This may seem like an unimportant topic, but let me tell you, it is actually one of my largest concerns when in a place I've never been before. It used to really stress me out. Now I know where to look for public restrooms and how to beg my way into less public restrooms.

If you are going to ride on a second class bus, go to the bathroom before you board. Really long trips in southern and northern Mexico, over fifteen hours or so, have rest-stops planned into them every seven to ten hours. These busses stop for about thirty minutes at the side of the highway in the middle of no-where, where there are little roadside restaurants, bathrooms, and sometimes souvenir stores just for the purpose of bus rest stops. On short trips you just have to hold it until the end of the trip. Bus terminals always have at least one restroom. The cost is usually one or two pesos. You hand your change to an attendant who will help you navigate the coin-op turnstiles controlling the entrance to the restrooms. On your way in, if no one has handed you a small folded pile of it, look for a large roll of toilet paper mounted near the doorway.

Often the only paper available is there by the door where everyone sitting around waiting for their bus can watch you roll it out. Learn to estimate your potential messiness. Once you are in the stall and dealing with traveler's revenge, you will have to make do with whatever you allotted yourself there in the doorway. If the paper is handed out by the attendant, it is all right to request more. "*¿Me da mas, por favor?*" is all you have to say and you will get a second folded parcel.

So what if you aren't in the terminal? Parking lots always have restrooms. Ninety percent of these are too gross for words (and still charge two pesos) but if you are in a real situation, you can try anywhere you see a sign with a capital letter "E" for *estacionamiento*. PEMEX gas stations also have restrooms—for the typical four pesos, and these often have paper and soap provided. Small restaurants, like *comida corrida* [Mexican home-style fast food] establishments have strange little mini bathrooms tucked away in the back, so don't be shy to ask your wait-person before you leave. The sink may be in the bathroom or outside along the wall where all patrons should feel free to wash their hands before they eat. Don't use the towel—they never seem clean. I usually air dry my hands. Internet cafes have facilities similar to the ones in *comida corrida* restaurants. In downtown areas of large cities you can try a large department store, where they are hidden way at the back just like home, but free and clean. No, there are no "feminine napkins" available in vending machines. You would have to stop at a pharmacy for those. You can buy toilet paper by the roll at pharmacies too, for that matter.

When traveling throughout southern Mexico I continually managed my pee breaks and always felt stressed about them. It is one thing not to drink water for an isolated four-hour trip, but if you are on the road and traveling long, hot, distances, you have to stay hydrated. That means you have to go to the bathroom. On some trips I would wait until we were one hour from our destination then drink my quart of water. I got so tired of wondering if I would be able to make it to the next rest stop, then wondering if there would be a functioning bathroom when I got there. So often I felt like I was a bother, interrupting a walk through an interesting tourist attraction in order to go find whatever obscure little inadequate public bathrooms were provided. It was probably misdirected anger, but I used to get so upset at such a male-oriented system, where women can't go when they need to. Yes, you do occasionally see men taking matters into their own hands (literally), peeing in out-of-the way spots – something women can't do. Still, once you master the strategies, going to the bathroom in unfamiliar towns in Mexico is a manageable issue.

You behind the Wheel (Driving)

It took me four years to get up the guts to drive in Mexico. I have seen more accidents, ranging from fender benders to all out smashes, since I've moved to Mexico than I had seen in all my years living in the Pacific Northwest. The other day, a taxi driver commented to me that he sees about nine accidents on Friday nights!

Driving habits and conditions range as widely in Mexico as they do in the U.S. (think New York City vs. Portland, OR). Some cities in Mexico have wide roads laid out in a grid pattern. Other places have narrow, winding roads. Some places have more population density than others. In Cuernavaca the roads are narrow and there are few cross streets, a situation that forces people to take extreme measures if they miss a turn or find themselves in a traffic jam. The lack of space also means you have to learn to look for signs in new places. One-way arrows, for example, are often mounted on the walls of buildings, rather than sign posts. Sometimes no-parking zones are under-labeled and you might only have a red-painted curb to clue you in.

There are many uncontrolled intersections and to an outside observer at rush hour they seem to become impossible tangles of people trying to turn left in front of people trying to sneak around the right hand side of yet other people who are waiting for people blocking the lane because a taxi is loading passengers right in the middle of the road.

Often roads are constructed in dangerous ways. I don't know whether it's due to lack of funds, lack of education on the part of those designing the projects, lack of studies of the traffic flow needs prior to project planning, or probably most likely skimming money allocated to the projects, but there are so many onramps and off-ramps without weave lanes, left turns without a turn lane, uncontrolled intersections, roads without access, etc. that you feel like you are driving in an obstacle course.

Despite the obvious peril involved, two main factors finally made me decide to try driving. The first was that my husband sincerely encouraged me to do this because he believed I would enjoy myself more if I could get out more often and more easily. He generously promised to loan me the truck whenever I wanted it and has stuck to that promise. The second factor was that as I branched out and became more involved in a variety of activities in Cuernavaca, I was stretching the limits of what can conveniently be done on the bus and I began taking taxis more frequently.

To put it bluntly, taxis are scary. The drivers take unnecessary risks and they never have seat belts in the back seat. (One time I did get into a taxi that had a seat belt, but only that once. This was a strange experience because I commented to the driver how nice it was that he had seat belts and he responded as if all taxis have seat belts in them. I think it must have been some kind of hidden camera thing to get footage for a reality-show version of the Twilight Zone.)

Before I decided to drive, I considered some other options, including riding in the front seat of taxis where there is a seat belt, but decided against it. It would be easier and cost less to just drive my own car and I would at least have a seat belt on if I ever do get into an accident.

Well, much to my surprise driving in Mexico isn't as hard as I thought it would be. Since the majority of stupid things happen at slow speeds, you have time to wiggle your way out of them. It all happens through the process of "nudging." I learned how to "nudge" by observing other drivers and it works like this. If there is no traffic officer or light to stop traffic in the lane that you need to enter, no one will ever let you in, so you have to nudge your way out until traffic can no longer go around you. (This will make more sense when you see rule number one of "Julia's Rules for Driving in Mexico" below.) Once you've won the lane, it is yours. Just in case your nudging skills aren't up to speed you can benefit from other drivers' skill in this area. If a car in front of you nudges its way out and claims the lane and you are so close to that car that others can't nudge in and take the lane back, the lane is yours. This is how I've learned to get through turnabouts and other uncontrolled intersections (discussed in detail below). I'm not so good at being the first one to nudge my way out, so I attach myself to the bumper of an experienced Mexican. If he/she cuts in front of other cars, I do too. If he/she stops, I do too.

In order to successfully drive in Mexico you must un-learn everything you think you know about driving. (You don't necessarily need a Mexican driver's license. See Getting Your Mexican Driver's License on page 123 for more information). For example, if I ask you the question "is it OK to pass on the right?" you would answer, "No, it is never OK to pass on the right." Well, in Mexico that is the wrong answer. In Mexico you must answer, "While I only pass on the right when I'm in a total traffic snarl, other people pass on the right at any time they want to and this is OK with me. I simply allow them to cut in front of me and continue on my merry way." Note the chipper attitude implicit in that reply. It is important to be totally at peace with the new driving rules. (Don't worry those kinds of questions aren't on the test. Mexicans pretend that they follow the same rules that we do in the U.S. and Canada. Actually, you don't even have to worry about the test. In some cities foreigners don't have to take it!) So what rules do you need to know? Here they are.

Julia's Rules for Driving in Mexico

1. **Whoever is already in the lane has the right of way**. (Memorize this one because this is the most important.)
2. If nobody is in "your" lane, it's yours and you drive as normal.
3. If someone else is in "your" lane – no matter what they are driving or riding, no matter in which direction their vehicle is pointing, slow down, move over, or stop to allow them to complete whatever maneuver they are

attempting to complete (because rule one applies to everyone at all times).

4. If there is some obstruction in "your" lane you can go around, but first you must wait for your turn to "take control of" the other lane (because rule one is always in effect).

5. In **turnabouts**, people entering from the busiest roads—even if they are to your left—have the right away.

Turnabouts:

Each turnabout [*glorieta*] has its own traffic flow characteristics and you learn them by driving them. As my husband so sagely put it, "If people honk at you, you know you're doing it wrong and the next time you do it differently." Once you are inside the turnabout you may have to stop to wait for cars that have the right of way to clear the area, but that's the only time you should stop in a turnabout. If you follow the rules for four-way stops and stop to "let someone in" someone else may rear end you. No one would expect you to stop unless there is a snarl of cars ahead. Ideally, you don't stop in turnabouts. If there are other cars in the turnabout that are going where you want to go, use my trick of gluing yourself to the bumper and let them do the "nudging" until you get the hang of it.

As you enter a turnabout you may be on the left, yet have the right of way. It's almost painful to drive in front of a moving vehicle that is on your right, but sometimes you have to do this. Try chanting, "This is not a four-way stop. This is not a four-way stop," to get yourself through it.

The last concept that you have to grasp about turnabouts is the "lane" layout. Here's a good Mexican concept for you: turnabouts are not round as they may appear, they are in fact square or rectangular. If Mexicans were to paint the lines for the lanes in the turnabouts these would be straight, not curved. Here's a drawing to help you out:

Correct:

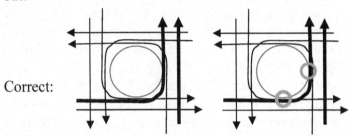

Notice that, at one or two points, you will be driving very close to the curb on the inside of the turnabout (as indicated by the two circles above right).

Wrong:

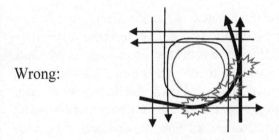

Do not follow the contours of the circle in the middle as in the drawing above. You can see that if you are turning left and you do this, you will be entering into the "lane" of the people who are going straight through the intersection. You will be crowding them and since everyone has their attention focused on the cars that have already entered the turnabout and the cars that are entering from the right, there is a real possibility of getting into an accident. Also— not pictured above due to the complexity of the drawing—

if you were to do this, a taxi driver would see the open space on your left and move in and take it. By the time you realized your mistake you would be sandwiched in between two cars, the drivers of both of which would not be feeling very gentlemanly at the time.

On highways, the obstacles in the road design are much more dangerous because of the speed at which you and everyone else are supposed to navigate them. What's my tip for highway driving? Try lots of prayer... and maybe wear a helmet. Expect people to stop at the end of an onramp, right in front of you. Expect abrupt drop offs on the shoulder (heck, don't expect a shoulder because there usually isn't one). Expect tailgaters and "cutter off-ers." Expect cars puttering along at the speed of a tractor. Expect busses passing as if they were cars. Stay alert. Don't talk on your cell phone—though everyone else might be.

Despite these challenges, sometimes having a car is the most convenient method to get somewhere, especially if you have a family. It's worth it to have a car in Mexico, but don't forget to learn to use the public transportation. Riding public transportation allows you learn about your city from the angle of the average person. You spare yourself parking-related risks and frustrations. You free yourself from the distractions of your car and all of your possessions in it. You enjoy a healthy, relaxing walking experience. Best of all, you get to interact with Mexicans and Mexico, rather than driving through it.

Note: for information on licensing and insurance see "Getting Your Mexican Driver's License," on page 123 "Licensing Your Car from the United States or Canada," on page 166 and "Why You Must Insure Your Car—There Is No Truth," on page 182.

3   Health Care in Mexico

Private vs. Public Health Care

It's helpful to understand the health care "system" in Mexico so that you can successfully chart your own health care course. I put "system" in quotes because it's not as systematic as in the U.S. and definitely not as systematic as in Canada—which has its advantages and disadvantages.

I'll start by describing the basics of how people who live in Mexico access health care services and branch from there into specific topics. You can decide how you might fit into the picture once you arrive in Mexico. Having a general understanding of how it all works will help you to make a smooth transition and to take advantage of the advantages while softening your exposure to the disadvantages.

Mexico has two different types of health care, which are referred to as private (*particular*) and public (*seguro*). You can decide in which you want to participate and to what degree.

Private Doctors

Private health care in Mexico can be terrible or it can be wonderful. It depends on what you make of it. When you retire in Mexico you could have the kind of personalized, professional care that you can only dream of in Canada or at your HMO in the U.S., but it will take a bit of effort to find really professional and dependable caregivers.

On a service for service basis, the cost of care in Mexico is much lower than in the U.S. That's the good news. The bad news is that you have to pay for it out of pocket (unless you opt to pay for health insurance), which can be quite expensive if you are earning in pesos.

Private health care in Mexico isn't a formal system at all. Doctors set up their own offices, often in loosely affiliated groups where they share a waiting room and receptionists. They find clients through client referrals or the sign hanging outside their office door and their yellow pages advertisements. This is similar to the way dentists are organized in Canada.

Many doctors have two jobs. They work in a public clinic during the day, then hold office hours for private clients throughout the evening.

They generally have few enough clients that you can get in to see them within a week of your call, sometimes that same day. It's common to have appointments between 7:00 and 9:00 p.m. and is very convenient to be able to go to the doctor at night, after you get off work.

For urgent care, drop-ins are welcome. Private doctors also give out their cell and home phone numbers for emergencies. If you call with an urgent care question, you don't have to talk to an on-duty "advice nurse," you get to talk to your doctor him/herself. Many doctors will "prescribe" a medication or direct your care right over the phone. In cases where people are too ill to come to the office, some doctors will do house calls.

Due to all of this personalized attention, the wait times at doctor's offices are often long, even if you have an appointment. I've been to some doctors' offices where they make an appointment at an arbitrary time, say 6:30, but you consistently don't get seen until 8:00 p.m. Other doctors are more conscientious about maintaining their schedules and have their receptionists plan the appointments in a way that does allow them to receive people with a minimum wait time.

There is a lot of variety in the cost, style, and quality of doctors. Once you are actually retired and living in Mexico it'll be important to find one that fits your expectations. There is more about this later in this chapter, but generally, the best way to do this is by getting a referral from someone else who has similar expectations.

Public

There are three major groups in the public health care system. They are IMSS (*Instituto Mexicano del Seguro Social* or Mexican Social Security Institute) which is available to many people working at private institutions as well as immigrants to Mexico—including retired people, ISSSTE (*Instituto de Seguridad y Servicio Sociales de los Trabajadores* or Security and Social Services Institute for Workers) which is available to employees who work for the state and other public institutions, and *seguro popular*, for all those not covered under IMSS. These services are organized on a national level and most employers who provide benefits—as they are legally required to—pay into IMSS for their employees. Beneficiaries can receive their services without paying anything in addition to what their employer pays on their behalf. Retirees who opt into IMSS pay for their own coverage. *Seguro popular* is available for retirees, and provides services on a sliding scale.

In my humble opinion IMSS is to be avoided. In fact, despite the fact that they are free, Mexicans who have IMSS or ISSSTE generally pay out of pocket for a private service rather than using their public service. No matter how good the doctors and others who work at IMSS might be on an individual basis, they can't provide adequate care. In my personal experience it is only through corruption and luck that a person can receive good care at IMSS.

I'm always amazed when Mexicans defend this service, saying that if

See also "*IMSS--Instituto Mexicano del Seguro Social* Report for retirees living in Mexico" by Rick Lewis at [http://www.mazinfo.com/infofiles/IMSS.htm].

Lewis, who has retired in Mexico and uses IMSS as his health care provider, gives an in-depth description of the IMSS system with personal anecdotes. You'll notice that even though Lewis has used his IMSS, his anecdotes still talk about NOT getting the service he needed. I rest my case.

they ever really needed it, IMSS would be there for them. Yeah right! After they kill you by not treating the little stuff they might get around to treating the big stuff for you.

Watch Out for IMSS

My personal wish for everyone who comes to live or retire in Mexico is that they don't have to use IMSS. I had IMSS as a "benefit" when I worked as a regular, full-time employee (this is called *nomina*) at a language school in Cuernavaca.

In Cuernavaca, at least, all IMSS personnel and facilities are serving about five times as many people as they should be expected to serve. Under these conditions even professional, kind people cannot give good care. You will hear that the best doctors work for IMSS, which I don't doubt is true, but because of the under-staffing and under-funding and Mexican version of the good-old-boy network, those doctors end up serving their acquaintances and clients who know them through their part-time private practices.

I was quite under-joyed with my so-called benefits. For retired people from the United States and Canada, the reality of IMSS is quite shocking; even dangerous.

If you want to, stop reading right here and skip ahead to the next section. I don't have anything good to say about IMSS—especially not for retired people, who may actually need to use the service. In fact, you may not even qualify for it. To read about the exclusions see "IMSS Insurance Terms & Conditions" at http://www.mexconnect.com/articles/3288-imss-insurance-terms-conditions.

If you feel the need to read the bad news, let me start by describing the clinic to which I was assigned.

The line for the administrative office at my clinic is usually long. You have to stand in it in order to enroll or do other paperwork. A thirty-minute wait is normal. You'll see elderly people standing there on their swollen feet.

Once you get inside, there is one row of plastic chairs along the wall, facing the little reception desks for each little doctor's office. The plastic chairs are full, and people who can't get a seat stand up. The receptionists are grumpy.

The floors are so dirty it looks like -- I can't think of another place where I've ever seen floors so dirty except the market downtown. You can see black dirt caked thick wherever people's feet don't keep it thin. The chairs are dirty too.

There is one women's bathroom to serve at least two hundred people. I'm not exaggerating. Guess how many toilets are in the bathroom? One.

The bathroom is worse than any gas-station bathroom I've ever seen with dirty toilet paper piled up and falling out of the garbage can. There is often poop on the seat. I'm young enough to squat. What do the little old ladies do? Do they have to sit down? The toilet paper has all been imported by savvy people because none is provided. There is no soap. This bears repeating because we are talking about a *medical facility*. There is **no** soap.

If you are more than a minute late to your appointment the receptionist will bark at you and put you on the waiting list for walk-ins for which you will wait hours, but if you are on time you will wait at least forty-five minutes for your appointment (and the receptionist will treat you with strained indifference).

How do you get an appointment? You call them at exactly 8:15 a.m. the day before you want to go. If you get a busy signal you hit redial until someone answers. They transfer you to the receptionist for your area and she will give you whichever time slot she is up to. If you're first to call, your appointment will be at 8:00, if you're second to call, it'll be at 8:15, etc. etc. Your doctor may arrive at 9:00.

Your doctor may be great or he/she may not be great, like mine wasn't. If your doctor is not there that day you won't know until you walk in and find a substitute sitting there. Every time you go, the doctor will ask you the same basic information and put it into the computer, but never refer back to the computer in the future.

To avoid treating you, you are referred from clinic to clinic while no one actually takes on your case. Canadians and Americans alike may say, "That happens here." Trust me; it's orders of magnitude worse.

This is all kind of funny in my case, since I'm not sick. A fellow teacher was telling me that her husband had undergone a surgery to remove malignant cancer. They waited months for their assigned check-up appointment that would allow them to move on to chemical treatment.

At the check-up the doctor told them that the critical time-window for testing to see if the cancer had been successfully removed had passed. Therefore, he stated, they would do nothing and wait to see if the cancer came back. If it came back, they would do the surgery again and see if they could get it treated in time the next time around. Can you imagine this?!

> For more bad news about IMSS, read my article "IMSS almost killed my husband" at [http://www.home-sweet-mexico.com/retire-in-Mexico-healthcare-IMSS.html]

The teacher and her spouse yelled and explained that it wasn't their fault and bullied the guy into referring them to the hospital in Mexico City that everyone says is actually good. (I've never had the honor of going, but I hope it's true.)

Seguro Popular

Seguro Popular was with the objective of ensuring those who are poor and unemployed, or who are self employed and not otherwise part of IMSS. In short, the goal is to insure everyone in Mexico! One of the program's main focuses is on healthy pregnancies and children.

It is very easy to sign up, with only three documents required and there is no screening for preexisting conditions. I have no experience with this system of health care, though those I know who have used it like it. If you are considering joining, see if there is a facility near where you will be living and visit it. To find the location nearest your home go to http://seguro-popular.gob.mx/index.php?option=com_content&view=article&id=64&Itemid=121 and click on your state. This lists the managers, but for some of the locations, the address is included in the column in the middle along with the name of the hospital. Also talk to people to see what kinds of comments they make about it.

The 2011 sliding scale for the premiums for *Seguro Popular*, ranging from zero pesos to 11,378.86 pesos per family, is posted on the *Seguro Popular* web site (see link below). What is not clear is how they determine on which level each family falls.
[http://www.seguro-popular.gob.mx/index.php?option=com_content&view=article&id=83&Itemid=175]

Finding a Private Doctor You Can Communicate With in English

At first I was nervous that the doctors here would not be up to date. The Mexico-wide lack of concern over cleanliness and hygiene along with the worn out furniture and the absence of that antiseptic hospital smell in consultation rooms made me feel as if somehow the medical treatments would also be old and worn out. This of course, is not true.

The potential for an ongoing, personalized working relationship directly with your doctor is one of the greatest advantages of going to see private doctors in Mexico, but it is somewhat of a double-edged sword. At first I found that I really liked the service I got from local doctors, but over time, changed my mind about certain individual doctors after more experience with them. Of course switching doctors is easy when you are paying them out of pocket and there are no rules created by a health insurance company and not as much scarcity as in the Canadian system.

I found all of my doctors and my dentist through personal referral. Just as there are good doctors here, there are plenty of bad ones, too. Ignorance in the general population drives dishonesty and lack of professionalism among some so-called professionals in Mexico. Talk to people you trust about where they go for medical care. If you can, get two opinions before you visit a new doctor. In the end you can have a better experience in Mexico than in your overpriced American Health Maintenance Organization (HMO) (or have shorter wait times than with your public health care in Canada).

Due to their common expectations, other expatriates are generally the best people to ask for referrals (though in the end, my best referrals came from Mexicans... once I had met the right Mexicans to ask). Of course, when you first arrive in Mexico, you might not know anyone, so you could start with the yellow pages under "medicos" (and there are tons; over sixty pages in the Cuernavaca yellow pages!). Those who speak English list that in their advertisement. Another good option is to see if there is a Newcomers club in your town and ask them for a referral. You can also put up a post on an expatriate forum. (See "Links to Forums on Mexico and the Expatriate Experience" in the Useful Links companion to this book.) Once you find a professional, honest doctor then

> Newcomers clubs in Mexico:
> [http://www.newcomersclub.com/mx.html]

they can become an excellent resource for referrals to specialists in other fields.

One doctor, who I still visit for simple issues, has a consultation room at her house only a five-minute walk from here. I have her phone number and can call her any time day or night. When I call her I usually get permission to come right up. She only charges 100 pesos a visit, so Luis and I don't hesitate to visit her when we are in need. This is a great advantage, but (there's always a "but") now we have learned that she always wants to prescribe some kind of medication (like many of her colleagues all over the world!) so we don't always choose to go to her.

Our son's pediatrician is exceptional! We found him by referral too, and the key comment the referrer made that convinced us to go see him was that he will not overuse antibiotics.

Like my neighborhood doctor, my dentist is also a five-minute walk from my house and uses the same modern equipment my dentist uses back home. He sends me to a special clinic to get x-rays first and then does the work in his neighborhood office. At first I was thrilled to be his patient, but after working with him for multiple visits I am starting to have doubts. On the good side, his schedule is flexible enough to make appointments within one or two days. He has worked in Chicago as well, so he can understand what I'm talking about if I use the English words for parts of my mouth. He charges a lot less than my dentist back home and provides a more relaxed and personal service. On the other hand, he appears to be getting complacent and I think I'm in the market for a new dentist. Recently, he cut corners with a filling he put in for me and it popped out a few months later. When I went back he re-did the filling but cut corners again. When it pops out again, I'm going to try someone else. Anyone know a good dentist?

If you don't like the first doctor (or dentist) you find, try another. I've gone to some doctors based on referrals and felt like they were just stringing me along to get me to come back and pay them more money. I've also found a couple of doctors who are professional, helpful, and give help over the phone without charging, like our son's pediatrician.

I don't think that it's necessarily true that more expensive doctors are always better, but so far I've had better experiences with the doctors that charge more. One of my favorite doctors is also an expatriate from the United States (and she charges on the higher end of the scale).

Honesty and Professionalism among Doctors

Without getting into details, I'll tell you one of my experiences with a dishonest doctor so that you'll know what to watch out for when you are choosing your doctor in Mexico.

I got a referral for a private doctor from a fellow expatriate from the U.S. The doctor charged a moderate amount on the pay scale (300 pesos per visit in 2005) and was a gentle, friendly person. My acquaintance absolutely raved about him and at first I was very pleased with this doctor, but eventually came to a crucial cross-road with him. I asked him for information about a condition that I thought I might have. He used that opening to recommend that he perform an expensive, invasive, and unnecessary surgery, while withholding information from me about tests available from local laboratories that would have told me if I had the condition or not. Luckily, another contact (one of the right Mexicans mentioned above) advised me to get a second opinion from a second doctor (who is, coincidentally, an expatriate from the United States).

That's when I found the expatriate doctor that I mention above in the section "Finding a Private Doctor You Can Communicate With in English." I was more than glad to pay the slightly higher price (500 pesos) for the office visit to this second doctor, who ordered the appropriate tests—which ruled out the need for surgery— and gave me the results over the phone, without charging for a second visit.

I have since been able to call this second doctor on her cell phone and ask her questions, which she gladly answers without requiring that I come in for an office visit.

In addition to the huge difference in the morals exhibited by these two doctors, there was a difference in the professionalism demonstrated by their receptionists. The former doctor's receptionists would make appointments for times such as 6:30 and 7:00, but when I got to the office, I would wait until 9:00 p.m. to see the doctor. If it was because he was regularly detained, why did they not use my phone number which they had in their appointment book to call me and ask me if I'd like to arrive later or reschedule my appointment? I was tired of sitting for hours and getting flat-butt in his waiting room.

At the honest doctor's office, I wait about ten minutes. The receptionist is professional in her manner, easy to work with, and calls the day ahead to remind me of the appointment. She has assisted me by relaying messages and requests to my doctor who then calls me when she has a break in her schedule.

When you live or retire in Mexico, get referrals from friends and acquaintances, but be your own advocate. It may be necessary to switch doctors (or dentists) in order to get the kind of care you deserve.

Private Hospitals

So now, since you are a savvy person, you are asking where these private doctors treat their patients in emergencies. The answer is that there is an extensive system of private hospitals at which private doctors provide services. Just like doctors, the hospitals vary in cost, quality, and variety of services provided.

At first, these hospitals will strike the recently retired in Mexico as more like clinics. They are generally small, often converted buildings with jury-rigged ramps, etc. Each hospital hires its own receptionists, nursing staff, and cleaning staff. They also own the equipment there, such as x-ray machines and other things that most of us take for granted will be at hospitals.

One of the reasons Mexicans give for having IMSS insurance is that the large IMSS hospitals in Mexico City are better equipped than private hospitals. They reason that, if they are at a hospital, they want to be sure that the necessary equipment will be available on location and I see what they mean. If you suddenly seizure one day, you'll need an MRI or CT scan to get a diagnosis.

If you have a special condition, such as diabetes, it would be smart to list all of the hospital equipment that you may need and check to see at which hospitals in your new area it is available. I recommend that you don't ask if the hospital has "X" equipment. Rather you should ask if "X" equipment is working and available for use. Hospitals often advertise special equipment, then when it breaks, don't stop advertising it and don't get it fixed.

Your doctor will be the best source of information about hospitals. Since s/he works there, you can ask her/him about the quality of the hospital. Of course, this happens after you find a doctor that you like and trust. Remember that living or retiring in Mexico is a process and doesn't get set up all at once.

While it's smart to be savvy about which hospitals have what equipment, for some things it really doesn't matter. In my anecdote about IMSS, "IMSS Almost Killed My Husband" [at http://www.home-sweet-mexico.com/retire-in-Mexico-healthcare-IMSS.html] we didn't need any special equipment, we needed trained staff that had the time and basic equipment to treat the fractured bones in Luis's arms.

Many private hospitals are small enough that there isn't always a doctor "on duty." If you have a private doctor, you should call them on their cell phone while you are on the way to the hospital, so that they can meet you there. If the emergency will require a specialist, I'd call your doctor anyway and then get to the hospital where they will call the correct "on call" doctor to come in and help you. In our broken arm experience, we waited about an hour for the doctor to come in and be ready for surgery.

I was with my husband as they prepped him and even got to meet the surgeon around the corner of the entrance to the surgery. He shook my hand, knew my husband's name, and had already looked at the x-rays that we had snuck out of the IMSS hospital. I felt very relieved to meet the confident, relaxed surgeon and know that my husband was safe.

Even in private hospitals you may still need to advocate for yourself to get the service you need. In our broken arm experience, during the first surgery, they tried to do a non-invasive intervention for my husband's arm, which was a nice try, but unsuccessful. Later, though, the doctor was dragging his feet about putting in pins, etc. With twenty-twenty hind sight it appears that he didn't want to do the work for the relatively small amount of money that the insurance agency would pay him.

We broke the stalemate unintentionally when my husband went to see the best trauma doctor in Cuernavaca (through a referral from a co-worker of mine) for a second opinion and mentioned that person's name and opinion to the original surgeon. After some hurt feelings and huffiness on the doctor's part and some Mexican smoothing of feathers on my husband's part, the real surgery got

scheduled and was a success, as was the post-op therapy…
and no, we didn't pay any additional money on top of the
insurance allotment.

The Cost of Private Doctors in Mexico

As mentioned above, in Cuernavaca, there are private
doctors that charge between 100 pesos and 500. My
favorite doctors charge 500 pesos per visit ($45 USD).

I have always been asked to pay for private medical
services in cash. If the amount to be paid is large, the
doctor is usually willing to break the payment down into
parts, each part being paid at a new stage in the process.

When you need to have lab work done, private doctors
will send you to a private laboratory to get your samples
taken and analyzed. Depending on the analysis needed, lab
work can cost anywhere from 250 to 1000 pesos (please
remember this is a ball park figure).

Private doctors and private hospitals get paid through
"*pagos por evento*" which means that everyone who takes
part in treating you (anesthesiologist, x-ray tech, surgeon,
etc.) and everything that is used (facilities, x-ray machine,
sutures, etc.) is listed and you are charged for each item on
the list. The prices are much more reasonable than those
charged in the United States. A room at a hospital can cost
500 pesos a night, for example. Sometimes doctors
establish "packages" for certain procedures, such as
deliveries of babies, and if this is the case, you pay the
doctor a lump-sum and he or she pays the hospital. You
can ask your doctor for general price estimates before you
need their services in order to have an idea of what the
costs might be in case of an emergency.

I wish I could give useful ballpark figures here but the prices vary so much by procedure and by region that it wouldn't give you any real information. Once you think you know where you'll be living you can stop by hospitals in the area and ask them about prices that relate to your own potential medical needs.

Consider Keeping Your Coverage in the U.S. or Canada

If you can afford it, you might consider being a snowbird, living in Mexico only part time and maintaining your health coverage back home, especially if you are already over 64. Canadians, remember that you must remain residents (more information on this topic can be found on page 154). When you are making your plans, please remember that illnesses aren't something we plan on and they can present themselves quite suddenly. Aneurisms are an example of the type of critical, sudden onset health issues that would negate a plan to simply mosey home for treatment. If your plan is to depend on your insurance from the U.S. or Canada, be sure to have coverage for medical evacuation from Mexico, should you need it.

Also consider the costs and logistics of bringing a partner back north, closing up the "vacation" home and opening up the home in the north, when one person of a couple becomes ill. One friend needed pituitary surgery and she went north by herself, while her husband stayed home in Mexico. This couple had no choice about being separated, but I personally wouldn't want to be separated by so many miles if one of us becomes ill. It would be wise to plan your safety net so that this need not happen to you. The experience of one of my family members really demonstrated to me, first hand how unexpected illnesses can change a person's life in an instant. She suddenly had a seizure and after many tests and more seizures, was diagnosed with a deadly brain cancer. If she had been an expat living in Mexico and keeping her medical coverage in the U.S. she would have been in a much worse situation than that created by the disease alone. I include these scary stories, not to frighten you, but to really make a strong point that we don't have control over illnesses and the way they may affect our lives. We must plan our safety nets accordingly.

Health Insurance Coverage in Mexico

If you don't feel comfortable taking all of the risk for payment of your health services through out-of-pocket private coverage, you could opt to pay for a formal health care insurance plan that would cover you in case of unforeseen, large expenses. These plans are sold by insurance agents and paid to large companies such as ING or Mapfre.

Retired people will know that when you are over 64 you can no longer qualify for coverage. It's the same in Mexico. If you are under 64, here is a basic outline of formal health care insurance in Mexico.

There are two plan types, which are generally sold as separate policies. The first is "*Gastos Medicos Mayores*" (Major Medical Expenses) and the other is "*Gastos Medicos Menores*" (Minor Medical Expenses).

Gastos Medicos Mayores

"*Mayores*" is for the big stuff like accidents and long term sicknesses. These plans have a deductible and some have upper limits for total expenditures on one particular illness.

I went in to an insurance agent and asked for a quote for coverage for a healthy, 60-year-old woman (no high blood pressure or anything of that nature). The quote was around $13,000 pesos (approx. $1,200 USD) annually with a 20,000 peso (approx. $1,800 USD) deductible. Not so bad if you have dollars to spend! If you are earning in pesos it's a lot. That could easily be two month's salary.

Canadians, if you choose not to maintain your residency in Canada (see page 149), you may wish to consider purchasing a policy to cover *Mayores*. You know those horror stories Canadians tell about Americans who lose it all when they become ill? Without coverage, that could be you.

Gastos Medicos Menores

"*Menores*" is for the yearly stuff such as doctor's visits, preventative health, lab tests, etc. – the stuff that is relatively reasonably priced in Mexico. There are a variety of plans that have different rules, but since it is similar to plans in the United States you can imagine that there is a percentage of coverage for lab work, a network of doctors from which you can choose or a set amount allowable for visits to doctors outside the network. This could severely limit your options in medium and small towns. Canadians, think this through before you purchase. The responsibility will be on *you* to figure it all out, and you'll still pay something out of pocket for each and every service.

Pharmacies

Everybody wants to know about the famous pharmacies here in Mexico. Can you really get your medicine over the counter at a fraction of the cost? The answer is yes... and no.

Pharmacies here don't always stock their inventory as "well" as they do in the U.S. Luckily I don't take any prescription drugs so I don't have any of my explain-the-situation-anecdotes about medicines, but I do wear contacts and have one about buying hypoallergenic contact solution.

I found the rare type of solution that I use in the case at a drugstore near my house. There were two boxes covered in dust. I bought one box. About two months later I ran low and went back to buy more. There was one box covered in dust. I bought it. It kind of made me wonder....

Sure enough, two months after *that*, the drug store was out of the solution. So I went all over town and finally found a drug store that had the solution. I bought it.

What happened two months later, you are wondering? Well the first store still didn't have more and the second store was out too, so I went all over town. I was getting worried. I didn't want to have to give up my contacts but I couldn't find any store that stocked the solution. Multiple pharmacy employees kept looking at my box that I brought along to show them as an example and telling me the product they carried was "*lo mismo*" (the same). Right, the only difference between the two products was that theirs would make my eyes swell up and get itchy because I am allergic to one of the ingredients. I found a privately owned pharmacy and the owner tried to order it, but neither of his suppliers carried it. Anyway, this story has a happy ending. Finally the drug store near my house has caught up with the demand and regularly stocks the solution.

As a retiree in Mexico, if you are a regular prescription user, it would be wise to find a family-owned pharmacy where you can get to know the pharmacist and communicate your needs to him or her. Still, they are limited to what their suppliers carry. The big chain pharmacies tend to hire bored teenagers who can't really provide good customer service.

Antibiotics

It seems that one of the biggest fears people have when they come to Mexico to live or visit is getting sick from the food or water. It is true that you are at a higher risk of contracting a food-born illness, in Mexico than Canada and the U.S. – mostly due to poor hygiene and food handling techniques, but it is not necessary to avoid eating foods that you really like out of fear. In all honesty, unless you are only here for a week and an afternoon is a critical amount of time for you, being sick really isn't all that bad. A regimen of antibiotics is available over the counter at any pharmacy for only a couple of dollars. I was pleasantly shocked at the price of my first antibiotics.

Because antibiotics are sometimes available over the counter it can be tempting to self medicate[†]. Remember that self-diagnosing is not OK. In this section I include some options and information that you can use to help you to find medicines when you are sick, but the information should be used **in addition to** the information given to you by a **licensed doctor** who is trained to diagnose your

---

[†] There has been an increased focus on making sure pharmacies don't sell drugs to people who don't have a prescription, so don't come planning to avoid the law.

illness. **The information in this section in no way replaces the need for you to see a doctor**.

You could consider informing yourself about antibiotics before you come to Mexico. Try talking to your doctor in the U.S. or Canada about types of antibiotics and the number of days you should take them to be sure that you don't breed a resistant strain. Get the chemical names of the ingredients and the amounts of each because those are almost the same in Spanish, but the brand names aren't. You can read the ingredients of the antibiotics before you purchase them.

Before you purchase antibiotics you can ask the attendant at the pharmacy to let you look at the "*enciclopedia de farmacéuticas*." This book is a well-kept secret, but all pharmacies have one under their counters. If the people at one pharmacy won't get it out for you, go to another. The book contains all of the medicines available, along with their indications and side effects. Even if your Spanish isn't very good, you will still be able to decipher the meanings of the medical and scientific terms, since they are very similar to English (well, Latin actually). From this book you can make sure that the antibiotic is right for you.

One very cheap way to see a doctor is to go to a consultation at the *Farmacias Similares*, a chain pharmacy that sells generic medications. Every *Farmacia Similar* has a consultation room attached to it. You go into the stark-white, painted waiting room outside of the consultation room and wait your turn. When it is your turn, you go into the consultation room and pay the doctor the thirty pesos in cash required for the visit. That's right, just over three U.S. dollars. You will describe your ailment (in Spanish) and he or she will write you a prescription that can be filled in the pharmacy right outside the door.

If you are like me and deny that you are getting sick until you can't risk a trip away from your toilet, someone else can go purchase your medicines. Luis even went to see the doctor at *Similares* for me! While *Farmacias Similares* has gotten Luis and me out of a couple of jams, I would be remiss if I didn't warn you that I've heard of some people having had very bad experiences with them. Be smart and use your own sense of what is right when you use this service. Don't take any medications that you don't think are right for you.

The thing is that antibiotics can be miraculous. As long as you get promptly and properly diagnosed and don't have a resistant strain of bacteria, in only a few hours they will have you back on your feet and moving around. Just remember to take your whole regimen. We really don't need to fear bacteria.

Sometimes taking a full regimen of antibiotics is overkill, but you still need some help getting your intestinal tract back to normal. My doctor told me about a thick suspension, containing an antibiotic that you drink as soon as you feel stomach pain after eating something. It's a useful thing to have on hand so that you can take it before you have an over-exploding population of bacteria in your intestinal tract. Ask your doctor about it, once you find one. In fact, this is a good type of conversation to have with your doctor. I personally believe it is important to find one of the rare doctors who refuse to participate in the overuse of antibiotics. Find out where your doctor stands on this important public health issue.

Remember, it is also possible to have severe irritation in our digestive tract that may make us falsely believe we have an infection. The spicy, greasy diet and stresses of a profound life change can easily throw an innocent intestine into fits. One time I swore I had contracted some invincible bacteria and went to my doctor. She had me take a sample of you-know-what to a nearby lab and I was shocked when the results came back negative for harmful fauna. I had a second test done, just to be sure. Negative. I made appropriate dietary adjustments.

Make sure not to blindly take a medicine that a friend or acquaintance offers you. Self-medication with antibiotics is rampant in Mexico and the potential for the growth of resistant strains of bacteria is a real and present danger. Public education on the topic is woefully lacking and pharmacies benefit financially from ignoring laws prohibiting the sale of antibiotics to people without a prescription[‡].

People often want to share medications that have worked for them. Once, when visiting a small town, I found that the water was giving me diarrhea. I had brought some Imodium AD with me from the U.S. and usually just one dose of this would stop the problem. When I ran out of Imodium, I asked someone where I could get more. He mentioned that a neighbor sold medicines for diarrhea and purchased me a couple of bubble packed pills, cut from the larger sheet. He told me they worked well for him (yes, Mexicans get sick from the water too). I took one and found that it worked as well as the Imodium had. It became my savior. About a year later, as I was explaining my diarrhea history to the *Similares* doctor, I told her the name of the medicine that had helped me before. "That's an antibiotic," she said. "No. It's for diarrhea," I said. "No, medicines with that type of name are antibiotics," she explained. Oh. Well duh. I would not have chosen an antibiotic and wouldn't have taken it if I had known that it

___

[‡] There has been an increased focus on making sure pharmacies don't sell drugs to people who don't have a prescription, so don't come planning to avoid the law.

wasn't the equivalent of Imodium. I certainly would have taken a full regimen if I had known that it was an antibiotic.

After being here for a while, you may get amoebas or other parasites in your digestive tract. Don't self-diagnose. Go to a doctor and they will help you figure out if that's what you have or not. The medicines for amoebas and parasites are "strong" and should not be taken if they aren't what you really need. There are two different types of medicines for amoebas. The first time I had them I went to IMSS (the national health care provider) and was prescribed a seven-day regimen of some killer medicine that made me so spacey I could barely remember where to get off the bus to go to work. I would literally zone out and later "come to" with my mouth hanging open. To me, the cure was worse than the illness so the next time I suspected I had amoebas I tolerated it for about a year. Finally I went to a private doctor and was prescribed a one-time only medicine that cured me in one day with no noticeable side effects. If your doctor says that you have amoebas ask them about the different types of medicines available to treat them. Better yet, get the lab test to be sure you actually have them.

How to Get Sick (Luckily, I'm not really an expert in this)

Living in the city, milk products can be plenty safe. You and everyone else can buy Lala or Alpura milk products. These are pasteurized and sealed at the factory just like back home. True, they may be transported to the point of sale in the open back of a pickup truck and sit outside the store stacked on a hand truck waiting to be stocked, but if you consume them within a few days of purchase you won't get sick. We have not gotten sick from any of these packaged milk products even after keeping them in our fridge for over a week. If you are in the country, the same pasteurized products are available, but so is fresh milk, which is not pasteurized.

The food that gets me is cheese—even cheese used on food I prepare for myself at home. I have been doing a little investigation of cheese handling methods and I think I have identified the contributing factors. One, cheese is transported uncovered. It is passed from bare hand to bare unwashed hand. It is left outside of stores, still uncovered, awaiting shelf space inside. Two, it is displayed in stores at room temperature (and you can guess how hot room temperature can get). Third, it is grated in huge meat grinder-like cheese graters which have never seen a bleach-water soaked rag in their entire usage history. I don't eat much cheese here. It's not a great loss, because Mexican cheese tastes like it ought to after being handled the way it is. If we do buy cheese, we go to the store in our neighborhood that is the most consistent about refrigeration and uses plastic bags over their hands to weigh it, and we eat it within a day or two of purchase. Sometimes, I allow myself to go to the supermarket with a friend, where I purchase good ol' oily Cheddar Cheese… or Brie… or Gouda.

One of Mexico's tastiest street treats is off limits for me: fruit chunks bathed in yogurt and sprinkled with granola. The yogurt is purchased by the shop owners in large industrial sized containers and kept out on the counter all day. I just can't bring myself to eat yogurt that may have been out all day, or all day the day before, or the day before that. It doesn't seem like the concept of keeping things cool to reduce bacterial growth has really reached popularity, even in the cities. Because of this, *crema*, which is a cross between heavy cream and sour cream may also be on your off limits list. You decide.

Veggies can be a danger too, since they may have been irrigated with polluted surface water and may not have been properly disinfected. At home you can use disinfectant drops, which are widely available at the grocery store (see Drinking Water <u>on page 56</u>). If you are going to be here a while, you can experiment with the tap water. In Cuernavaca, the tap water hasn't ever made me sick. We buy bottled water in huge five gallon containers, called *garrafones,* to drink, but the inconvenience of disinfecting every little carrot that I want to eat has caused me to wash my veggies in tap water, then dry them on a towel and eat them. So far, knock on wood, this hasn't made me sick. I also eat veggies willy-nilly in restaurants and taco stands. I use the, don't-picture-where-they-have-been-and-you-won't-get-sick method. This is a personal choice. I'm sure the risk is different in different places, so be careful, but don't be paranoid.

4 Eating in Mexico

Drinking Water

Getting sick from ice is probably one of the biggest unnecessary fears of people who come to Mexico from the north. We have been traditionally warned not to accept ice in our drinks. I find that we have no need to be afraid. My experience is that the ice served in restaurants is safe (usually the round kind with the little hole in the middle). Some people still do use the block ice that is delivered to the doorstep, but they use it for keeping things cool or in street foods where you will be able to see if they have a block of ice in their preparation area.

There are many factors that could cause us to get ill. The reasoning for the fear is logical enough and is as follows: our digestive tracts haven't been exposed to very many different micro organisms, causing us to be extremely susceptible to them. That's inside our bodies. On the outside are all of the Mexican factors, which are highly variable and generally dangerous. Despite all of this, the good news is that clean drinking water is available everywhere in Mexico. Unsafe water is unsafe for Mexicans, too, so good water is provided in stores and restaurants throughout Mexico. You just have to become accustomed to differentiating between the water that comes out of your tap and potable water, which comes out of a sealed plastic bottle.

When walking around town you can pick up bottled water from any small store, of which there are about two on every block. You can choose cold water (*frío*) or room temperature water (*al tiempo*) in sizes ranging from half liter to one and a half liters. If you have the time, ask the price of the water. On the street in a non-touristy area, a half liter bottle of water should cost you five pesos, a liter ten pesos, and one and a half liters 15 pesos. Restaurants charge twenty pesos for a half liter with your meal, but I've never been asked to put my personal water bottle away, so I try to buy my water before going in.

At home you can buy a *garrafón* of water. This is a blue plastic five-gallon jug of purified water, like those used in many offices up north. It would be pointless for me to include a price estimate for these because the prices vary across the country, mostly based on what the companies who sell them can get away with charging. If there is only one company selling *garrafones* or if the municipal water supply is un-clean, the prices can be three times what they are in other places. If you live in a city you can arrange for delivery of your water. This will involve paying a deposit for the returnable water jug to the delivery guys. After that you just buy the water, trading the empty jug for a full one. If you can't arrange for delivery and you are strong enough to carry it, you can pick up your own jug at your corner store. If you can't carry your jug, I'm sure you can find some nice young man to do the job for you. Tip him ten to 20 pesos to make it worth his while. There are a wide variety of pumps and tipping racks that you can purchase to facilitate the pouring of your heavy water jug.

I bought a portable backpacking water filter, knowing that I would be staying in the homes of extended family, who live in the country and might not always buy bottled water to have in their homes. I didn't want to bother them with my need for clean drinking water. In the end, I found that I only used the pump about three times in a month of traveling and it wasn't worth the expense of purchasing it, nor carrying the extra weight. Clean drinking water is so easy to purchase, even in tiny little towns, that it was easier than pumping it through the filter.

Disinfecting drops can also do the trick. Pick up a bottle of disinfecting drops at a grocery store here in Mexico (displayed in the vegetable section) and carry this with you. One of the brands available here in Cuernavaca is "*microdyn*" which comes in a small blue dropper bottle, reminiscent of an eye drop bottle. The instructions on the back state how many drops to use for disinfecting washed vegetables and for drinking water as well as how long you have to wait for the chemical reaction to take place. I find that there is no bad flavor associated with these drops, though the water does look a little yellow. If you would like to come to Mexico ready, you could buy disinfecting tablets from your local outdoor store back home. This would buy you some time to find a grocery store in your first days in Mexico and you would have these with you in case you ever get into a pinch later.

If you like to live sustainably, you may prefer the filter or tablet/drops option to lower your carbon footprint and to avoid disposing of so many non-returnable plastic liter bottles. It is even possible to install a water purification system into your home. Avoiding bottled water is also preferable from a human rights perspective since it keeps the focus on good municipal water for all, rather than supporting a system in which the rich buy bottled water and the poor live with unsafe, unreliable municipal water.

Grocery Shopping and the Art of the Market

When we moved to Mexico, we both brought with us very negative viewpoints about large-scale grocery stores with their oversized parking lots. This had grown out of reading much of Wendell Berry's writing[§] and enjoying some of the local market outlets that are available in the Pacific Northwest. Despite my relatively young age, I have watched the farm fields in my home county succumb to isolated, walled housing developments surrounded by four-lane roads and shopping

[§] It was *The Unsettling of America* that opened my eyes to this topic, but here are two short articles that show what Mr. Berry has been teaching for years.
"The Pleasures of Eating" by Wendell Berry:
http://www.ecoliteracy.org/essays/pleasures-eating
"The Agrarian Standard" by Wendell Berry:
http://www.orionmagazine.org/index.php/articles/article/115/

areas with acres of parking lots. When we got here, we both wanted to buy local and to support Mexico's wonderful small-business market. Living in the States we had been disgusted with the necessity to hop into the car and drive through congested intersections in order to pick up something so simple as eggs and butter to make cookies. Mexico's neighborhoods sprout small businesses selling fruit, snacks, staples, meats, school supplies, tacos, full meals, among many other things like carpentry shops, and hardware stores. In our Mexican neighborhood we have all of those things and need only to peek out our window to see if the veggie store is open before we go out to buy avocados and tomatoes for guacamole.

Not wanting to promote Mexico's decline into U.S.-like consumer patterns, we began our grocery shopping at "the market." The Adolfo Lopez Mateos Market of Cuernavaca, named after a former president, is a huge football-field sized concrete building containing hundreds of tiny stalls selling fruit, vegetables, meats, eggs, household goods, etc. and surrounded by hundreds more semi-permanent stalls erected all around the market selling shoes, batteries, clothes, kitchen wares, and in my favorite section, flower arrangements.

A Mexican market can be an overwhelming thing to someone from the United States or Canada and the Adolfo Lopez Mateos Market is one of the dirtiest I have ever been to. The floor of the market is covered in thick, black grime. The drain grates are clogged with unidentifiable objects. In some isles you slip on rotten tomatoes and onion peels. In the four-foot-wide isles, people of all sizes, shapes, and disabilities jockey around you. The only section of the market that doesn't smell bad is the isle where the flower arrangements are sold, though the floor there has almost as much gunk on it. In the chicken isle everything is covered in chicken slime. I haven't seen the fish isle in a while because it smells quite fishy and I avoid it. The beef isle is permeated with a stench that, well, you know. The entire place hasn't been clean since it was constructed. As a whole, the vendors are grumpy and a little tricky with their scales. You have to lug a heavy bag with you everywhere you go and the crowd that forms on Sunday makes it hard to maneuver. Mexicans have a habit of crowding into every inch of available space. They set boxes out in front of their stalls and stack their wares on those. I guess the idea is that you will be inclined to buy things after you have tripped on them or been shoved into them by the passing multitudes.

For months I couldn't go there without Luis. I was slowly acclimating myself to the layout, rhythm, and smells of the market. At first I couldn't bring myself to buy meat in the meat section. I had to hold my breath just to get through it and the gray slime built up around the floor drains almost made me gag.

We tried a couple of grocery stores which reminded us of grocery stores back home—until we looked for products commonly sold in the Pacific Northwest, but completely unheard of here. Eventually we settled on Superama (an upscale branch of Walmart) where we went for meats, most of which are sold in Styrofoam packages. Next we would go to the market for the fresher, less expensive veggies. The first time we walked into the clean, air conditioned, familiar "grocery store" layout of Superama, we both breathed deep sighs of relief. In my mind I was in a Fred Meyer back home and my mother might just pop out of the next aisle in a pleasant surprise encounter just like used to happen to the three of us. We splurged on balsamic vinegar and bought meat in tidy little Styrofoam bundles. Luis discovered that the shrimp there was fresher than we could ever lay hands on back home. So, for a while we had things worked out. We hit the market for veggies which were sometimes half the cost of and mostly fresher than the veggies in the grocery store and on another day we would go to the supermarket for hygienic looking meats and Top Ramen (the market has over-packaged Maruchan but no Top Ramen).

I should take a moment to warn you that there are no chocolate chips (though after months of searching I have found semi-sweet chocolate chunks of acceptable quality sold in one particular stand in the market), no rice milk, no three bean dip, no frozen dinners, and no dill pickles sold in Cuernavaca.[**] This list could be longer, but hopefully those items will give you the idea of the seriousness of matters here. These things surely must be available in Mexico City, but I wouldn't waste my time looking for them in other places. An American friend of mine has told me of a day wasted, at her mother's insistence, looking all over Cuernavaca for tofu. I have similarly wasted

See "Shopping for … Hassles" to learn how it took all day to buy a sorry pot with a broken lid at [http://home-sweet-mexico.com/retire-in-mexico-shopping.html/]

much time in a vain search for chocolate chips at every super market I have entered. Surely, it is one of the world's

---

[**] Later, I found that soy milk is very rarely available at Sam's, but a membership costs two or three days wages. I think there are also frozen dinners in the supermarket, but I honestly haven't checked to see what's available because I don't have a microwave. I still haven't seen dill pickles, but I've heard you can buy a two gallon jar of them at Costco. How many memberships do we need here? Anyway, they wouldn't fit in my fridge.

greatest ironies that a cacao producing country cannot boast one tiny chunk of decent dark chocolate. All of the chocolate I have tried here tastes like last year's Easter candy, although, to their credit, *Ibarra* brand chocolate for drinking makes the best hot cocoa I have ever drunk. Sometimes people will insist that a product is available, but once you find it, it will be so different from your expectations, it might as well not exist. For me, this product is soy milk. There is a brand of soy based fruit juice called *Ades* that includes a plain flavor. The plain is so spiked with imitation sugar it will curl hair. It just doesn't hold a candle to the brands available to us in the Pacific Northwest. While with every passing year more and more products become available, once you arrive here, you may discover a few products you personally miss and will have to work out the shipping details with friends and family back home. I wonder if my friend's mother brought tofu with her in her carryon luggage… until the post 9/11 rules gave us a 100 ml fluid limit.…

One day it all came to a screeching halt when we rounded the corner heading to our favorite Superama, only to find the doors boarded up and a sign declaring its closure. At first I tried denial. Surely the store was only closed for remodeling. After reading the sign three times we had to come to grips with the permanency of the change. We did mental calculations on every other supermarket we knew of but none of them were within range of only one bus… and the market was. I had already been playing with the idea that Mexicans are Mexicans whether they work for Superama or in the market and that they would probably handle meat in about the same way— whether or not I could smell it. This concept was blaringly confirmed once at another store called "Mega" when I returned a package of meat that smelt bad the day I bought it. The store employee opened the package, handled the chicken in question with both hands, smelling it to confirm, then reached straight for the fresh chicken in the display case to give me replacement pieces! When I stopped her and asked her to please wash her hands first, I realized with horror that there was *no* sink installed in the meat preparation area. So, in the end, I have become accustomed to the meats section of the market[††] and have even developed a habit of buying my beef from a particular vendor, who can figure out my strange American requests for thick cuts of steak. Sometimes I even forget to gag. I guess it's only the floors that stink.

There is an art to shopping at the market and I can't say that I have it entirely worked out, but I have a system that works for me. Once I got my bearings, I found it more pleasant to shop by myself than with Luis. It is difficult to navigate the over-packed maze with someone else, and we would sometimes gripe at each other because we didn't have a system worked out for choosing at which stall to buy which things. My current system works well for me now and I enjoy feeling independent again. I bring my backpack and my indestructible, reusable, plastic Mexican shopping bag (originally purchased in the market, of course). Get yourself one or two of these as soon as you

---

[††] You will have to make your own choice about meat safety in light of the high rate of contamination of meat in Mexico with Clenbuterol. A friend has stopped purchasing meat in the market in favor of packaged meats at Sam's that appear to have been packaged for sales in the U.S. (the label is all in English as well as having the FDA symbol on it). I'm not so convinced you can trust the packaging. It's possible that products that can't be sold in the U.S. are "dumped" on customers in Mexico. In 2007, I purchased from Sam's in Cuernavaca recalled peanut butter tainted with Salmonella because I had no idea about the recall happening in the U.S. I was quite ill. If you're not vegan and not a rancher, you'll have to make your own difficult choice.

arrive in Mexico. I start with heavy items first, like chicken and beef. You can get your beef cut any way you would like and even smashed flat (*aplanado*). The chicken vendors will pull the skin off and even de-bone at your request. Now that's service!

As a foreigner you are sure to find a vendor or two who can handle the fact that you don't know the names of the beef cuts and will put out the extra effort it takes to communicate with you and prepare you what you want – like thick steaks. In central Mexico people don't "get" thick steaks. While you wait for the vendor to cut your meat you also have the pleasure of breathing directly on the meat that he will be selling to clients who come after you, since the meat is considerately stacked at nose height for your inspection. You can also amuse yourself by looking at his families' collection of disposable plates of leftover lunch, lucky animal feet with the fur still on the shins, and slightly dried out special cuts which are found in the refrigerated display case by your knees.

You can also purchase garlic, matches, *nopales* (delicious cactus leaves), avocados, cinnamon sticks, and flowers for tea called *jamaica* from pushy native ladies wearing checkered, ruffled aprons. They will tap your forearm with their wares and jam them into your face asking you if you would like whatever they are selling. They will stay there for a while, telling you the things are good until they are completely sure that "no gracias" means "no." If you don't want to buy what they have you have to stare straight ahead, making it a point not to look at them. If you do want to buy what they have, you ask the price, pay, and add your purchase to your shopping bag. I like to buy avocados from them.

After the meats, I usually cruise the vegetable section until I see one of the vegetables that I want looking good and labeled with a good price. I reconfirm the price (sometimes the price of the lower quality pile is labeled and the good stuff has a slightly higher price) and request the amount that I want. The best vendors give you an appropriately sized plastic bag and let you select what you want (*escojer*). They weigh the veggies—I used to try to keep an eye on the scale to be sure they don't cheat, but have since given up. They always take the tray off of the scale, put the veggies in it then hang it up together so you can never see the zero mark. They never back down if you point out something might not have been weighed correctly and after one particularly feisty day in which I had to walk away from some tomatoes I wanted to buy and ended up spending more at another stand, as well as had to keep track of which vendors I had pissed off, I decided to let it go. What are a few pesos, anyway?

As my bag fills up, I find a spot that isn't filled with people and has a dry—no part of the floor is clean—area to transfer heavy things into my backpack. After meats and veggies I head to fruits and granola. Most bus routes have a stop in the area out back of the market, so I catch my bus home from there.

When you come you will have to decide where to shop and how much running around you want to do to pick up items sold only by a single vender. Honestly, most people shop in supermarkets and are quite happy doing it. If you have a car, the market isn't quite as convenient as a supermarket, where you can pay 2 or 3 pesos to park your car out front, although there is a car parking lot at the market too. Also, not all markets are the same. Cuernavaca, like other cities, has many smaller markets which are generally cleaner, calmer, and have more room in the isles. Some of these smaller markets are overpriced while others have prices similar to those in the larger one. Additionally, some neighborhoods have weekly temporary markets that form on a particular day of the week. You can scope out the various marketing options near your house and pick the ones that suit your needs. Really, the main reason I continue to shop at Lopez Mateos is that I have direct transportation to and from it. If our neighborhood had its own, smaller market, I would gladly go there. After you find a market you like to shop at you will have the pleasure (and I'm NOT being sarcastic here. I mean it) of getting to know your venders and supporting their locally owned businesses.

If you come to Cuernavaca, you can also buy freshly ground coffee—organic or with pesticides, at the market. I still haven't discovered all of the market's wonders. In fact, after living in Cuernavaca for one year and one month, I spotted powdered soy milk (9% fat) in the back of a stall at which I like to buy granola and semi-sweet chocolate. After living here for one year eleven months, I discovered flax seeds on display among a bunch of dry goods in gunny sacks. Don't give up even if you ask someone where to find something and they say it's not available. Depending on how you describe it, sometimes they just don't know what you mean. The surprises never end, so take the time to really comb through the market near you and do it every few months, because as you become more attuned to Mexico, you will "see" more and more.

Even better yet, throughout Mexico there are itinerant sales people who sell everything from bulk shampoo out of fifty-five gallon drums in the back of a pickup to mobile vegetable stands and butcher shops. To get a feel for the quality of their products, you can try buying from them or ask your neighbors about them. At first it can seem dangerous to buy meats from the back of a truck, but sometimes these products are actually better because they are fresh. In our neighborhood there is a man who drives an ancient green station wagon around selling fresh, cold chicken every morning except Sunday morning. When he opens the back of his station wagon I can smell the bleach that he uses on his rags, which are freshly cleaned every day. Though he doesn't carry ice, he keeps the chicken covered with clean rags and when he gives me my chicken it is still cool to the touch. I prefer to buy chicken from him rather than from any other vendor I have found. Now that he knows me as a customer I can make requests for particular cuts of chicken a day in advance.

A Mexican friend shared with me her perspective on buying chicken. It is one that might surprise someone from the north because our initial reaction to meat in the back of a battered vehicle is a negative one. She doesn't like to buy chicken from the supermarket because it is not fresh and not of good quality, whereas someone like our "chicken guy" sells a superior product. I have to agree with her, the chicken purchased from "the chicken guy" lasts longer in the fridge than chicken purchased at other stores. The final advantage is that he brings it to the customer's very door step!

In Cuernavaca, there are also a couple of stores that specialize in items from the U.S. They sell things like boxed CousCous, rice noodles, pickles, and the thing that really made my mouth water, canned Oregon blackberries. They don't sell chocolate chips; I looked. These items are very expensive, though, so whether or not you can indulge will depend on your budget.

As a postscript I should add that there is a Superama in a rich neighborhood here in Cuernavaca that does stock bars of semi sweet chocolate for baking and occasionally stocks tofu. It took me two years to find these because without a car and with my low earnings in pesos, I never went to that store. I went shopping with an Italian friend who shops there and asked about tofu, which was out of stock, but on order. If you have a car and the income to shop in the most expensive super markets, you may be able to find things that are among the items I listed as impossible to find. The thing is that on a drastically reduced budget it's easier and smarter to eat like the Mexicans. A friend of mine from the states commented on her cookbook of Mexican recipes. She said it was the only one that was useful since the others have so many ingredients that she can't find here, anyway.

My Italian friend also uses a service that I'm not sure why I've never used. If she or her kids get sick and she can't go out to the store, she calls the grocery store on the phone and requests a delivery of her groceries. The store sends them to her with the only additional cost being the cost of the taxi, which delivers the groceries right to her door! It doesn't get more convenient than that.

Getting Some Fiber

One thing I miss a lot is fiber. I miss salads, I miss raw carrots, I miss veggie plates at parties, I miss whole wheat, I miss brown rice. Between the chili in the food and the complete absence of fiber in the diet here, one's digestive tract gets, well, dysfunctional.

Even though I love salad, I find that I rarely make it. It is smartest to disinfect lettuce and other veggies in a bowl of water for 10 minutes (instructions are on the bottle of disinfectant, which is available at the supermarket or at a few stalls in the market) or to at least rinse them with drinking water. Since I don't have a sink that can be plugged and filled and since my jug of drinking water was on the floor on the other side of the kitchen for years until we had a local carpenter make a special cupboard for it, this involved getting out a bowl and filling it, then washing it afterwards. Somehow the inability to just rinse and go makes making a salad a chore and I just don't do it. However, I have discovered other ways to get some fiber into my body.

The author's sink. The drain is new because Luis replaced the old one to make it nicer.

First, there are always beans, which are loaded with fiber. There are a few types of whole wheat bread available. The really good ones cost the equivalent of five dollars a loaf, so those are out of our budget range; besides, they are a little on the dry side. Wonder and Bimbo, the two brands of sandwich bread sold here, both have a whole wheat version of white bread. I prefer Bimbo's double fiber in the green bag. After growing up on rye and multigrain bread with seeds in it, it still tastes like white bread to me, but supposedly there are almost five grams of fiber in there. You can buy brown rice at one or two supermarkets here and at one or two stalls in the market. You just have to ask around. The key word for foods like whole wheat and brown rice, is *integral*. You can ask for *pan integral* [whole wheat bread] or *arroz*

integral [brown rice]. One warning: people don't really seem to talk about the makeup of food. I find that if I mention that I want more fiber or less carbohydrates people tend to look at me with a slightly confused look on their faces. You don't have to talk about it, just ask for *integral*.

A doctor in our neighborhood recommends making a *licuado* (smoothie) out of a half of a cored apple with the skin on, 2 tablespoons of quick oats, sugar to taste, some ice cubes, and milk (or water, if you don't like milk). This is a delicious way to have a snack and still eat some fiber. Now that I have discovered flax seeds in the market, I put them into the blender. I often use chilled hot cocoa made with chunks of Ibarra chocolate as the liquid base for *licuado*. Let your imagination run wild—just don't forget to add some fiber in there.

Over time my *licuado* recipe has evolved into an ultra-healthy, thick fruit sludge. Key ingredients are almonds for the calcium, flax for their fiber, bananas or mameys for their natural sweetness, water (I don't drink milk) and imitation vanilla. Apples, pineapple chunks, and fresh squeezed orange juice are among the other fruits that I like to put in the blender for a filling, healthy breakfast. Really it would be crazy not to make the many fresh, ripe fruits available in Mexico a daily staple in your new diet.

To learn more about toxic vanilla fakes sold in Mexico, see [http://www.vanilla.com/index.php/TROPICAL-FOODS/VANILLA/vanilla-from-mexico-central-american-and-the-caribbean.html] and [http://www.snopes.com/food/ingredient/vanilla.asp]

Another source of fiber recommended to me by the doctor was cereal. She recommended bran flakes, but I like

Fibra Max (which is like Fiber One and not like Fiber Max back home—go figure). She says she makes sure she eats a bowl a day in order to stay regular. This may sound trivial to you now, but after you've been down here a couple of months and are suffering chronic gas pains and constipation you'll remember this little chapter.

5 The "Bennies:" Some Ways

to Live it up in Mexico

Benefit 1: Ice-Cream

While you are in Mexico, there are a number of things that will be difficult or uncomfortable, but at the same time there are pleasures that can only be enjoyed here. For me, most of these things involve food. Ice cream

A typical outdoor ice cream

and sorbet are simply award winning here. They are chock full of real fruit chunks. Once we were selecting the flavors we wanted from a private vendor selling hand made ice-creams in Mazatlán. I was debating between lemon, which is made with a water base and always at least good, and usually great, and guava. When the sales lady took the lid off of the guava container, I could smell the guavas from where I stood. That made the choice for me. I ordered a scoop of guava on a cone; it was simply unforgettable.

When you go into an ice-cream store there are two basic categories of frozen treats from which you can choose: those made with milk as their base (*de leche*) or with water (*de agua*). Of these there are two more decisions you have to make: Scoops or on a stick. You can get scoops served into little plastic cups (*vasos*) which you eat with little plastic spoons or on cones (*barquillos*). You can get ice-cream or sorbet bars on sticks (*paletas*). If you can drink milk, I recommend the "nut" (*nuez*) ice-cream on a stick. Sometimes you get one so full of nuts that it is like a little snack, great for afternoons hiking around downtown.

In addition to the ice-cream shops, there are also people, mostly old men, who I think of as "*los dones de nieve*" who push ice-cream carts around the *Zocalo*, and even through the neighborhoods selling scoopable, on sticks, and even frozen flavored water in sealed plastic bags. You nip off a corner of these and suck the juice off as it melts. Don't be afraid, try these guys' treats too.

Because there are so many flavors, including some with chili, and because all of the stores are different, I recommend conducting your own personal experiment when you arrive in Mexico. Try different flavors and different stores. Please, skip the stores that say Nestle on the coolers; the more local the better. And you're hearing this from a chocoholic: skip chocolate. It's the fruit flavors that will knock your socks off.

Benefit 2: Lemonade

Another benefit of living in Mexico is the abundance of limes and the "lemonade." The most common type of *limón* here is a small green fruit that has an exquisite flavor. You will eat these limes squeezed over tacos, on salad, whatever, but you *must* make yourself lemonade (actually limeade). To facilitate this, you can buy yourself a lime squeezer, which works like a garlic press. The lime squeezers keep the seeds inside them and keep your hands dry.

Benefit 3: Italian Food That Will Fit into Your Budget

Some things that are too expensive back home aren't so far beyond one's means once one gets here. As a tourist especially, one can treat one's self to a nice sit-down meal at an Italian restaurant. Once you are earning in pesos, and not dollars, you may not want to go out frequently, but you will find that you can still treat yourself every once in a while.

Benefit 4: Fresh Fruit

Another food related bennie is all of the wonderful fruit available here. There are fruits here that I had never even heard of growing up in the Pacific Northwest – and each region of Mexico has its own – especially throughout central and southern Mexico. Sometimes it is hard to know how they are best eaten. Luis has created some good memories for my family and me teaching us about the wonderful flavors that literally grow on trees here in Mexico. Below is a list of fruits that you ought to give a taste test when you get here:

Name: *chicozapote* (sapodilla, fruit from the gum tree)
Description: salmon colored flesh in a thin woody cover
Consumption: Cut in half and eat with a spoon.
Julia's Rating: Almost too sweet with a hint of nutmeg.

Name: *ciruela* ("plum")
Description: Grape textured flesh and skin. Incredibly juicy and sweet.
Consumption: Wash and bite in. Spit out pit. There are a number of different varieties and all are delicious.
Julia's Rating: The first time I tried these, I thought I hated them. It took me years to try again and then I was sorry I'd missed so many years! I *love* them!

Name: *granada* (pomegranate)
Description: Hard pink husk around flesh covered seeds
Consumption: So fun to break the geometric seed pouches out of the husk
Julia's Rating: Enjoy these as they should be eaten – ripe and sweet.

Name: *granadilla* (passion fruit) - see also *maracuyá*

Description: Like a fragile gourd with juicy seed packets inside

Consumption: Break open the outer shell, put your lips to the soft, sweet, flesh and suck up mouthfuls. Dainty seeds add a light crunch. This fruit is similar in appearance to *maracuyá*, but is sweeter.

Julia's Rating: I could eat ten myself if I didn't have to share.

Name: *guanábana* (soursop, prickly custard apple)

Description: warty green skin over soft, white flesh

Consumption: Pry open the soft fruit. Pick out soft chunks of white flesh. Suck seeds clean of flesh then spit them out.

Julia's Rating: A worthy adventure.

Name: *guayaba* (guava)

Description: usually yellow

Consumption: Take a bite, swallow seeds.

Julia's Rating: One will do you. May cause constipation.

Name: *huauzontle* (a type of goosefoot)

Description: Green flower buds

Consumption: Pick small branches off of the stem and simmer in red chili sauce, preferably covered in egg and with salty cheese in the middle.

Julia's Rating: I know this is not a fruit, but it is so delicious, you must try it if it's available in your region.

Name: *liche* (liche)
Description: Dragon balls
Consumption: Peel away outer skin and suck on fruit, separating the pit with your tongue.
Julia's Rating: They sooth your mouth and you want another and another.

Name: *limón* (lime)
Description:
Consumption: Squeeze over everything from tacos to green mangos. Make into lemonade.
Julia's Rating: These tiny fruits are to die for. See benefit 2.

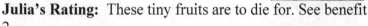

Name: *mamey* (*none*)
Description: rough, oval fruit with a pointy end. The peel is brown, like tree bark and the flesh salmon colored. That color is named *mamey* in Spanish.
Consumption: slice the long way, pry the peel away from the slice and bite into the flesh. Excellent in "shakes."
Julia's Rating: Heavenly and filling.

Name: *mango* (mango)
Description: yellow, green or gold skin. Ranges from almost tear drop shaped to mini-footballs.

Consumption: Eat slightly green with chili and limón or ripe any way you want. Try the different varieties, to see which ones you like best. Some varieties are *manila, ataulfo, criollo* and *petacón*. To prepare a bowl of cut mango cut down into it on both sides of the pit so that the knife just misses the side of the pit (see the photos). Next,

score the flesh both horizontally and vertically, cutting almost to the skin. Push up against the skin so that it pops inward forcing the flesh up. The cubes

will be sticking up like hair on a play dough toy. Slice them carefully off of the skin. There will still be some flesh on the pit. Peel the skin off and try your best to slice more of the fruit off.

Sometimes I give up and just use my teeth.
Julia's Rating: grrrreat!

Name: *maracuyá* (passion fruit) – see also *granadilla*
Description: like green ostrich eggs on a stem.

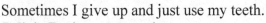

Consumption: Makes a delicious fruit "water." Slice in half. Scrape the flesh and seeds into a blender with a spoon. Puree with water and sugar. Strain the seeds out.
Julia's Rating: Refreshing.

Name: *níspero* (loquat)
Description: Slightly overgrown, fuzzy, yellow grapes
Consumption: peel or rub the skin to remove some of the fuzz. Spit out seeds.
Julia's Rating: The best. Eat them by the handful.

Name: *nances / nanches* (none)
Description: yellow, marble sized "eyeballs"
Consumption: Pop them in your mouth like grapes, then spit out the pits.
Julia's Rating: The smell knots my stomach. They're not going bad. They're supposed to smell like that. Rinsing reduces the smell.

Name: *naranja* (orange)
Description: orange or green
Consumption: Don't let their thin, tough, green peels fool you. They are better than what we have at home. Cut in half and squeeze for juice, or slice and eat.
Julia's Rating: More juicy than you can imagine. Best when in season.

Name: *papaya* (papaya)
Description: Like a pear-shaped, blotchy melon.
Consumption: Slice the long way, scrape out seeds and bite like a watermelon slice. Reportedly very healthy.
Julia's Rating: Yuck.

Name: *pinzán, guamúchil/huamúchil* (madras thorn)
Description: White cotton
Consumption: Pick the white cottony
material out of the pod. Pick or spit out
the seeds.
Julia's Rating: This tastes neat and is a
special part of being in Mexico. May cause gas.

Name: *pitaya* (wild cactus fruit)
Description: egg-sized, prickly, maroon fruits
Consumption: Cut off ends and slice, then peel like a
tuna (see below).
Julia's Rating: Wildly sweet, wild fruit. You *must* try
this, but you might not get a good one unless you can get it
ripe off of the plant.

Name: *plátano macho* (plantain)
Description: huge bananas
Consumption: Peel, cut into thick slices and fry. Good
with sweetened, condensed milk or with rice.
Julia's Rating: Take it or leave it, but it's fun to eat "fried
bananas."

Name: *plátano tabasco* (bananas)
Description: these are the ones sold in North America
Consumption: peel and eat.

Name: *plátano manzano* (bananas)
Description: tiny, chubby bananas a little bigger than
dominico
Consumption: peel and eat
Julia's Rating: I like these better than the ones we get in
the north.

Name: *plátano dominico* (bananas)
Description: tiny, chubby bananas a little smaller than *manzano*
Consumption: peel and eat.
Julia's Rating: I like these better than the ones we get in the north.

Name: *sandía* (watermelon)
Description: look the same as they do up north.
Consumption: Cut up just like at home or put chunks into the blender for an amazing *agua*.

Name: *toronja* (grapefruit)
Description: look just like the ones we get in the north
Consumption: Try them, they are sweet.
Julia's Rating: It's amazing what the right amount of time on the tree will do for a fruit! This was my "craving" when I was pregnant and nursing and my son developed a love for them as well.

Name: *tuna* (prickly pear)
Description: duck egg sized, light green with invisible thorns
Consumption: Hold with a dish towel to avoid the rare spine and cut the ends off, slit the skin, and peel. You can swallow the seeds (don't let them deter you from eating this cool, refreshing fruit).
Julia's Rating: Eat every day when they are in season. The thought of living without this fruit is enough to keep me in central Mexico!

Name: *zapote negro* (black sapodilla)
Description: green skin over soft
black flesh

Consumption: Peel, then mash the
black flesh. Top with lemon juice and a
tiny amount of honey. Eat with a spoon.
Julia's Rating: Refreshing and delicious.

If enjoying a variety of fresh fruits is important to you, you may want to live in Central or southern Mexico. The middle of the desert is not the best place for year round fruits. In Los Cabos, for example, the fruits are not nearly as plentiful and cost much more than in Cuernavaca. I doubt you'll ever find chicozapote, for example.

Note: I've included the names in Spanish that I know. Names differ from region to region and people from one region may not have heard the names from other regions. Find yourself a local friend who likes to share the wonders of Mexico and have them help you prepare and sample fruits. You will find so many people who want to share their special Mexican treats.

Benefit 5: Tacos

tacos al pastor

You will have many opportunities to eat tacos here. Tacos *al pastor* are strips of spiced pork loaded onto a vertical roaster. The meat is rotated in front of a huge gas flame. As the meat cooks, the sweating *taquero* cuts perfectly thin slices off of the roaster and a small piece of warm, juicy pineapple, mounted on the tip of the roasting bar. If you want your tacos *con todo* he will put finely chopped onions and cilantro onto them. You can add any of the selection of salsas available and squeeze some lime juice onto them.

A variety of salsas and fresh lime is the key to delicious tacos.

Tacos de barbacoa are also available. Despite what you may think based on their name, they are nothing like our barbeque. These are made of incredibly soft, steamed goat or sometimes mutton. Wait, before you take this off of your list, you have to try it. Pick your taco stand based on visible cleanliness. Order tacos *de maciza* (pronounced, mas-ee-sa) so that you will get the best meat and the least fat. You can also buy it by the kilo and take it home to enjoy with your whole family.

Tacos de cabeza are another steamed meat. This is literally the skinned head of the cow steamed above a salty soup called *consumé*. The *taquero* will select a piece of meat and chop it into tiny pieces on his chopping block. You can have these with onions, cilantro, lime, and salsa too. They are so soft and warm—perfect for a cooling evening. You will never have to see the head of the animal from which the meat was cut. I recommend that you ask for *de maciza* also because this is a less fatty part of the head. If you are feeling really adventurous you can have the nose (*trompa*), area that surrounds the eye (*ojo*), the tongue (*lengua*), the cheek (*cachete*), and I'm sure many more "parts." Make friends with your *taquero* and he will help you to try all the best tacos.

Of course, there is always the old standby, beef tacos (*de asada*). These are always good and perfect for the squeamish. Another good choice for the squeamish are *tacos de canasta* literally, "tacos in a basket" (a regional treat, not available everywhere). These are small, pre-made tacos loaded into a basket or cooler, all wrapped in cloth to keep warm. These have many different fillings, such as beans, chicken, potato, or *chorizo* (spicy sausage). Since they are small you can buy a number of them and try lots of different fillings. I like to choose beans in at least one of them to be sure I get extra protein. Here in Cuernavaca, people also sell tacos made with beef or chicken that contain Mexican rice right inside the taco. These are called *acorasados* and will fill you up.

> For other delicious traditional foods, see my article *Morelos's Exotic Foods for the Brave at Heart* at [http://home-sweet-mexico.com/expatriate-author-exoticfoods.html/]

If you move to a city different than Cuernavaca you will have to figure out what their regional tacos (and *tortas* or hot sandwiches) include. In Michoacan I have eaten *memelas* and *pambasos*. Guadalajara is famous for its *tortas ahogadas*, made of white bread with chicken inside, dipped in a pot of red sauce made with *chili guajillo*.

Benefit 6: *masa*

Traditional foods made with *masa*. *Tamales, sopes, huaraches*....

Benefit 7: Sun

It is always sunny here. Only typhoons and hurricanes can keep the sun away. Even during the rainy season, it only rains for an hour at most, then it clears back up, leaving the city newly refreshed. This is true for all of Mexico; you will rarely have one of those days that are gray, drizzly, and overcast, but you will have times when it pours down so hard, the streets run with inches of water. (In Los Cabos be ready for hurricanes.)

Benefit 8: Walking Lifestyle

There is a store in every neighborhood. You can easily walk to the store when your food stocks run low. You can buy staples such as milk, yogurt, tortillas and pop (to many Mexicans, this is a staple) as well as fresh baked bread, candy, and ice cream bars.

You can hang out in the *Zocalo*, eating corn on the cob. Some *zocalos* tend to have a circling movement with many walkers strolling together, while others have deeply shaded benches from which you can watch children playing, lovers kissing, old men chatting, and native women selling lovely handicrafts. Often you can catch a free concert. We have been treated to high quality, memorable

A large crowd gathers to listen to drummers in Tepoztlan's *zocalo*.

free concerts in Merida, Puebla, Oaxaca, and Palenque. We just moseyed down to the *Zocalo* and found ourselves drawn into wonderful music.

The excellent public transit all over Mexico frees you from bondage to a car. Walking around you stay strong, healthy, and in touch with life. While all my friends were getting fat back in the U.S. (I can get away with writing this because they all got bored with this book half way through the first edition.), I maintained the same weight. I was surprised when I went back to visit and saw how much bigger they all were than when I'd moved to Mexico. I think my walking lifestyle was as large of a help as the differences in our diets. (Oooo. That's another "bennie." It's easier to eat a healthy diet in Mexico.)

Benefit 9: Your Position of Prestige (if you are white)

Mexicans often surprise me with their racism and class-ism. Paleness is widely considered superior to dark skin. Female blondness induces stares and whistles from passing cars—yeah, I know, this is *not* a benefit. If you are a young woman, people will want to hang out with you, talk to you, buy your beers (see, it is a benefit), and ask you on dates. If you are a young man, girls will hug you, compliment you, practice their English with you, and giggle a lot. When you walk in the door to get a job, people will listen. If you are African-American or African-Canadian and reading this, I have to say, you will just have to test Mexico out for yourselves. Mexicans won't let their manners and hospitality be overshadowed by preference for paleness. They will still honor you as Americans or Canadians. English skills are highly valued here and will be your ticket in the door for many work opportunities, and even spontaneous friendships with people who want to practice their English or learn about the U.S.

As I have been beginning my career as an English teacher I have sometimes felt bad because it is so much easier for me to get a job as an English teacher than it is for Mexican teachers. I have never been to an English school where I was not instantly offered a position—whether or not I was offered an hourly rate I would accept is another story. If you choose to be an English teacher (more about that in the Teaching English section) you are in control of your options. You can choose the schools that pay the best, that have the smallest classes, that offer you the best hours, and that provide whatever benefits you find most important. If you are French Canadian you can also find plenty of opportunities to teach French.

Basically, coming from the United States or Canada automatically opens doors for us that will ease our paths into Mexico. I am always grateful to Mexico for the opportunities and acceptance that I have received here.

Benefit 10: Travel within Mexico

Mexico is a culturally and ecologically rich country. There are so many wonderful places to visit – all reachable via excellent long-distance bus service. My personal travel wish list includes: migrating hawks in Veracruz, the Copper Canyon, whale watching near Guerrero Negro and  Magdalena Bay, and the monarch butterflies in Michoacan again.

Does warm sun and sparkling water sound wonderful? See my free Morelos travel guide at [http://home-sweet-mexico.com/expatriate-author-articles.html/]

6 Working: Yes, It's A

Developing Country

When we first arrived in Cuernavaca I was discouraged to notice that the normal work week includes the better part of Saturday. I was frightened to see how my buying power had decreased. Suddenly, I was earning about $4 USD an hour, but only able to work about four to six hours per day as a teacher! With that I could live—and just barely, but I sure couldn't call the folks back home nor go out for dinner. Suddenly, buying contact lens solution and deodorant, which sell here at the same price or more than they do back home, became a serious budgeting matter. Let's see: fourteen dollars for disinfectant solution and eight for saline... that's... five and a half hours of work... as an English teacher, that's one full day. As time has gone by, I have increased my income. I have received permission to live and work in Mexico from immigration (see "Getting Documentation" on page 95) and found a stable place to work. I even receive benefits. But it doesn't happen over night and even when you do get to this stage, you will still have only a Mexican buying power (See "A Mexican Income" on page 94). For the young, growing a retirement fund is mostly impossible. The financial giant north of us looms large.

Teaching English

I think the most common and quickest way to find a job here in Mexico is as an English as a foreign language teacher. Some areas of Mexico are more into language studies than others and Cuernavaca has to be the hotbed of language study. Here, there is an English school, or bilingual daycare on every corner. Americans and Canadians come here to study Spanish and Mexicans living here study English, French, Italian, and German. Mexico City also has many language schools and language teachers there get paid more than in Cuernavaca. Queretaro is also a good city for teaching English due to the many international companies located there. Most large cities have language schools.

I am blessed in that I have an aptitude for teaching and really enjoy it. When I left the United States I left my life of field work on wild salmon preservation behind and have learned to be a teacher on the job. I have been lucky enough to teach at a professional school which is dedicated to offering classes taught with leading-edge teaching techniques. I have received training and opportunities to develop and advance.

If you are already a teacher, you are in even more luck than I was. If you go to a large-enough city you can find a bilingual school, where the various subject matters are taught in English. You can potentially teach high school chemistry, for example, in English, and get paid twice as much as the average English language teacher. With your master's you can teach at one of the universities and also receive a higher salary.

English teachers can work with students of all ages from pre-school through adults. Adult classes are offered in a variety of settings from universities, to private classes, to small language centers that focus exclusively on offering language classes to independent students just as aerobics classes are offered back in the States. The students don't get credentials, but if they learn enough English they can take an internationally recognized exam to prove their skill level. Most language centers also offer classes to large companies, called "*impresas*." In these cases the teacher is itinerant, traveling from company to company, offering on-site classes to engineers, administrative assistants, salesmen, etc. Teachers are paid by the hour in the classroom and don't receive payment for their prep time.

One of the potential limitations of teaching English is the schedule. Most adult English students have to work and therefore require their classes before and after work. English teachers generally work from 7 a.m. to about 9 or 10, then again from about 4 p.m. until 9 at night. If you can handle children's or high school classes, then you can work from 7 or 8 a.m. until about 2 p.m. Adult classes are generally preferred by foreigners because they don't require as much teaching technique. Also, adults tend to appreciate the value of having a native speaker and participate in stimulating dialog.

I have covered the topic of Teaching English in Mexico in the following series of articles published on Mexico Connect and subsequently in the articles section of my web site. How to Make Teaching in Mexico a Reality…

- Part 1: Making Plans and Gathering Documents

-

-

-

Uh-Oh, I Hate Teaching

You hate teaching? Well, you are not alone. What can you do if you don't want to teach? The first thing you will have to do is plan to live in a tourist area such as Los Cabos or Cancun. Here in Cuernavaca I have known people who didn't want to teach and either ended up teaching anyway, going home, or moving to tourist cities because they couldn't find jobs where they earned enough money outside of teaching.

In tourist places, business owners like to hire foreigners to fill positions where relations with the tourists are the main aspects of the job. Speaking English is more important than experience and a friend who lived in Los Cabos wrote[‡‡], "[T]hey will hire you with virtually no experience to do just about anything. Concierge, restaurant hostess, activities person at a hotel, or anything were you can be the front person for their business.... [One North American woman] came here and worked as a concierge and now ... is the sub-director of the hotel and head of guest services. I knew another girl who worked in a coffee

---

[‡‡] This was before the recession. It is now much harder to find a job in tourist areas, though the information remains basically true.

shop. There are also lots of foreigners working at the golf courses as cart drivers, caddies etc. and getting good money with tips. One [young woman] works in reservations at the golf course." It is important to be able to speak a little Spanish, too, as not all tourists speak English.

A Mexican Income

It is hard for me to include a comprehensive review of salaries here since they vary from city to city and job type to job type. I include here comparisons between Cuernavaca and Cabo San Lucas to try to give a comparison between a wealthy city and a tourist area. One way that you can learn about salaries is to get onto the web site of an international temporary job search agency, such as Manpower and see what salaries are listed in the city or field you are considering working in.

Generally, elementary school teachers earn between 4,000 and 8,000 pesos a month in Cuernavaca, which breaks down to about 35 pesos per hour. Elementary school teachers can earn even less sometimes as low as between 3,000 and 4,000 pesos a month. In Cabo San Lucas, which is a very touristy city, an elementary school English teacher can earn 120 pesos per hour. Teachers who teach adults are usually paid by the hour and work for either a language school or give private classes. Language schools in Cuernavaca pay anywhere from 30 pesos per hour up to 110. Schools that pay on the lower end of the pay scale are much more common than those that pay more. Schools never pay for the preparation time required to give good classes and often won't even pay for photocopies. The going rate for private classes in Cuernavaca is 100 to 150 pesos per hour, though many people charge as low as 60. In Cabo San Lucas a native speaker can earn up to 230 pesos per hour for private classes given to a group. For the few people with their masters in teaching, there are opportunities to work for universities, which pay at least 110 pesos per hour. Classes for *empresas* (companies) pay between 140 and 200 pesos per hour but require the teacher to travel to the company campus. It is important to keep in mind that because of commute time and peak demand hours, it is rare for a teacher to be able to give classes for more than 6 hours a day.

Administrative type positions in Cuernavaca usually pay between 4,000 and 6,000 pesos per month and may require work on Saturday. If sales are involved and commission paid, they can be as low as 2,000 to 3,000 pesos per month. In Cabo San Lucas activities representatives at a hotel earn about 8,000 pesos per month for a 6 day work week. Time share sales people earn 12,000 per month. Remember when comparing the salaries between Cuernavaca and Cabo San Lucas that tacos in Cuernavaca cost 5 pesos each and in Cabo San Lucas cost 10. While you can earn more in a tourist area, the cost of living is much higher.

Getting Documentation

Coming here as an employee of an international company is a good way to secure your ability to work. You won't have the many frightening months of finding and settling into a new job. You will know your salary and benefits. You won't have to give up your 401K and you will have help getting your work visa.

A precedent has been set by many North Americans of overstaying tourist visas and working under the table. This is still done, but I wouldn't recommend it—particularly if you live in a city that has its own immigration branch office. Here in Cuernavaca I have heard a couple of stories of inspection by Mexican immigration agents. Your overall success and stability warrant honest dealings. You deserve to travel internationally without wondering what kind of trouble awaits you at the border and Mexico deserves the respect and honesty due any country.

Formerly, most people, including myself, have entered Mexico on a tourist visa. I never considered going to the Mexican Consulate where I lived in the U.S. to ask them for information on working in Mexico prior to coming here. Now we are going to have to change our ways. Mexican immigration laws are similar to those of the U.S. and Canada, and in fact, the temporary residence visa can only be applied for from your home country (more on the new immigration laws on page 102). To enter Mexico as a tourist, all you need is your passport. As you are entering Mexico, you will pass through an immigration checkpoint where an official will ask you how long you are staying. Ask for the maximum of six months, which will give you time to get settled and look for a job if you need or want one. Once you are in Mexico, if you decide to stay longer than your visitor visa allows and you want to work, you can apply for the permanent residence visa. This is the new version of the "non-immigrant visitor with 'lucrative' (that word kills me) activities" (*No Inmigrante Visitante con actividades lucrativas*) visa.

This requires patience and diligence as well as the payment of some fees, but is not a difficult process—especially if you compare your experience with that of Mexicans who want to live and work in the US! The immigration office here in Cuernavaca is much more comfortable then any U.S. consulate I've yet been into. My waiting time has varied from 15 minutes to two hours—which sure beats the eight hour ordeal with no food or water the United States immigration office in Ciudad Juarez put us through. My fees included a first time processing fee of under 400 pesos (in 2001) and a yearly fee of 2,356 pesos (for 2012). This yearly fee seems to increase by about 150 pesos a year.

In order to get your visa (the kind that allows you to work in Mexico), you must have an employer that is willing to write a letter to immigration stating that they would like to hire you. Some employers are not willing to do this. They enjoy the benefit to themselves of not paying taxes on your income and don't want immigration to see their tax files (which is necessary for an employer who wishes to "help" you get your work visa)—which is fine, but doesn't help you with your long term stability. Once you find an employer that doesn't mind hiring you and documenting you with immigration, they still won't want to pay your fees. You can make it clear to them that all you want help with is the documentation and that you will be responsible for your own fees.

See "Getting Your Immigration Documents" on page 102 for how-to information on getting your visa.

Paying Taxes

Once you have your visa, you will have to apply for two numbers from the Mexican government so that you can pay your taxes. One is your *CURP* (see "Getting Your RFC and CURP" on page 122), an individual number which applies only to you, which is like your Social

Security Number, if you are from the United States or your Social Insurance Number if you are from Canada. The second is your *RFC* (a tax payer ID number), which is used when charging your employer for your work and in paying your taxes. Ask the people at immigration and at your school for information on where and how to get these documents (and see below).

Paying your taxes requires more responsibility on your part than it did back home. Here your employer will withhold only part of your taxes due every month. You will have to make monthly trips to a bank to pay the other part, then make a yearly declaration before April 30th, at which time you will find out if you can receive a refund of some of your taxes paid. In order to reduce your monthly tax expenditures, you can collect *facturas*, which are special receipts issued by businesses that show your *RFC*. You can ask for *facturas* for things that are related to your job and for gas and other expenses. Every month you list the expenses documented by these *facturas* to reduce the amount of tax you owe.

Hacienda, or *SAT*, the government agency responsible for charging you taxes, will help you to get your *RFC* and explain to you how to pay your taxes and the guidelines for *facturas*. Most Mexicans seem either to pay an accountant or avoid paying taxes, but I have been successful at completing all of my tax responsibilities by myself. The *SAT* office here in Cuernavaca has been a dream. They have people at help desks who explain every step to you— often one step at a time, so remember that patience is more than a virtue….

7 How To Do Paperwork in

Mexico

The Basics

Whenever you go to do any official paperwork, these are the basic documents that you almost always must have with you.

1. **Your passport or Mexican immigration document** as a photo ID.
2. **A proof of address** (*comprobante de domicilio*). This is a <u>recent</u> telephone, electric, or water bill or something like a bank statement mailed to your house. Surprisingly enough, your name does not have to appear with the address, but the address must be exactly the same as the one that you are giving for the paperwork and must match the one on your ID card. These are required for almost every

official transaction. I've learned through experience that they are almost always necessary so I bring it even if I'm not told that one will be necessary. Most of the time I'm very glad that I did, because they end up asking for it.

3. A *croquis*. This is **a map showing the location of your house** in relationship to the nearest cross streets[§§]. These are required for paperwork that may involve someone coming to you house, such as for a telephone installation, official tax documents, or a delivery. The maps (created by you) are needed because street names are often painted over, lost, or otherwise impossible to read. With a *croquis* anyone looking for your house can use the nearest cross streets as a reference.

4. A set of **photos** of yourself. These are required for paperwork that will somehow identify you, such as an ID card for your work or getting a permit of some kind. There are all different sizes of photos and it never seems to fail that if you have an extra one of any size, the next time you need photos a different size will be required. If you have the correct size, it'll be in color and sure enough, black and white will be required. Photo sizes are standard, so you just have to remember the key word for the particular size requested, such as *infantil*, and ask for that size from the photo shop where you go to get them taken. Don't forget to determine

---

[§§] I'm amazed at how much mapping has improved since we moved to Mexico. I used to have to draw these by hand, but nowadays you can print out a satellite image of your house and nearby streets!

if they should be in color or black and white
before you go to the photo studio. Be at peace
with going to get your photo taken. It's all part
of the process.

It is wise to come with a set of two photocopies of the
documents listed in numbers 1 through 3 above. Often the
official person processing whatever documents you are
getting will need to keep copies and they never make the
copies for you. Instead, they send you back out to the street
to find a stationary store and get them yourself. It's easier
to have the photo copies already made. If you don't use
them, keep them in an accessible place for future use.

Another thing you should be aware of when doing
paperwork in Mexico is that if you have to pay fees for
whatever you are doing, you sometimes have to go to the
bank with a special form. The special form is usually
provided by the people with whom you are doing the
paperwork and is increasingly available online to print
from home. Government offices can't accept payments on
site. Instead, people pay at a bank of their choice.
Basically, the idea is simple: you take a special form to the
bank and pay there, where they stamp a copy of the form
for you as proof that you have paid, which you then turn in
to the proper authorities. In practice, it's a little more
complicated than that.

Don't be surprised if you have to make two or three
trips to get something done. When you are expecting a
simple, one-step, streamlined experience you might feel as
if doing things in Mexico is "hard." It's really not so bad as
long as you have planned ahead for enough time and
energy.

Getting Your Immigration Documents

In order to live in Mexico you need to get a visa from the *Instituto Nacional de Migración* (INM, National Immigration Institute). According to *El Universal* on April 29, 2011, a new immigration law was passed, protecting the rights of immigrants and controlling the flow of immigration to and from Mexico.

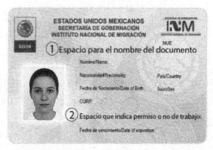

New post-November visa card
source: http://www.visasmex.com

Additionally, this legislation substitutes more than 30 immigration classifications... with only three:

Visitor (*Visitante*) – immigration status granted to foreigners who will remain within Mexico for short time spans for the purpose of tourism or business; visitors with permission to receive payments on stays of less than 180 days; and visitors or workers in the border regions.

Temporary Resident (*Residente Temporal*) – granted to foreigners wishing to stay in Mexico for less than four years. Included in this category are students, who can remain in Mexico for the duration of their studies.

And **Permanent Resident** (*Residente Permanente*) – granted to foreigners wishing to reside in Mexico indefinitely [including to live with] family.

(You can see the original article in Spanish http://www.eluniversal.com.mx/notas/767674.html)

Many people have been saying that one of the goals of the new law was to simplify the immigration process, and, at least on paper, it has done that. Between April 2011 and November 8, 2012, people were working behind the scenes to publish the regulations for this new law.

Old style FM3 booklet

I've combed through the regulations to the best of my limited ability and this section summarizes the main points that will be important to the majority of my readers. I am NOT an immigration lawyer and this section of the book should only be used for a general idea of what the new rules are. It is in no way to be taken as legal advice or guidance. The guidelines for immigration documentation and procedures *(LINEAMIENTOS para trámites y procedimientos migratorios)* and general guidelines for issuance of visas by the Ministries of the Interior and Foreign Affairs *(LINEAMIENTOS generales para la expedición de visas que emiten las secretarías de Gobernación y de Relaciones Exteriores)* are found on line at http://dof.gob.mx/nota_detalle.php?codigo=5276967&fecha=08/11/2012 and http://dof.gob.mx/nota_detalle.php?codigo=5276966&fecha=08/11/2012 and I encourage you to comb through them yourself if you can read Spanish. Of course, there is no substitute for going to the embassy or consulate nearest you and finding out for which type of visa you should apply based on your particular circumstances and then getting the list of requirements.

In the past there have been differences in the ways that each of the various immigration offices and consulates process visas. In previous editions of this book I recommended that once you started your process at one office you should finish it there, because each individual entity that processes immigration applications interpreted the law and established procedures for their own office. The differences between offices were not large, but they made a difference in exactly what you needed to turn in with your application such as whether or you need black and white or color photos, and the forms that you filled out. The variations from office to office have been increasingly ironed out by INM as they develop a streamlined process using a web-based application system. The guidelines published November 8, 2012, may have finally put these variations to rest, but only experience will tell.

It is probably still a wise idea to ask the exact procedures established by the consulate/immigration office through which *you* will be getting *your* visa. Keep in mind that if you talk to another expat who already has

| Immigration Hotline |
| 01-800-004-6264 |
| Available 24/7 |
| *Sí, se habla inglés.* |
| (Yes, English is spoken.) |

their visa and they describe a procedure different to the one you are experiencing you shouldn't be alarmed. This does not mean that the procedures are random. Each office requires about the same things because they are all following the law. It does mean that you must get the requirements *in person*, straight from the horse's mouth.

Below I include a simplified summary of the main aspects of the three major categories of visas for Mexico to help you get a general idea of which visa you might apply for and some of the requirements you would have to satisfy.

Visitor [*Visitante*] Visa

The Visitor visa (formerly the FMM, FMT or Tourist Visa) can be valid for up to 180 days, if you request it, and is issued to U.S. and Canadian citizens at any border crossing or on the airplane if you are flying into Mexico. It has been common practice to enter Mexico as a tourist, requesting the maximum of 180 days, then go to an INM office and apply for a visa that will allow you to live in Mexico. Now you should contact the Mexican embassy or consulate nearest your home before making any solid plans. As a first time applicant you are only allowed to apply for a permanent residence and not a temporary residence visa from within Mexico and must be sure you meet the requirements as described in the following section.

Temporary Resident [*Residente Temporal*] and Permanent Resident [*Residente Permanente*] Visas

The Temporary Resident visa is similar to what were formerly the Non-Immigrant (FM3) and the Immigrant (FM2) visas. The Permanent Resident visa is most similar to what was called the Immigrant visa. Please keep in mind that this section is just a summary I created by reading the guidelines posted by INM. This chart will give you an idea of what you may prefer, but **make sure you get the most current information <u>directly</u> from INM, as it relates to your personal context**.

Temporary Resident	Permanent Resident
For those who wish to live in Mexico for more than 180 days and no more than four years. Note: This visa can be extended or lead to a permanent residence visa. If this is your desire, be sure to check with the officials about what will be involved.	For those who wish to live in Mexico indefinitely. Note: foreigners who are spouses, or common-law partners of Mexican citizens or of holders of permanent residence visas cannot hold permanent residence visas and must apply for temporary residence***.
Apply from: Apply from your home 3country. A change of status from an existing FM3 or FM2 can be made from within Mexico.	**Apply from:** Within Mexico or your home country.

Continued....

*** I can't find anywhere where it talks about couples who want to immigrate to Mexico together, so double check that this is true.

Mexico: The Trick is Living Here 3rd edition
available on www.home-sweet-mexico.com
106

Temporary Resident	Permanent Resident
Requirements:	**Requirements:**
For retired or Pensioners:	For retired or Pensioners:
1. Original and copy of investments or bank accounts showing proof of an average monthly income over the previous 12 months equal to 20,000 days of the current minimum salary (see more <u>on page 112</u>) in Mexico City, or	1. Original and copy of investments or bank accounts showing proof of an average monthly income over the previous 12 months equal to 25,000 days of the current minimum salary (see more <u>on page 112</u>) in Mexico City, or
2. Original and copy of documents proving that the applicant has a job or pension providing monthly income – free of encumbrances - equal to 400 days of the current minimum salary in Mexico City, during the previous six months.	2. Original and copy of documents proving that the applicant has a pension providing monthly income – free of encumbrances - equal to 500 days of the current minimum salary in Mexico City, during the previous six months.

Continued….

Temporary Resident	Permanent Resident
Family Members of a Mexican citizen or of someone who holds a <u>temporary</u> visa:	For family of Mexican Citizens:
1. You must prove economic solvency (I'm not sure if it's the holder of the visa or the applicant…).	1. Original and copy of documents proving the relationship (for example, spouse, common law spouse, sister, parent, etc.) as appropriate.
2. Original and copy of investments or bank accounts showing proof of an average monthly income over the previous 6 months equal to 300 days of the current minimum salary in Mexico City, or	2. Proof of economic solvency to maintain the family member during his or her stay in Mexico. With Original and copy of investments or bank accounts showing proof of an average monthly income over the previous 6 months equal to 300 days of the current minimum salary in Mexico City, or

Continued….

Temporary Resident	Permanent Resident
3. Original and copy of documents proving that the applicant has a job or pension providing monthly income – free of encumbrances - equal to 100 days of the current minimum salary in Mexico City, during the previous six months.	3. Original and copy of documents proving that the applicant has a job or pension providing monthly income – free of encumbrances - equal to 100 days of the current minimum salary in Mexico City, during the previous six months.
Family Members of a Mexican citizen or of someone who holds a <u>permanent</u> residence visa: 1. You must prove economic solvency the same as for holders of temporary residence visas (above).	Points System: 1. Will be published in the official Federal Journal [*el Diario Oficial de la Federación*].
Obligations:	**Obligations**:
To notify the National Institute of Immigration about any change of status, i.e. change of marital status, nationality, change of address, employer etc. The notification must be made within 90 calendar days of the change.	To notify the National Institute of Immigration about any change of status, i.e. change of marital status, nationality, change of address, employer etc. The notification must be made within 90 calendar days of the change.

Temporary Resident	Permanent Resident
Allows Employment:	**Allows Employment:**
Yes, for adults, if the application is accompanied by an offer of employment or if the forthcoming jobs quota list allows it. The quota list will be published in the official Federal Journal [*el Diario Oficial de la Federación*].	Yes, for adults.
Entries and Exits from Mexico:	**Entries and Exits from Mexico:**
When you first arrive with your visa, you will be allowed only one entry. Once you have completed the paperwork for your residence card (you have 90 days) multiple entries and exits will be allowed.	When you first arrive with your visa, you will be allowed only one entry. Once you have completed the paperwork for your residence card (you have 90 days) multiple entries and exits will be allowed.
Duration:	**Duration:**
May have duration of one to four years, depending on the request of the applicant. In the case of an offer of employment, the expiry of the visa will coincide with the term of work and can be extended.	This visa does not expire as long as you live in Mexico. If you need to live outside of Mexico for an extended period of time, check with the immigration office how long you can remain away and still maintain it.

Temporary Resident	Permanent Resident
Renewal: Can be renewed. When a renewal is requested based on an offer of employment, a letter from the employer on letterhead specifying the term of work is required.	**Renewal:** Does not need to be renewed.
Fee: $3,130 for one year (~$242 USD) $4,690 for two years (~$362 USD) $5,940 for three years (~$458 USD) $7,040 for four years (~$543 USD)	**Fee:** $3,815 (~$294 USD)
Adapted from the Guidelines published November 8, 2012 http://dof.gob.mx/nota_detalle.php?codigo=5276967&fecha=08/11/2012 and http://dof.gob.mx/nota_detalle.php?codigo=5276966&fecha=08/11/2012	

Minimum Salary

The pensioner or retired person must prove economic solvency in amounts expressed as multiples of the minimum salary. These are subject to change, but the chart below will get you started.

Minimum Salary as of January 1, 2012	Required Multiple	Amount in Pesos	Approximate Amount in U.S. dollars*
$62.33 pesos	400	$24,932	$1,870
$62.33 pesos	500	$31,165	$2,338
$62.33 pesos	20,000	$1,246,600	$93,518
$62.33 pesos	25,000	$1,558,250	$116,898

*Assuming an exchange rate of 13.33

Minimum Salaries
(Salarios Minimos) are posted on the SAT web site, and are subject to change. You can check for the current ones here.
[http://www.sat.gob.mx/sitio_internet/asistencia_contribuyente/informacion_f recuente/salarios_minimos/] Note: The minimum salary used for the purposes of visas is the one for *Distrito Federal*, which is Area "A."

To find out the value of Mexican pesos in your own currency go to a converter such as http://www.xe.com/ucc/

Changing from Temporary Resident to Permanent Resident

The guidelines specify that the holder of a temporary residence visa will be able to apply to become a permanent resident based on the points system, being a pensioner or retired person with sufficient funds (investments or bank accounts over 20,000 times the minimum salary for the previous 12 months, or monthly pension of 500 minimum salary days over the last 6 months), or after being a temporary resident for four years. In the case of the application being based on four years with a temporary residence visa, the application must specify that this is the reason.

The required monthly income for a temporary residence visa is approximately $500 USD less than that of the permanent residence visa therefore I expect that some people will choose this route. Of course, you must plan ahead for the greater fee(s) and the subsequent fee for the application for the permanent residence visa, but if your monthly income is limited you'll have to do what you have to do. Double check with the officials to be sure you'll be able to apply for a permanent residence visa after four years and what that will entail. Don't make any assumptions about it.

Changing from FM2 and FM3 to Permanent Resident

If you have been in Mexico with an FM2 or FM3, you will be brought into the new system upon renewal. If you wish to apply for permanent residence, the time on a FM3 does not count toward the four years required. Time on a FM2, on the other hand, does count towards permanent

Mexico: The Trick is Living Here 3rd edition
available on www.home-sweet-mexico.com
113

residence. This doesn't surprise me because that was one of the main differences between the two visas when the older system was in effect.

Bravely Begin Your Paperwork

Your immigration office will give you a checklist of documents required for your application packet. Sometimes the person helping you wants to just give you the list and send you on your way. Ask them some questions about the items you must bring and **take notes**. The documents may include letters in Spanish from you to immigration officials. The person at the desk can help you with general wording for the letters. There are standard wordings that Mexicans know and we northerners would never dream of, so bring a pen and paper.

All of the forms are right up on the internet. Ask at the immigration office which would be the correct form for you. The names of the forms are wordy, so I would recommend writing it down word for word when they tell you which one(s). The main web page for the *Instituto Nacional de Migración* (INM, National Immigration Institute) is http://www.inm.gob.mx/[†††]. From the home page you click on "*Trámites y Servicios*" then on "*Migrantes*" next on "*paso a paso ingresa tu trámite.*" [‡‡‡] This page gives you a choice of the type of visa you would like to process. Try clicking on the "English" link at the top right of the page. (As of January 2013, the new information has not yet been translated into English but INM is

---

[†††] If you have trouble viewing the text on the web site, try a different web browser, such as Internet Explorer.

[‡‡‡] I apologize if these instructions become outdated. INM is really working to streamline the visa application and renewal process and consequently the rate of change on this web site is astounding.

frequently updating and changing their web site and I'm sure it won't be long before they have some of the pages translated into English.) Deactivate any pop up blockers you may have so that you can **write down the control number**, which pops up after you have submitted your form.

Please see the section "Links for Visa Information in Mexico" in the companion *Useful Links* that you downloaded along with this e-book. Those links take you to immigration and consulate web sites that will tell you what you need to know without the danger of transmitting any inaccuracies in this text. Even after carefully reading the information you will have to go to the office in which you will process your visa application and **get specific instructions from the personnel there**.

As you are embarking on your immigration paperwork journey, it will probably be encouraging for you to know that there has been a solid push for paperwork reduction and processes streamlining that will result in a better and better experience for immigrants. For example, you no longer have to stop at the immigration console in the airport to get your document stamped. The processing times for visa applications have been reduced to near two weeks and there is much more information available on line. You can even check the status of your paperwork on a tracking web site (not that you'll know what the steps actually mean, and if you really need to know you'll have to go in to the office to ask in person).

If you are going to process your permanent residence visa application inside of Mexico, you should prepare the necessary supporting documents before you arrive in Mexico. Following are the documents that you <u>may</u> need in order to get your permanent residence visa (I've included documents required by a variety of visa applicants):

- Passport (and photo copy/ies of all the pages)
- marriage and divorce certificates (depending on your circumstances) with Apostilles (see section on Apostilles below)
- college degree with Apostille
- college transcripts with Apostille
- birth certificate
- recent bank statements with Apostille
- letter from an employer (if applicable)
- photos of yourself – of course you can easily get these in Mexico if that is where you are applying (ask the size and view required).

Some of these documents will need to be apostilled then translated by an *official* Mexican certified translator once you are in Mexico.

Apostilles

An apostille is an authentication of official documents by your state government for international use. The apostilling (U.S.)/legalizing (U.K.) process involves two steps. The part that is called apostilling/legalizing is actually the second step in the two-part process. Your state government office can tell you what you will need to do in order to get your apostilles. See the box to the right to go directly to the correct institution in the U.S., Canada, or the

U.K.. **Do this before you head to Mexico**, or your lucky mother/brother/best friend will be doing it for you and Fed Ex-ing your documents to you.

U.S. and U.K.

For those of you in the U.S. or U.K. the steps are the following:

Step 1: get a **notarized** copy of the document. (Notaries in the U.S. can be found at banks, credit unions, and lawyers offices, among other places.)

Step 2: find out how your state processes requests for apostilles by checking their web site or calling the **apostille** office and get it done (allow a couple weeks and plan for a small fee for processing). (See the Useful Links!)

Canada

For those of you in Canada, you must go through a slightly different process called authenticating:

Step 1: Unless you are sending the original, get a photocopy notarized by a Canadian notary or commissioner of oaths.

Step 2: Send the documents to Foreign Affairs and International Trade Canada in Ottawa.

Step 3: Have the documents certified by the Mexican Embassy in Ottawa or the consulate that has jurisdiction over the region in which the documents were produced.

If you are applying from inside of Mexico, some of your documents in English will have to be translated by a local, certified translator. Immigration will give you phone numbers of the certified translators in your area. Only use translators from this list. There will be a cost for this service, but it is something you will have to pay for once you are in Mexico because only some translators are certified to translate documents for immigration. It must be *official*!

If in doubt about whether or not you will use a certain document, get an apostille for it. I recommend doing birth certificates, adoption papers, diplomas and/or transcripts from school, marriage certificates, divorce papers, and any other type of document that proves something vital about you or your family. There is a cost for international authentication, but *don't be tempted to skimp*. Even if you don't need a particular document for your visa application, you may need it in the future for some other reason. Once you are in Mexico and earning in pesos you definitely won't want the cost and stress of getting it done from thousands of miles away. You can also get documents notarized and apostilled at the Embassy or one of the consulates for $50 a document by requesting an appointment with the "Notarial Service." Again, I really recommend that you just bite the bullet and get it done before you move. If you need them, you'll be glad that you have the documents.

Once you have gathered all of your documents and gotten them apostilled/authenticated/legalized you will already be half way done with your application for immigration. It's really not as hard as it seems when you first get started.

Special Information on Applying for a Visa within Mexico

One Spanish word you need to know for this and other official processes is *cotejar* or *para cotejo*. This is similar to what we call "notarization." Often you need to bring one or two copies *para cotejo*. This means you bring the original document and the required number of copies to the official office. The official will go through them page by page and stamp the copies as the same as the original. You will keep your original and they will keep copies that they are sure are exactly the same as the original. Often, one of the copies is for you to keep in your records.

In the "old" days the government office would tell you which forms to use (the number of the form were specified after the letters "SAT": *forma SAT-#* on your checklist) and you would purchase these at a special stationery store. I'm including this here just in case they are still used in some smaller towns. For some official processes handwritten forms are not accepted and you have to type these out yourself or pay someone at a stationery store with a typewriter to do it. This is Mexico: remember there are no self-serve typewriters. I use one at my school so that I don't have to pay. Probably, the fee isn't very much and may be worth it just to reduce stress and time. I just have this thing about doing things myself (That's how we are in the Pacific Northwest—In Washington and British Columbia we even pump our own gas!). Anyway, the Cuernavaca office of immigration has always filled out my forms for me once I buy them and bring them with me. The checklist says *en blanco*, which means blank forms. You turn the blank forms in with your initial packet of information.

When your request for documentation has been approved, you will go to the office for the filled out forms[§§§], take them to a bank, and return to the office with your forms stamped "paid." Then the immigration officer will give you your paperwork. Once you have all of your

---

[§§§] I can't believe it but the new web-based forms will soon make this history. I'm almost nostalgic. What will expats do without all the character building practice at being patient?

official paperwork signed and translated by the proper authorities, getting your visa is just a matter of going around and around and around gathering everything you need, like special photos, letters, etc.

After turning in the complete packet of paperwork, you should allow at least three times as much time for the processing of your paperwork than they promise you. In Cuernavaca, they always tell me that it will take two weeks, but it seems to take about three months from the time I turn in your paperwork to the time I can come pay my fees and pick up the official identification card. When doing paperwork in Mexico, patience is not just a virtue it is the only survival tool which can lead to success.

Permission to Bring Your Household Items

If you plan on moving your personal belongings across the border and into Mexico, in addition to getting the visa, you will need to get permission to bring your "stuff." This permission is called a *menaje de casa* and it requires great feats in organization. Some consulates/immigration offices process the visa and *menaje de casa* at the same time while others do it in a two-step process.

When you make your initial inquiries about the visa, tell them that you would like to move your household items and ask them how and when you should apply for this permission. Also, ask them about the rules that you will have to follow after receiving the *menaje de casa*. There is a time limit to how long you will have to move your household items into Mexico and you'll need to know the specific time requirements established by the office through which you process the document. Likely, it will coincide with the 90 days you have to arrive in Mexico with your visa, but you should ask just to be sure.

Mexico: The Trick is Living Here 3rd edition
available on www.home-sweet-mexico.com
120

Most people who have moved their things to Mexico say that using a professional moving service is the best option, due to the rules about what individual people can bring across the border. Please also see the section "Links for Information on Moving Household Items to Mexico" in the companion *Useful Links*. These links give you access to lots of information that will be invaluable in preparing your "*menaje de casa*" and deciding if you will use a professional moving service or not.

Tips for the Visa Process

Finally, keep in mind that the key to a successful and pleasant experience at your immigration office is patience (especially if you do your paperwork from inside Mexico). Bring a good book and a snack with you. Bring extra sets of copies for everything. Be ready to spend all day. Be ready to run out to the stationary store or bank. Be ready to come back the next day. Don't expect your documents to be returned to you when they say they will be. Greet the person attending you warmly. Ask a lot of questions and take notes (because they often forget to tell you that you will need something, then when you get there without it, they ask you to come back the next day to give it to them). Most importantly, start the process early, especially if you will be traveling and will need your documents done by a particular date. Though you can get a special permission to travel while your documents are in processing, why put yourself through this extra step if you can prevent it? Remember, *you* may be in a rush, but *they* aren't.

Once I was in my immigration office and a European woman was told that her document wasn't quite ready yet. "What?" She demanded in Spanish. "You said 1:00 today. It's 1:20. I don't understand why my document isn't

Mexico: The Trick is Living Here 3rd edition
available on www.home-sweet-mexico.com
121

ready." I almost burst out laughing right there. My experience has been that my documents are ready *weeks* after they say they will be. It would never have occurred to me to expect them to be ready at a particular time of day! On the other hand, I've heard from others that at their immigration offices and consulates the process goes quickly, smoothly and is done in a matter of days!

Getting Your RFC and CURP

You will get your *RFC* (*Registro Federal de Contribuyentes*) from SAT (*Secretaria de Hacienda*, the branch of government that collects taxes). They can give you both your *RFC* and *CURP* (*Clave Única de Registro de Población* / unique population registry code) if you show up with your visa (including the text that gives you permission to work) and a proof of address as explained in "The Basics" on page 99 . You can supposedly save time by preregistering on the internet, but since you have to go into a SAT office to complete the registration you might as well just let them walk you through the process. Offices often provide computers to complete the new-fangled web-based forms because not all households in Mexico have computers.

If you aren't going to pay taxes and need your *CURP* for something else, you can get it from the nearest *Registro Civil* (civil registry office). To find the one nearest you, there is a link to a directory on this government page (in English, imagine! You are so spoiled. When I moved to Mexico, there weren't useful web pages – let alone in English!):
http://www.gobernacion.gob.mx/en_mx/SEGOB/Consulta

_tu_CURP_. Bring your immigration document with you as official photo identification.

Getting Your Mexican Driver's License

You can drive in Mexico with a current license from a foreign country, but if you'd like to get a Mexican license, they will be happy to take your money. Non-resident Canadians may also need to get a Mexican driver's license. I chose to get one because it seemed that it would be easier to deal with police officers if I just had the normal thing that most Mexicans have. Go to the municipal transportation office (*transito municipal*) in your city and bring with you your immigration documentation, your driver's license from your home country, a proof of address (see The Basics on page 99), and some money.

Licenses are issued for one year, five years, or ten years. You pay the corresponding fee and fill out the forms provided. You will be putting down your *blood type*, so make sure you know that before you come. Gee, do they have a lot of car accidents in Mexico? In Los Cabos you can get your license for more than one year, but in Cuernavaca, even if you live and work here, foreigners are only allowed to get 1 year driver's licenses and they always expire in December even if you get your in November. Cha-ching (cash register noise).

Each city will have slight variations on the rules for getting a driver's license, so even though you've read this section of the book, you'll still have to go to the municipal transportation office (*transito municipal*) in your city and find out how to get yours. First ask how to get to *transito municipal*, then inside ask for *placas y licensias* (license plates and driver's licenses). In Cuernavaca, they have their computers set up with little electronic cameras, so you don't have to bring photos with you. This may not be true in the more "Podunk" areas of Mexico, so you may need to take an initial scouting trip to find out ahead of time if you need photos. In Mexico City you can go to a *Módulo de Licencia y Control Vehicular* [Office of Licensing and Vehicle Control], but I recommend using one of the conveniently located *Centros de Servicio de la Tesorería* [Treasury Service Centers] found in grocery stores in almost every part of the city. These are similar to the Canadian vehicle licensing and insurance service desks open for extended hours in grocery stores. You can pay the fees and do the paperwork for your license in less than thirty minutes, enjoying the personalized assistance of a real person. The customer service representatives will help you and can answer your questions about a variety of transactions. Here is the link to the page about them, from there you can click on a link that shows the various locations

http://www.080.df.gob.mx/tramites/importante/centro_serv icio_01.html

A friend of mine had a funny experience when she got her Mexican driver's license in Los Cabos. Unlike in many other places in Mexico, in Los Cabos you actually have to show documentation proving your blood type. She knew her blood type, but didn't have any documentation to prove it. It was something she'd known since her youth in Canada. Anyway, the person said that it was not enough that she knew her blood type. She would have to take the test. No, not a blood type test, the written driving test! Well, so there she was with the driver's test in front of her, but she couldn't read Spanish well at the time, so they told her that her husband's uncle, who had accompanied her could help her. Uncle Roberto didn't know some of the answers and soon about five men were helping Uncle Roberto take her test! She never even got a chance to fully read any of the questions because her team of impromptu assistants was blurting out the answers before she could stumble through the Spanish. The public servant watched this entire process then granted my friend her license, still without showing proof of her blood type.

My friend's experience is unusual in that she actually saw the test. Most foreigners who go to get their driver's license are never given a test as long as they have a valid driver's license from another country. Don't worry about studying before you go, just take your current foreign driver's license. If you find out you do have to study for the test, cram for a night and go back the next day.

Mexico: The Trick is Living Here 3rd edition
available on www.home-sweet-mexico.com
125

8 Passport Renewal and

Citizenship for Children

Citizenship for Children Born in Mexico to Canadian Citizens

If you or your spouse are Canadian citizens and your child is the first generation born outside of Canada (as of April 17, 2009), that child automatically acquired Canadian citizenship at birth[****]. (To learn more about the new

---

[****] In this section I include a number of links. I keep *Mexico: The Trick is Living Here* up to date, but the rate of change to web sites is quite rapid and links soon become "broken." If you find there are broken links, don't be dismayed, Canadian government web sites are always very user-friendly and an internet search using the key words included in this section will get you to the correct web pages.

citizenship rules which came into effect April 17, 2009, see the Useful Links companion to this book.) In order to be able to prove this citizenship you can apply for a citizenship certificate from Citizenship and Immigration Canada. As of October 2012, the fee is $75 Canadian dollars.

The CIC web site (http://www.cic.gc.ca/english/citizenship/proof.asp) describes citizenship certificates this way:

- A Canadian citizenship certificate is a document that proves that a person is a Canadian citizen.
- The citizenship certificate is an 8½ x 11 paper size certificate that contains:
  - your certificate number
  - your Unique Client Identifier
  - your name
  - your date of birth
  - your gender
  - your effective date of Canadian citizenship
- **A citizenship certificate is not a travel document. Any Canadian citizen wanting to travel outside Canada should <u>obtain a Canadian passport</u>.** [see: http://www.ppt.gc.ca/cdn/index.aspx?lang=eng]

The Embassy of Canada in Mexico City requires the following documents in addition to the Application for a Citizenship Certificate from Outside Canada:

1. a notarized copy of a document proving that one or both of the parents was a Canadian citizen when the child was born (citizenship card or Canadian birth certificate);
2. each parent should submit a notarized copy of one piece of **valid** personal identification (i.e. a passport, driver's license...); and
3. original birth certificate of the child which lists the parents (issued by government authorities in the country where the child was born), with an official and certified translation* into English or French.

*To see a list of translators organized by location, click on the link "official and certified translation" or go to [http://www.canadainternational.gc.ca/mexico-mexique/consul/trans-trad.aspx]

The embassy also provides the following warning:

- Citizenship applications submitted at the Embassy are forwarded to the Registrar of Canadian Citizenship in Sydney, Nova Scotia, Canada. Please be informed that the processing time for Canadian Citizenship Certificate applications is approximately 12 months.

I summarize the requirements in this section, but it is imperative that **you read the appropriate web sites yourself and ask questions if needed**. It is also imperative that you clear your calendar for a couple of weeks. This will be a full time job for a little while. To get started, download the application for the citizenship certificate from the Canadian Embassy in Canada's web site at http://www.canadainternational.gc.ca/mexico-mexique/consul/citizenship-citoyennete.aspx. Since it can take up to a year to get the Canadian Citizenship Certificate (CCC) and you can't get a passport without one, your travel may be restricted. Read the information on the Passports page of the Embassy of Canada in Mexico City so that you can plan accordingly. Under some circumstances it is possible to apply for both a CCC and a passport at the same time, but the trip must be "justified." See http://www.canadainternational.gc.ca/mexico-mexique/consul/ppt.aspx.

Confused? Here's a checklist you can use to stay focused.

Your New-Born Canadian's CCC and Passport in 9 Steps:

1. Get Baby's **Mexican birth certificate**. (See the section "Getting Mexican Birth Certificates" Below.)

2. If you aren't close to the Embassy in Mexico City, find the nearest Canadian Consulate or consular agency at:
   http://www.canadainternational.gc.ca/mexico-mexique/offices-bureaux/index.aspx?lang=eng.

3. **Authenticate and Translate** Baby's Mexican birth certificate.
   Translating the birth certificate is a *major* undertaking -- let's be honest here -- but you can handle it. I have broken it down into sub-steps for you.

Mexico: The Trick is Living Here 3rd edition
available on www.home-sweet-mexico.com
129

a. Before you have the document translated, it must be authenticated. Here is the instruction on that process straight from the Canadian Embassy in Mexico's web site:

> Documents issued in Mexico to be used in Canada must first be authenticated by the Mexican Ministry of the Interior (*Secretaría de Gobernación*) and the Department of Legalizations of the Mexican Ministry of Foreign Affairs (*Secretaría de Relaciones Exteriores*) having jurisdiction over the region where such documents were originally issued. Once authenticated, documents can be legalized by the Canadian Embassy in Mexico City or the consulates in their area of jurisdiction, and finally can be officially translated into English or French....

> Please note that Notarial Services are only provided from Monday to Friday from 9:00 a.m. to 10:30 a.m.

> (source: http://www.canadainternational.gc.ca/mexico-mexique/consul/leg-jur.aspx?lang=eng#notarial)

I recommend that you plan at least one whole day for each step b through e below...

b. You have to ask around to find out where the nearest Mexican Ministry of the Interior

(*Secretaría de Gobernación*) is located and go there to find out what they require for authentication. This is likely to be the classic Mexican go-to-office-for-forms-and-requirements,-bank-for-payment,-and-back-to-office-to-complete-forms kind of deal. Go in the morning when they are more likely to be open. Don't be surprised it you need to leave your documents (and copies of it) with them and go back to pick it up on a following day.

c. The people at the *Secretaría de Gobernación* will be able to tell you where the Mexican Ministry of Foreign Affairs (*Secretaría de Relaciones Exteriores*) is. It shouldn't be too hard to find because it is where Mexicans who want to travel go to get their passports. You are likely to do another classic Mexican paperwork routine at this office. Don't be surprised if the Mexican officials ask you to do even more than the Canadian Embassy specifies. Take paper and pen to take specific notes on exactly where you must go and what you must do. Don't be afraid to tell them a sob story to see if there is "any other way" to get it done, but don't feel pressured to bribe anyone. Bribes are the way of the past. I've done lots of paperwork in Mexico and never had to bribe anyone.

d. Once you have your document legalized by the two Mexican offices, you must get it legalized by the Canadian Embassy or nearest consulate. Ooooops, yes, you read that right. Plan an extra trip to the Embassy, consulate, or consular agency. You have to plan to be there at the right

Mexico: The Trick is Living Here 3rd edition
available on *www.home-sweet-mexico.com*
131

time of day. If you are going to a consulate or consular agency contact them directly to find out at what time notarial services are provided; in the case of the Embassy, the following applies:

"Please note that Notarial Services are only provided from Monday to Friday from 9:00 a.m. to 10:30 a.m."

e. Now you can finally find a translator who will translate your document, **then come to the Embassy with you**.
The Canadian Embassy in Mexico's web site states the following: "**Important:** to certify any translation, the translator who did the work must **personally** come to present the document at the Consular Section of the Canadian Embassy or one of its points of service. No certifications can be made if the translator is not present." See http://www.canadainternational.gc.ca/mexico-mexique/consul/trans-trad.aspx for information on finding a translator.]

4. Fill out the **CCC application form**. You can pick it up at your nearest consulate (when you are there getting your document legalized) or download and print it from http://www.cic.gc.ca/english/information/applications/certif.asp

5. If you are going to apply for a passport simultaneously, fill out the **passport form**. You can pick it up at your nearest consulate or download and print it from http://www.canadainternational.gc.ca/mexico-

mexique/consul/ppt.aspx Note: it will say (abroad) on top.

   a. If you apply for the first time for a Canadian Citizenship Certificate and a passport for a newborn or a child under 2 years old, the applicant **must** provide a proof of travel or a written statement explaining the emergency and complete the PPT116 PDF [*] (91 KB) form at [http://www.canadainternational.gc.ca/mexico-mexique/assets/pdfs/pptc116.pdf]. The passport will be issued for two years and its validity will not be extended.

6. Get **two sets of photos** of your baby. Follow the two different specifications that accompany the CCC and passport applications (in numbers 3 and 4 above).

7. Get at least one of the **photos and the section of your application labeled "Declaration of Guarantor" signed** by a guarantor. This is to prove Baby's identity. See http://www.ppt.gc.ca/cdn/section2.aspx?lang=eng&region=international for the requirements of who can be a guarantor (make sure you read the information for Canadians abroad).

8. Go to the **nearest consulate** with all of the above, plus **two pieces (and 2 copies of each) of official photo ID for each parent**. Bring the **Canadian parent's birth certificate** as proof of Canadian citizenship as specified by the embassy (above and at http://www.dfait-maeci.gc.ca/mexico-city/consular/assist1-en.asp#CITIZENSHIP). Remember to bring the person who translated the Mexican birth certificate. Bring enough **pesos in**

Mexico: The Trick is Living Here 3rd edition
available on *www.home-sweet-mexico.com*
133

cash to cover the equivalent of $20 CAD for the passport and 75$ CAD for the CCC.

9. Take a deep breath.

I have some experience with legalizing Mexican documents for Canada and I still carry scars. In order for the employees of the various Mexican government offices to fit all of the requisite signatures and seals onto the back of the legal-sized document, they taped on extra paper!

This is the folder I used to carry my documents as I was getting them legalized. The entire outside was covered with procedural notes as I kept adding more and more at each step.

Citizenship for Children Born in Mexico to U.S. Citizens

If you and/or your spouse are U.S. citizens and you have a child who was born in Mexico, your child receives U.S. citizenship but you must apply for a Consular Report of Birth Abroad (CRBA) at the U.sS. embassy in Mexico City or one of the Consulates prior to his or her 18th birthday. A Consular Report of Birth Abroad (CRBA) "is an official record confirming that a child born abroad to a U.S. citizen parent or parents acquired U.S. citizenship at birth and serves as proof of citizenship." The CRBA costs $100 (as of March 2011).

The following section is written based on the instructions on the Embassy web site, but you may apply for a CRBA and Passport at any of the consulates. To find the consulate nearest you see http://mexico.usembassy.gov/eng/main.html and click on the link that says "Citizen Services" from there finding the links for Consular Report of Birth Abroad and Passports. Each consulate presents the information in a different way and you'll want to follow the instructions provided by the agency that will serve you.

In this section I summarize the requirements as they are presented on the U.S. Embassy in Mexico City web site (see http://www.usembassy-mexico.gov/eng/eacs_birth_abroad.html). Again, it is imperative that **you read the site yourself and follow the instructions given to you**. Start by downloading the three forms (DS-2029 for the CRBA, DS-11 for the passport, and Affidavit of Parentage and Physical Presence) as well as the checklist (all available in pdf form) from the web page. Some consulates allow you to call, but the Embassy web site instructs people to do the following:

> The applying parent should email the completed DS-2029 as well as the the (sic) Affidavit of Parentage and Physical Presence to MexicoCitypassport@state.gov. In the email, please be sure to include the applicant's name, parent's contact information and the completed forms. Once the information has been reviewed, a reply email will be sent indicating how to schedule the appointment.

You will use the checklist to determine which documents will be required for your situation. Ultimately, it all boils down to that moment when you are standing across the counter from the official. It is the official who

Mexico: The Trick is Living Here 3rd edition
available on www.home-sweet-mexico.com
135

processes your application who will make the final determination about the citizenship of your child. You wouldn't want to go all of the way to Mexico City only to find that you should have brought a photo of yourself while you were pregnant. Don't make the mistake of bringing less documentation than you should have.

The affidavit might give you fits because you have to write down all of your entrances and exits from the U.S.! When we went for our appointment, I had to fill out the older versions of these two different forms, showing all of my entrances and exits from the U.S. since I was 18 years old! Luckily, all of the dates were stamped in my FM3 because I was not prepared for this. Now this information is included right in the forms that you fill out prior to the appointment, so you can do the necessary research ahead of time. On the new forms, the instructions for the two sections about physical presence in the U.S. (numbers 12 and 13 on the form) read as follows:

> 12. List periods of physical presence in the U.S. prior to the child's birth in exact detail. Do not include periods that will be mentioned in item 13. Vacation trips abroad, schooling in foreign countries, and any other brief absences cannot be counted as periods of a physical presence in the U.S.

> 13. List periods in detail. Official written evidence from the appropriate governmental department or international organization must be presented to support any periods shown. For names of qualifying organization, see consul.

You may wish to use a scratch paper and make a summary, like the following:

Enter X country from...	Date	Return to U.S.
Mexico	April 5, 1998	Mexico
Mexico	Dec. 12, 2008	Mexico
France	August 7, 2010	France
Mexico	May 5, 2011	I'm still here!

You should also get your child's **passport** on the same day that you are getting the CRBA. The cost for this is $105 U.S. dollars for children. Instructions on the Embassy web site can be found at http://www.usembassy-mexico.gov/eng/eacs_passports_general.html. Make sure you scroll down and read the long checklist of documents you may need to provide. If you will be applying through one of the consulates, refer to their web site.

In order to be ready to get the CRBA you need to already have your child's Mexican birth certificate. This can easily take a couple of weeks and I can imagine circumstances in which it could take more than a month. If you are going to travel with your child, start the process for the Mexican birth certificate, which, surprise, surprise, isn't simple (see Getting Mexican Birth Certificates) as soon as you are able to get around town.

Consider spending the night before your appointment in Mexico City to facilitate getting to the Embassy in plenty of time. There are lots of wonderful things to see in Mexico City and you can make it a fun trip. There is a special door and line up for U.S. Citizens -- but the professional and orderly door guards will orient you and get you in the right place. No food, water, belts or electronic devices are allowed inside. Last time we were there, cell phones were kept at the door for you in a plastic

Mexico: The Trick is Living Here 3rd edition
available on www.home-sweet-mexico.com
137

bag, but we were required to throw out our own food. Information from 2010 indicates that they are still keeping cell phones in zip-lock bags at the door, but I wouldn't count on it. What will you do if you get there and find out they've changed their rules? You should make prior plans about how to be at the door with only your clothing and the paperwork you need.

Be sure you are ready with all of your documents and either U.S. dollars or a credit card to pay the fees required. They will process the payment for you right inside.

On any given day there are always many people at the embassy (don't let the fact that you have an appointment fool you) and the whole process takes a few hours. The room is carpeted and there are comfortable chairs to sit in. The people are polite and helpful, so as long as you are relaxed and have your documents organized you will have a pleasant experience.

(Note for parents bringing babies: I don't know if they allow baby formula inside, so if you are not breast feeding your child you should ask about that when you make your appointment. The women's bathroom has a changing table in it, but the men's does not.)

OK. So fair is fair. I did it for the Canadian readers I'll do it for the readers from the U.S. Here's a step-by-step guide to help you keep the process in perspective.

Your New-Born U.S. Citizen's CRBA and Passport in 11 Steps:

1. Get online and **read the directions** at
    http://mexico.usembassy.gov/mexico/eacs_birth_abr
    oad.html and
    http://mexico.usembassy.gov/mexico/eacs_passports
    _general.html. OR find the nearest consulate and

read their directions starting at
http://mexico.usembassy.gov/eng/main.html and
"drilling down" from "Citizen Services."

a. The links on the above web sites take you to
   electronic forms. You can **print out forms** at
   http://www.state.gov/documents/organization/79
   955.pdf (DS-11) and
   http://photos.state.gov/libraries/libya/19452/publ
   ic/DS-2029_report_of_birth.pdf (DS-2029). If
   you want to be prepared I recommend that you
   fill out **"practice" forms** to see if you
   understand everything.

2. Get Baby's **Mexican birth certificate**. (See the
   section "Getting Mexican Birth Certificates" below.)
   You can probably fill out the forms and request the
   appointment at the embassy or consulate before you
   have the Mexican birth certificate in hand, but make
   sure you plan a LOT of time to get the birth
   certificate. Do not, under any circumstances, leave it
   for less than two weeks away from the appointment;
   a month would be preferable. Trust me.

3. **Fill out the forms** electronically.

4. **Email Embassy** with all of the forms attached. From
   the Embassy web site: "In the email, please be sure
   to include the applicant's name, parent's contact
   information and the completed forms."

5. Follow the instructions in the return email **to make
   an appointment**.

6. Get **passport photos** of baby. Follow the instructions
   on the consulate or embassy web site. This is fun.
   Can you get baby to smile?

Mexico: The Trick is Living Here 3rd edition
available on www.home-sweet-mexico.com
139

7. **Using the checklist on the web site gather all other documents** that you will need to take with you to the embassy on the day of your appointment. You might want to go to the local *papelería* and get a plastic document envelope to store them in. Again, I recommend that you begin this process *weeks* in advance. Here's that checklist from the Embassy web site:

b. **Original or Certified Copy of the Mexican Birth Certificate**, a provisional copy cannot be accepted.

c. **Proof of Parent's Citizenship**: Please show one of the following documents for one or both parents: U.S. Passport (valid or expired), original U.S. birth certificate or original Certificate of Naturalization.

d. **Proof of Both Parents Identity**: Driver's license, State ID card, School ID, Mexican Voting Card, Passport.

e. **Marriage Certificate**: If parents were married prior to the time of conception, please provide an original or certified copy of the marriage certificate and divorce decree (if applicable). If parents were not married at the time of conception, please provide proof of the existence of the relationship at that time (personal letters and cards, dated photographs, telephone bills).

f. **Prenatal Documents and/or documents from hospital where the applicant was born**: ultra sounds, prescriptions, medical records, identification bracelet, crib card, discharge orders, hospital bill, photos of the mother during pregnancy and in the hospital before and after the birth.

g. **Proof of parents' presence in Mexico**: Mexican visa or Mexican passport.

h. **If only one parent is a U.S. citizen, proof of the parent's physical presence in the United States**: The parent must prove at least 5 years of physical presence in the US, at least 2 of which are after the age of 14. The period of physical presence need not be continuous. Presence must be proven with concrete evidence (school records, tax forms with W-2, Social Security earnings statement, pay receipts, passport with entry and exit stamps, etc.).

i. Add your own notes here:

8. Get required **photo copies**. Be sure you know if you need to get the entire passport or just the ID page.

9. **Plan your trip to Mexico City**. Make it fun.

10. Go to Mexico City and **be in line at 8:00 on time** with both parents, all documents, no food, no belts, and no cell phones. (Take a taxi or plan where you'll park the day before.)

11. **Follow the instructions of the officials** inside. They are really helpful and will guide you through step by step if you are organized.

Mexico: The Trick is Living Here 3rd edition
available on *www.home-sweet-mexico.com*
141

You will **receive your documents** about a month later by registered messenger service. You pay for this service at the time that you pay for the CRBA and passport, so bring extra money.

Getting Mexican Birth Certificates

When your child is born, you will be issued a report of his/her birth with the signature and identification number of the doctor or midwife who delivered the child. You must take that along with additional documents which identify you (the parents) and two witnesses to the local registrar's office to apply for a birth certificate. The hardest thing about getting a Mexican birth certificate is finding two witnesses (*not* related to the child) who can spend the better part of a day at the registrar's office with you. Oh, and standing around with your newborn infant in a cramped, dirty office with insufficient seating and un-enforced smoking rules. If you don't register your child before he or she is six months of age you will be charged a fine. Some people may tell you that you have until the child is a year old, but the rule has been changed to six months.

Prior to going to register your child get a list of the documents required and be sure that the list includes what is required for parents who are not Mexican because there are additional requirements for foreigners. This means going there in person and getting/writing down the list of required documents. Each office will have slightly different requirements but passports (for foreigners) or electoral cards (for Mexicans), and birth certificates of both parents (translated into Spanish by an official translator if you are a foreigner) are definitely going to be required.

In Cuernavaca both parents have to be present along with two witnesses, all of whom prove their identity with an official ID card or passport, then sign the original birth certificate. We made an outing of it. We had our backpack with all of the documents (my neighbor had gone by on a previous day to get the list of requirements) and we all stood around filling out forms. My husband paid fees (you can pay them right at the registrar's office) while the rest of us took care of the baby.

There were some issues about my birth certificate because it didn't have all of the exact same information that a Mexican birth certificate has. In the end they left some blanks on my son's birth certificate because they couldn't know for sure his grandparent's nationalities. After about an hour it was time to sign the form (which they keep on record), then they told us to come back in a week for the certificates. Afterwards, we took our witnesses out to lunch. One of the parents has to pick up the birth certificates so a couple weeks later I took my mom, who was visiting me at the time, on an outing and we picked up the birth certificates that we had ordered and paid for on that day.

Be smart and pay **the fees for about five official copies of the birth certificate right at the get-go**. There are some institutions in Mexico which will require that you give an original birth certificate to them rather than a copy, so you will have to give away some of the originals. Additionally, as foreigners we always seem to be doing a variety of official documentation and it's easier to have extra copies on hand in your home. There is also more potential that you may move away from the city in which your child was registered – and you're not going to be able to get one through the mail. I doubt anyone will want to make a special trip just to get a birth certificate. Because of this same reason, you could consider keeping a copy of one of these in a secure place that is not your home, like you would do with a computer back up.

Still sound hard? Close your eyes, take a deep breath, and follow these steps.

Your New-Born's Mexican Birth Certificate in 9 Steps:

1. **Figure out where** the local Registrar's office (called *Registro Civil* in Spanish) is located. In larger cities there may be more than one office and you may have to go to one in particular.*

2. Stop by the local Registrar's office and **get the requirements** to register your child.

   a. Double check requirements for foreign parents.

   b. Double check any "rules" about translation of foreign birth certificates.

   c. If you don't have a Mexican marriage certificate ask if a foreign marriage certificate is acceptable.

      i. You may need to register your marriage in Mexico. If this is the case, get directions for that. Ours was already registered in Mexico as part of my original visa process. (If you have to do this, don't freak out. It's all the same thing; go here, go back, go there, get stuff translated, make lots of photo copies, pay, go back.)

   d. Ask if you should copy all pages of your passport or just the ID page.

3. **Find two witnesses** who are not related to the child.

4. If necessary, get foreign documents officially **translated into Spanish**.

   a. Birth certificates of foreign parents

   b. Foreign marriage certificates

5. Gather documents and take **2 photocopies** of everything.

   a. Passports for foreign parents

   b. Electoral cards (IDs) for Mexican parents (both sides of the card)

   c. **Electoral cards (IDs) for witnesses** (both sides of the card)

   d. Birth certificates for both parents (translated if not in Spanish).

   e. All other documents required such as proof of address, etc. (See step 2 above.)

6. **Go to the registrar's office** with all documents, both parents, two witnesses, and baby.

7. **Pay** for original and about 5 copies of the birth certificate.

8. Take witnesses **out to lunch**. This is fun! Celebrate.

9. Wait the indicated amount of time and **return to pick up birth certificates**.

   *In our case, there is a registrar's office within walking distance of our house. When Luis went to get the requirements for the birth certificate they told him he would have to "redo" our Mexican marriage certificate to an "updated" format. Of course this involved paying a fee. Someone suggested that we try another registrar's office on the other side of town. When he went there for the requirements he was assured that our marriage certificate was acceptable as is. We processed our son's birth certificate through this second office and all was well.

Getting Mexican Passports for Children Born in Mexico

If your child is born in Mexico you must get them a Mexican passport if you are going to travel internationally. When you travel to your "old home" country, they can enter with a passport from that country

Find the Mexican passport office nearest you here: http://www.sre.gob.mx/ index.php/donde-tramitar-tu-pasaporte

(see the sections on birth certificates for U.S. or Canadian citizens above to learn about getting those) then re-enter Mexico with their Mexican passport. They are a citizen going both ways the lucky dogs!

Mexican passports are processed in one day – but it does take almost all day. You bring all the required supporting documentation to the

Passport fees, payment forms, and instructions for first time passports: http://www.sre.gob.mx index.php/primera-vez/248

passport office in the morning, fill out the application, go to pay the fee at the bank, return to the office and turn in the completed application form, paid fee, and supporting documents (such as IDs). A few hours later you will receive the passport. Mexico will only issue passports that are valid for a year to children under three years old, so you really don't need to get one until you know that you will be traveling.

When you want to get your child's Mexican passport find the nearest *Secretaria de Relaciones Exteriores* [Ministry of Foreign Affairs] office and stop in to get the requirements or check on the web site at http://www.sre.gob.mx/pasaportes/. Surprisingly enough the web site is easy to navigate and includes all of the requirements, costs, and special instructions -- but you must be able to read Spanish because the English translations on the site haven't quite gotten to the nitty-gritty pages. You can even download the forms on line and come with them filled out, though our office in Cuernavaca prefers to give personal instruction on how to fill out the forms, which is helpful because there are a few blanks that are a little unclear as to what they want you to put down.

These requirements are all listed at http://www.sre.gob.mx/pasaportes/primeravez/menoresedad.htm for minors getting their first passport.

One of the most confusing requirements of the first-time passport application is that of a photo ID for your child. How do you prove your child's identity when they still don't have a photo ID? Well, you get your doctor to write a letter on letterhead stating for how long he or she has known your child and that he/she knows that the child is yours (including everyone's full names). The doctor glues a photo to the letter and places his/her seal partially over the photo, signs the letter, and attaches a photo copy of his/her *cedula* (official doctor's license) to the letter.

Both parents and the child must be present on the day that you go to get the passport, so you can make it a semi-fun family day. In 2011, a one-year passport for a child under three years old costs $410 pesos, a three-year passport for children over three years old costs $850, but passports can cost more at different offices, so you have to ask your local office exactly how much it will be. You can download and fill out the payment form from home so that you can pay at the bank ahead of time. The web site requires that you get a photo copy of the completed payment form for yourself after going to the bank and prior to turning it in to them. This type of requirement is typical and explains why there are always photocopying businesses next door to passport offices.

Bring with you your child's Mexican birth certificate, a letter signed by your doctor which identifies everyone in the family (as described above), three passport photos of your child (follow specifications on the web site), and parents' IDs (Mexican visa and foreign passport for the foreigner and electoral card if Mexican). Note: Each person's name must be written *exactly* the same way on every piece of identification.

9 Giving up or Retaining

Residency

for Canadian Citizens

When deciding to move to Mexico, Canadian citizens must carefully consider whether or not they should become non-residents of Canada or maintain their residence status. Becoming a non-resident of Canada potentially affects three crucial aspects of being a Canadian citizen. These aspects are taxes, health care, and banking. Other aspects potentially affected are driver's license renewal, safety deposit boxes, lifestyle, family connectedness, etc.

To find out more about this situation I talked to Rod Burylo BACFP (www.rodburylo.com), a financial advisor and recipient of the 2004 Advisor of the Year Award as well as the educational director of Canadians Retiring Abroad Ltd. (www.canadiansretiringabroad.ca), a collection of advisors who specialize in helping Canadians

Mexico: The Trick is Living Here 3rd edition
available on www.home-sweet-mexico.com
149

interested in retiring abroad. He says that many Canadians don't understand the factors that contribute to either maintaining or giving up residence in Canada—even when they think they do! (Watch out, we don't want you to be one of these unknowingly ignorant folks.) Additionally, while for some Canadians it is financially beneficial to give up their status as a resident—mostly due to savings in taxes, for others it is actually beneficial to **keep** their status as a resident. He and a handful of other professionals throughout Canada can help you to plan your retirement in Mexico. Not all financial advisors can advise you on retiring (or living) abroad due to the complexities involved in the concept of residency as it applies to Canadians so you have to find one who specializes in this area.

Rod told me that a Canadian's residential status is determined by whether or not they sever their residential and social ties to Canada. (Go to the web sites discussed below and follow the link to IT-221 to see how the government explains it). Residential ties include things such as houses, apartments, and furniture. Social ties include things such as dependent children, safety deposit boxes, bank accounts, and financial portfolios. It is possible for you to choose a few key things that you would like to keep active in Canada, such as a bank account with a credit card in which you receive your pension(s) (C.P.Ps or Registered Retirement Savings Plans) as well as an investment portfolio by severing all but approximately five "minor" ties to Canada. You can receive your Canadian Pension Plan as a non-resident, but there are some cases in which you cannot receive your Old Age Security. The Canadian government makes it's determination of non-residence on an individual basis. This is why it is so important to get the help of a qualified advisor.

It may seem expensive to pay an advisor, but I urge you to ignore that independent, pioneering spirit that makes you want to break out and live in Mexico, just for one aspect of the move, and learn as much as you can about this topic. You don't want to jeopardize your financial solvency, nor have inadequate health care after moving to Mexico when the potential exists for you to have tax benefits as well as excellent health care and just the right banking and portfolio management for your situation. While some advisors do charge for their services others, provide the advice as part of their service, earning commissions from products, and do not charge clients. You can find the right advisor for you.

6 Factors Unique to Canadians Living in Mexico:

Rod Burylo told me that there are about six factors unique to Canadians in Mexico. Those factors are the following:

1. Canadians are taxed on their residential status. If a Canadian determines that they wish to move into a different **tax situation,** he or she can become a non-resident. In order to become a non-resident, you must sever most, but not all social ties to Canada. You must then reside outside of Canada for a cumulative total of at least 6 months and 1 day. (I know you are doing the math. Is it enough to avoid those long winter months?) When you wish to visit Canada, you must do that as a tourist. (Don't worry, you can stay in your children's or friend's basement.)

Before leaving Canada it is important that you

Mexico: The Trick is Living Here 3rd edition
available on www.home-sweet-mexico.com
151

carefully analyze the advantages vs. disadvantages of becoming a non-resident. Will your tax savings offset the costs of private health care in Mexico? Is it worth it to give up most of your social ties to Canada and make some changes to your financial assets? Will you sell your house outright or take other steps to give up access, such as renting it to an arms-length party through the services of an independent rental agency? Which social ties will you keep, such as a bank account or investment portfolio? For a more in-depth description of how non-residency may or may not benefit you see the section "Douglas Gray's Pointers on Taxation" below.

2. When Canadians live abroad it changes their **banking and financial services** and relationships. Many financial institutions will not offer non-resident Canadians the same service as resident Canadians due to the complexity of the situation. Even though they may not give advice, they may still keep your money for you. You will have to ask at your current financial institution what services they offer for non-resident Canadians. As stated above you can keep one bank account in which to receive your pension payments as well as maintain a financial portfolio. I highly recommend doing this.

   See the section "Banking" for more information. Also see the Companion: Useful Links for links to Canadian banks that offer international banking services.

3. When Canadians give up their residential ties they give up their access to **health care**. Because Canadians are accustomed to the health care system

Mexico: The Trick is Living Here 3rd edition
available on www.home-sweet-mexico.com
152

in Canada they often don't understand private health care and what the services are all about. When living in Mexico it is important that you be able to choose and manage your health care options because the public health care system is not of high quality (see the section "Health Care in Mexico" for more information) while there are excellent private options available. It is important that you choose the health care that will give you the breadth of coverage and quality of service that you require. In order to do that you must budget for the costs of that care. This is not the place to be cheap because your health is crucial to your wellbeing. It is expensive, but remember this is where the tax benefits of being a non-resident can pay off.

There are some links to health and insurance related web sites for expatriates in the companion Useful Links.

4. **Climate**. Need I say more?

5. **Accessibility and Access to Mexico**. Because the United States separates Canada from Mexico, most Canadians don't drive straight to Mexico. Sometimes they bring a car (see "Licensing Your Car from the United States or Canada"), but they do that later, after they have established themselves in their new home. You will probably use air travel as your most common way of coming and going to Mexico both during your "scoping" period of visiting Mexico prior to moving and after you have selected a new home and officially moved to Mexico.

This means that moving to Mexico is more

challenging than moving within Canada or even to the United States. The Mexican government requires that if you bring household items with you into Mexico you apply for a *menaje de casa* (see "Permission to Bring Your Household Items" above) and you will probably want to hire a mover with experience in transport to Mexico. Even if you do hire a mover and bring some of your most valued possessions, you will probably find it more economical to buy many of the larger items in Mexico.

6. There are **relatively few Mexican Consulates** and Mexicans in Canada. Additionally, Mexico is just starting to market itself to Canadians as a retirement destination (as opposed to a travel destination). This means that it is challenging for Canadians to get information and support during the planning stages of their move to Mexico. They may have to travel a great distances to get their visa. Also, if for example, they are purchasing real estate in Mexico, they may wish to have the support of a Mexican lawyer, but it is often difficult for Canadians to find people who know a lot about Mexico.

See the Companion: *Useful Links* for a directory of the Mexican Embassy and Consulates in Canada.

Information on Residency in Canada and Tax Responsibilities

Even if you do decide to become a non-resident of Canada there are some tax responsibilities for the first year that you move from Canada that you will need to know about. You can learn about those and other responsibilities at http://www.cra-arc.gc.ca/tx/nnrsdnts/ndvdls/lvng-eng.html. Below are two quotes from that web site to get you started:

1. "Generally, you are an **emigrant of Canada for income tax purposes** if you leave Canada to settle in another country **and** you sever your residential ties with Canada." Learn more at http://www.cra-arc.gc.ca/tx/nnrsdnts/ndvdls/lvng-eng.html#b.

2. "Severing residential ties includes:

   • disposing of or giving up a home in Canada and establishing a permanent home in another country to which you move;
   • having your spouse or common-law partner (see the definition in the General Income Tax and Benefit Guide [http://www.cra-arc.gc.ca/E/pub/tg/5000-g/README.html]) and dependants leave Canada; and
   • disposing of personal property and breaking social ties in Canada and acquiring or establishing them in another country.

   Other ties that will be taken into account in determining your residency status include:

   • a Canadian driver's license;
   • Canadian bank accounts or credit cards; and
   • health insurance with a Canadian province or territory.

   For more information, see Residency - Individuals [http://www.cra-arc.gc.ca/tx/nnrsdnts/cmmn/rsdncy-eng.html] and IT-221, Determination of an Individual's Residence Status [http://www.cra-arc.gc.ca/E/pub/tp/it221r3-consolid/README.html].

If you want an opinion about your residency status, complete and submit Form NR73, Determination of Residency Status (Leaving Canada) [http://www.cra-arc.gc.ca/E/pbg/tf/nr73/README.html]."

Douglas Gray's Pointers on Taxation

Douglas Gray, LL.B., is a Vancouver-based expert on retirement and tax and estate planning issues, and the author of *The Canadian Snowbird Guide*, 4th edition. He has several websites with helpful information on retirement planning, retiring abroad, estate planning and buying a home, both in Canada and abroad. They are: www.snowbird.ca, www.estateplanning.ca, www.retirementplanning.ca, and www.homebuyer.ca. In his article "Retiring Abroad? Some Pointers," Gray manages to make the complex understandable. The excerpt below is the part of this article that talks about taxation.

> You cannot terminate your Canadian citizenship or residency simply by living in another country. Moreover, becoming a legal resident of another country does not establish non-residence in Canada for tax purposes. You must demonstrate your intention to leave the country permanently.

The CCRA (Canada Customs and Revenue Agency) determines non-resident status on a case-by-case basis, so you should consult a tax advisor about the necessary steps you should take. *Retaining Canadian residency does not necessarily put you at a disadvantage* [italics mine].

Depending on your situation, your actual tax liability could be lower than the nonresident withholding taxes imposed on your Canadian pensions and investment income. For example, if you have a modest income and would not have to pay much tax under Canadian tax laws, you could be further ahead than if you relinquished your residency. There is a flat rate withholding tax for non-residents, which could be more than your taxes. [italics mine]

In general, absence from Canada for two years or longer is considered evidence of non-residence provided that you relinquish or terminate other key connections. These include:

- · Residences
- · Bank accounts
- · Credit cards
- · Driver's licenses
- · Health-plan memberships
- · Club or professional memberships.

Taxpayers who emigrate from Canada are generally deemed to have disposed of their assets at fair market value on the date they leave. Capital gains taxes, if any, are assessed at this time. Assets affected by this provision include shares in Canadian corporations, but not real estate. Deemed disposition is triggered by your declaration that you have left the country, which you make on your final income tax return, filed by April 30 of the year following your departure.

Canada imposes a withholding tax on "passive" income paid to non-residents from Canadian sources, including annuity payments, pension plans, CPP, and OAS. More information on taxation of non-residents is available from the CCRA at [http://www.cra-arc.gc.ca/tx/nnrsdnts/ndvdls/nnrs-eng.html]. You are eligible for OAS payments for your lifetime, as long as you were resident in Canada for at least 20 years before you leave Canada.

You are eligible to CPP payments for your lifetime as well, without a minimum residency requirement. The amount varies depending on the type of income, but it is 25 percent for pension payments. This tax may be reduced or waived according to the terms of tax treaties between Canada and other countries.

See the rest of Douglas Gray's article at http://www.50plus.com/lifestyle/retiring-abroad-some-pointers/29634/2/ to see how he talks about many of the six factors discussed above.

Your life in Mexico will be that much more pleasant if you invest the time and money required to form a plan that works for you prior to making the move from Canada to Mexico.

Maintaining a Canadian PO Box

You can get "mailbox service" through the UPS store in Canada[††††]. This service does what an expat needs, including providing you with a street address, not a P.O. Box number, package acceptance from all shipping carriers, package and mail receipt notification, and probably most importantly, mail holding and forwarding.

[††††] Information for U.S. citizens on page 203.

10 Bringing Your Dog or Cat to

Mexico

Of course you can bring your dog or cat with you to Mexico; it just requires some preparation and planning well in advance of the date of your trip to obtain the proper veterinary certification. On the other hand, here's a word to the wise. There is more than paperwork to consider. As anyone who has traveled in their home country with their pet knows, having a pet in tow greatly restricts the options available to you. Multiply that restriction by an order of magnitude of 10 and that's about how it will be in Mexico. I strongly advise that you leave your beloved pet at home until you are already experienced at traveling or living in Mexico.

First, in the unfamiliar environment it's hard enough to get around and figure out your options for yourself, without the added dificulty of finding pet friendly accomodations or leaving your pet outside in the blazing hot sun so you can eat in a restaurant. Second, pets are less accepted in public places in Mexico than they are in the

Mexico: The Trick is Living Here 3rd edition
available on www.home-sweet-mexico.com
160

United States and Canada. Pet owners in Mexico leave their pets at home. Period.

For those of you who are expert travelers, who have service dogs, or who just *must* bring your dog or cat along, the *Servicio Nacional de Sanidad, Inocuidad y Calidad Agroalimentaria* (SENASICA) [National Service of Health, Safety, and Food Quality] is the official group in charge of regulating the entry of small animals into Mexico. SENASICA and the Mexican Consulate in the United States both explain on their web sites what you need to bring. Not surprisingly, their recommendations don't exactly agree. Also, not surprisingly, the information on these official web sites doesn't exactly agree with that reported by pet lovers who travel in Mexico. See the Useful Links companion for more information about traveling in Mexico with pets. Below is a conglomerate list of the requirements to cross the border with your pet.

Bring with your dog or cat a letter from a licensed, professional veterinarian (or much better, your veterinarian should have an internationally recognized form called an **International Health Certificate**) as follows:

- No more than 10 days old on the date you travel. Set an appointment date accordingly.
- The veterinarian's name, address, and certification number. The medical center's letterhead will likely cover this requirement.
- Your name and address.
- The date of the animal's most recent rabies and other vaccinations as appropriate to your pet and the expiration date of the rabies vaccination. Animals under 3

months of age are exempt of this
requirement.

- The veterinarian's certification that the
animal has had preventative medication
against internal and external parasites
within six months of the date of travel to
Mexico, specifying the date the medication
was administered.
- The veterinarian's certification that the
animal has been inspected and found
clinically healthy prior to export.
- Bring the original and a photo copy when
you travel. I'd advise you have a second
copy for yourself, as well.

When you pass through customs with your pet, you
will present the documentation as above to the official,
who will review and, if all goes well, issue you a
Certificado Zoosanitario para Importación [Zoo-Sanitary
Import Certificate].

You can see the requirements in English (Thank you
SENASICA and Mexican Consulate) here
http://www.senasica.gob.mx/default.asp?Idioma=2&id=62
3 and here
(http://portal.sre.gob.mx/was_eng/index.php?option=displa
ypage&Itemid=67&op=page&SubMenu=)

You can bring up to three pets with you without
paying import fees. If you are traveling with four or more
pets you will pay a fee of $1,817.00 pesos **per certificate**
via internet or bank deposit. Use the form on the web site
before you travel and bring the proof with you. The
customs official will send you to the cargo area and you
will follow the procedure as if you were a commercial
importer.

SENASICA's web site explains that SENASICA permits you...

> ...to bring a single day's ration of pet-food and treats, in an unmarked bag, accompanying your pet while he travels. You can also bring with you dry or canned food and treats as long as they do NOT have ingredients of ruminant animal origin (beef, mutton, lamb, etc.). The bags must be sealed in their original packaging, labeled in Spanish or English with a seal from the sanitation authority. Remember, you can obtain healthy pet-food stamped with approval by SAGARPA (Mexican Dept. of Agriculture) when you arrive to Mexico.

It further advises...

> ...[y]our pet may be transported in a clean carrier, kennel or other bag suitable for travel, *without bedding or material accessories*, or these will be removed and a prophylactic treatment will be performed if the SENASICA OISA official considers it necessary to do so. [italics mine]

A friend recently moved with her cat from Canada to Merida. She had all of the necessary documentation (a letter from the vet and rabies shot certificate in original and two copies as well as the rabies tag on the collar) but she also had something very important. She brought with her just the right attitude. Here's how she described it:

Mexico: The Trick is Living Here 3rd edition
available on www.home-sweet-mexico.com
163

When I landed in Merida, they kept the original, and they may have kept one copy too, I can't remember. What I do remember is (as is always the case in Mexico) acting nonchalant, unworried, relaxed, like I'd done it all my life. Like it's no big deal; I always fly half way round the world with a cat. Well that goes a lot farther than freaking out, trying to ask questions that aren't important, or just in general looking like a stupid nervous gringo/a - those will be triggers that raise flags with immigration/customs and you will end up with a hard time on your hands. If/when they do ask me questions, I have always smiled, acted like everything is just peachy, and life couldn't be better. It always works.

11 Bringing or Buying Your Car...

Insurance & License

Bringing your car to Mexico doesn't simply boil down to whether or not the car will make the trip, as it would if you were relocating to another city. This is an *international* move and there are more aspects to consider. The first of which may be that it's likely a very long drive unless you're in California, Texas, or somewhere in between. If you're headed to Merida, it's a long drive, no matter where you're from!

The biggest consideration is your final destination in Mexico and whether or not a permit will be required to drive your car. There is a "free zone" of about 20 to 30 kilometers along the Mexico/U.S. border and including all of Baja California in which you are allowed to drive your vehicle from the U.S. or Canada without a permit – anywhere outside of that area, you will need to apply and pay for a special temporary import permit. Maintaining the permit comes with a set of requirements that may rule out the option for some expatriates. Still, after weiging the options, some people do choose to bring their car from the United States, or even Canada, into Mexico.

Licensing Your Car from the United States or Canada

Here's the down-low on what it takes to "temporarily import" your car into Mexico so you can make a carefully considered decision. If, after reading this section, you are thinking, "O-oh, that's not for me," just skip on down to "Licensing Your Car Purchased in Mexico" on page 177 or forgo car ownership all together. Living car-free is practical, if not preferable, in most Mexican towns and cities.

It is important to know that the Mexican government is very strict about bringing cars from the U.S. and Canada into Mexico. Here are some rules that you will have to follow if you decide to bring your car with you:

1. You can NOT sell your car in Mexico.

2. Only you, your spouse, parents, siblings or children can drive your car alone. Foreigners with proper immigration status may also drive your car alone. Mexicans who are not your relatives can drive your car *only* if you are a passenger. Mexicans who are your direct relatives would be well advised to travel with proof of your non-expired visa and their relationship to you. Consequences for disobeying this are seizure of the car and hefty fines. The car will not be returned if it is seized. [This rule applies to non-Mexican nationals. If the vehicle is imported by a Mexican national, other rules apply.]

3. The car must be in your name because the name on your visa must match that on the title. If a bank owns your car, you must get a notarized letter giving you permission to bring it with you into Mexico, including the VIN number in the letter.

4. When you exit Mexico with your car, you must stop and have a customs official cancel your permit and scrape the sticker off of your window, otherwise they will assume that your car has remained in Mexico and will charge you (see #5 below) and ban you from ever bringing a car into Mexico again.

5. You must either give your credit card or cash card number or pay a cash deposit of $200 to $400 U.S. dollars plus a one-time processing fee of 50 U.S. dollars in order to receive the permit. If you allow your car to overstay the permit (see #6 below) you will *not* receive your deposit back. The amounts of deposit are as follows: cars from 2000 and older are $200, cars 2001 to 2006 are $300, and cars from 2007 and more recent are $400.

6. Your car "rides" on your immigration status (pun intended). The permit for the car is tied into the expiration of whatever immigration document you have. If you have a visitor visa, the permit will expire in six months, as does the visa. If you have a current temporary resident visa your car is legal *as long as you don't allow it to expire* (even if the sticker on your window has expired). If you are caught in Mexico driving a car with an expired permit (meaning more than six months on a visitor visa, or that your temporary visa is expired) your car will be seized and NOT returned to you and you will be fined hundreds of dollars. In such circumstances, you

must not drive your car until you apply for a special permission, allowing you three to five days to remove your car from Mexico. As of November 2012 the rules for permanent residents of Mexico had not been published.

7. Since your car "rides" on your immigration status, you take on the extra paperwork related to informing a local customs office, in writing, of the changes in your migratory status so that they don't consider your car permit expired and take your deposit.

8. When you travel, you must always have the documents they issue you in the car, but would be in real trouble if they were lost for any reason, including if the vehicle were stolen. Keep a spare copy in a safe place.

9. In case of accident or theft of your car, you take on the responsibility of doing the paperwork to cancel the permit of the car. Read the section of the customs web site, listing all of the required documents so that you can make the appropriate photo copies as a preventative measure. Don't let your car be stolen or impounded with necessary documents in the glove compartment where you won't be able to get at them. (See http://www.aduanas.sat.gob.mx/aduana_mexico/2008/vehiculos/141_11258.html.)

10. Note: It costs about a third more to insure a car from the U.S. or Canada as it does to insure one from Mexico. Not all insurance companies insure foreign cars.

11. Your car must be properly insured for inside Mexico. If your insurance policy from your home country

doesn't cover you for Mexico, purchase insurance at the border.

12. Note: You won't have to pay expensive licensing taxes called *tenencias* on your foreign car (see "Licensing Your Car Purchased in Mexico" on page 177). Technically you are supposed to keep the licensing current in your state back in the U.S. but really there is no one to force you to do this (except maybe your insurance coverage). You could save money this way if you don't plan on driving in the U.S.

Aduana (Customs) Web Site

The information in this section comes from the section "Temporary Importation of Vehicles" (*Importación Temporal de Vehículos*) at http://www.aduanas.sat.gob.mx/ aduana_mexico/2008/vehiculos/ 141_10028.html and applies to non-Mexicans. If you are a Mexican national there are slightly different rules for you.

Note: The section "*Internación temporal de vehículos al interior del país*" applies to those who live in the narrow "free zone" and want to drive deeper into Mexico.

Stopping for a permit

As mentioned above, there is a "free zone" of about 20 to 30 kilometers along the Mexico/U.S. border and including all of Baja California in which you are allowed to drive your vehicle from the U.S. or Canada without a permit. If you are going to drive your vehicle into the interior of Mexico you must stop at the border to get the permit for it. If you are in Baja and want to take your vehicle on a ferry to the mainland, you can get your permit from the ferry officials. As with most things in Mexico, this isn't hard, but does require patience. It's all about standing in various lines. Depending upon where you cross the border, it could take a couple of hours to complete all of the necessary paperwork. Immediately after crossing the border into Mexico, stop and ask where *Banjercito* (short for "Bank of the Armed Forces" (*ejercito*)) is. That's the institution with whom you will process the application to bring your car into Mexico. It is located in different places at each border crossing, but is usually right after you cross the border. Once you find *Banjercito* you can commence standing in the various lines, such as the line for the initial application paperwork, the line to make the payment, etc. Your application will be granted as long as you have all of the required paperwork ready.

You may now use the customs and *Banjercito* web sites to prepare much or all of the paperwork ahead of time. As of 2011, the cost at the border is $32 and via internet is $48. Due to the absolute inflexibility of Mexican officials regarding any slight error or deviation on paperwork, I would not recommend trying to get the permission completely on line. Plan to go in to the *Banjercito* office and see someone *in person* no matter what. By the same token, using the on line resources is a really good idea because it will help you to ensure that you have exactly the right documents and information for their forms when you arrive at the border. No matter which way you decide to process your documents, look at the web site (more on this in the following section).

Preparing to Temporarily Import Your Car into Mexico via Internet

Aduana's English language instructions for application via internet can be found at http://www.aduanas.sat.gob.mx/aduana_mexico/2008/pasaj eros/139_10134.html, once you are viewing the page, click on "Passengers Arriving by Land" and read the various topics that will appear. If you can read Spanish, I recommend you also comb through the information in Spanish starting at http://www.aduanas.sat.gob.mx/aduana_mexico/2008/vehi culos/141_10028.html because there is more information included in this version, notably the procedures to inform *Aduana* of any changes to the status of your permit.

The real action happens on the *Banjercito* web site where you register the important information and pay the fee and deposit. Go to the web site, click on "Application for Temporary Import Permit for vehicles boats and RVs" – yes! It's in English! - and follow the instructions starting at http://www.banjercito.com.mx/site/siteBanjer/Bicentenario /index.html. I recommend that you "pre-register" rather than applying and paying online. If you do the entire registration on line, you must allow at least ten days for this because they then mail you your permit and the sticker for your window in the mail. As you are filling out the form take note of the part of the instructions that says "we strongly recommend you double check each entry;" they mean it. **No** errors will be accepted.

Make sure you have the following documents ready and in your car with you when you leave for Mexico.

Required documents to bring your car into the interior of Mexico

1. **Car title** or registration in your name (plus two photo copies of this).

    a. If the car or van is owned by someone else or is jointly owned by you and another person bring a notarized letter from the other person granting you permission to bring the car into Mexico. Include the VIN number in the letter.

    b. If you are still paying for your car, bring a notarized letter from the bank (or whichever institution holds the lien on your car) giving you permission to take the car to Mexico. Have them include the VIN number in the letter.

    c. If the car belongs to your employer, you will be required to produce a valid identification as his (her) employee.

    d. If the vehicle is rented, you should submit the rental contract with the respective authorization.

2. Valid U.S. or Canadian **driver's license** (plus two photo copies of both sides of this).

3. A **credit/cash/debit card** in your name *OR* a **cash bond**.

4. A **credit card or debit card**. This card MUST be in your name. The name of the person requesting the permit for the car and the name on the card MUST match. There will be a one-time only fee of 50 dollars to process the permit.

a. A **cash bond** plus a one-time processing fee of 50 dollars. The amount of the cash bond depends on the age of the car and will be at least $200 U.S. dollars.

- No matter how you pay the bond, when you leave Mexico, you must stop at the customs office to have them record that your car is leaving Mexico. If you check your car out of Mexico after the permission has expired, your bond will not be returned to you. It is still important that you check your car out because if you fail to record the departure of your car, you will **never** be allowed to bring a car into Mexico again in your life. Be sure **to keep the receipt** that they give you when you leave Mexico, just in case there is a computer glitch and your car's departure is not recorded by Mexican customs.

5. **Your passport**. (Bring two photo copies of this. At some border crossings only the picture page (of the old style booklets) is required but at others you must have two copies of the entire document including "blank" pages. It's easier just to have the copies ready in case you need them.)

6. **Your visitor or other visa**. (Bring two photo copies of this. At some border crossings only the picture page is required but at others you must have two

copies of the entire document including "blank" pages. It's easier just to have the copies ready in case you need them.)

7.   If you pre-registered via internet, bring the confirmation code you were assigned.

8.   If it applies, the document that proves the return of the last imported vehicle in the past.

Notes about the permission to bring your car into the interior

1.   You may bring your motorcycle, car, truck (as long as it weighs less than 3.5 tons), or RV (no weight limit). You can only bring one vehicle per person, except in the case that you are driving a motor home and towing a car.

2.   For RVs you can also get a 10-year permit for the motor home, renewable via internet if done 15 days prior to expiry. The motor home permit allows you multiple entries and exits. This does not apply to pickup campers.

3.   The rules for bringing a boat are similar to those for RVs.

4.   You may bring a trailer, but it must be registered in your name and you must show your ownership papers.

5.   If you are towing or carrying in your truck motorcycles, ATV or other single passenger vehicles you can register these as part of the "main" vehicle. You can bring as many of these single passenger vehicles as there are passengers in the

vehicle. You must show proof of ownership and they must all leave Mexico at the same time that the vehicle does.

6. If you leave and re-enter Mexico you will need to stop and have them remove the sticker from your car, then when you return you will have to apply for a new permit for your vehicle. No re-entries are allowed. (Keep your receipts and all of the required items numbers 1 through 5 above.)

7. The *Consulate General of the United States of America Ciudad Juárez, Mexico* web site* gives the following warning about **drivers other than yourself**:

> If you wish to authorize another person to drive your car, record the authorization with Mexican officials when you enter Mexico - even if you expect to be a passenger when the other person drives. Do not, under any circumstances, allow an unauthorized person to drive the vehicle when the owner is not in it. We caution American citizens not to loan their vehicles to Mexican citizens resident in Mexico (even when driving in the Border Zone). Your vehicle would be subject to seizure by Mexican authorities and such person would have to pay a fine amounting to a substantial percentage of the vehicle's value. If confiscated, your vehicle will NOT be returned.

8. The *Consulate General of the United States of America*
Ciudad Juárez, Mexico web site* gives the following information about **spare parts**:

> If you bring spare auto parts to Mexico, declare them when you enter the country. When you leave, be prepared to show that you are taking the unused parts with you or that you have had them installed in Mexico. Save your repair receipts for this purpose.

9. The *Consulate General of the United States of America*
Ciudad Juárez, Mexico web site* gives the following information about **driving in Mexico City**:

> All vehicular traffic is restricted in the capital city of Mexico City in order to reduce air pollution. The restriction is based on the last digit of the vehicle license plate. (This applies equally to permanent and temporary plates. There is no specific provision regarding plates with letters only.)

> Monday: no driving if license plate ends with 5 or 6.
> Tuesday: no driving if license plate ends with 7 or 8.
> Wednesday: no driving if license plate ends with 3 or 4.
> Thursday: no driving if license plate ends with 1 or 2.

Friday: no driving if license plate ends with 9 or 0. [The author believes that specialty plates don't circulate on Fridays.]
Saturday and Sunday: all vehicles may be driven.

10. The *Consulate General of the United States of America*
Ciudad Juárez, Mexico web site gives* the following information about **lost permits**:

Under Mexican Customs Law, if a U.S. Citizen loses the car importation permit, he has to file a police report with the PGR (Procuraduría General de la República – Attorney General's Office) and present that document at Customs so they can issue an exit permit.

This would NOT be a simple procedure. DON'T loose your permit.

*Note: I could not find information on the same topics on any consulate web site in 2011, but don't see any evidence that the information is not still pertinent and have therefore included it in the 3rd edition.

Licensing Your Car Purchased in Mexico

Tarjeta de Circulación

Licensing your Mexican car in Mexico is similar to in the U.S. and Canada. You have to pay a yearly licensing fee at the *Transito Municipal* of your state and in most states get emissions testing. Until December 31, 2011, you used to have to pay a tax, called *tenencia* in Spanish, which was based on the value of your car. This was a yearly responsibility (unless your car was ten years old or more), but the *tenencia* has been revoked as it was originally begun to pay for the Olympics and was supposed to be a temporary tax. For now – as long as you get your current *tarjeta de circulación* before March 31, you won't have to pay this, unless your new car costs more than $250,000. I won't be surprised if something

Man displaying his 2012 *tarjeta de circulación* in Mexico City.
Source:
www.aztecanoticias.com.mx

similar takes its place, but for now you just pay the yearly fee. (In 2012, the fee was $375 pesos in Cuernavaca and $237 pesos in Mexico City. Do not ever try to drive without this, and be sure to keep a copy in a safe place, just in case.

You also have to prove that you are not polluting the air by taking your car for an emissions test.

In previous years, they gave you a sticker to put on your car, rather than on your license plate, showing the year.

Emissions Testing

In Morelos you must get your emissions tested every six months – you are assigned two, two-month windows during the year to get this done. The testing is efficient and will probably only take 20 minutes or less. It consists of the attendant taking the paper from the previous emissions test (which he will keep), then entering your data into the computer of the emissions tester, and finally putting a cap on your tailpipe. The computer indicates if your vehicle passes or not.

Once your car passes, the attendant puts a sticker on the inside back window of your vehicle (you can peel off the old one). It is this sticker that a police officer would look for in the event that they pull you over. You will also be given a piece of paper that indicates when you need to return for your next test. You must keep this in your vehicle. You will turn it in when you go for your next emissions test.

The 2007 emissions testing sticker in Morelos.

You can find the mechanic shops that conduct emissions tests by looking for signs outside that say "*verificaciones*." You pull into one of these places with the following things on hand:

1. $120 pesos cash (You can pay the people who do the testing directly.)

2. A photocopy of the *Tarjeta de ciculacion*

3. The receipt from the previous emissions verification (If your vehicle is brand new, you won't have one of these yet. Just go in the month indicated and tell them that it's your first emissions test.)

If you miss the two month windows allowed for you to get your emissions tested you pay the $120 pesos for the test plus an additional $140 peso fine (*multa*). You will have to go to a bank to pay the fine, but don't go there directly. The emissions tester will give you a receipt to take

Mexico: The Trick is Living Here 3rd edition
available on *www.home-sweet-mexico.com*
179

with you to the bank to use to make your payment. You return with the receipt that the bank gives you when you pay and turn that in to the person who does your testing.

In some places emissions testing can be a joke because if a particular vehicle doesn't pass the test some people conducting them are willing to input the data of the vehicle, but put the testing equipment onto the tailpipe of a newer car that passes. They just ask someone to "lend" their tailpipe for a few minutes and the problem is solved. Oh well, at least it's efficient.

Emissions testing is also updating rapidly. Luis has seen a reduction in the items required to complete the testing (indicating increased streamlining of the process) in the two years that he has owned a vehicle. There may be some variation in the process in the area that you live from what I have described here due to variation in the streamlining in different areas, but hopefully the description will still be helpful to you.

Purchasing Your Car in Mexico

Another point to consider is that cars can cost more in Mexico than they do in the U.S. For example a 2013 Ford Focus is listed as starting at $ 227,300 pesos ($17,410 U.S. dollars) on Ford's Mexico web site (http://www.ford.com.mx/home.asp) and the same car is listed as starting at $16,200 U.S. dollars on Ford's U.S. web site (http://www.ford.com/). When you are deciding of you want to purchase a car in Mexico or bring one with you make sure that you find out the value of the car **in Mexico**.

When you purchase a used car in Mexico there are a couple of details that go a little beyond the things that you have to check in the U.S.

First of all, having a complete history of records for the car goes beyond a "good idea." It's necessary to have. Ask the previous owner to review their file of all of the documents for the vehicle. First check to make sure that the receipt for the original purchase is included in the file (called the *factura*). You must have this when you go to pay your *tenencia* (see "Licensing Your Car Purchased in Mexico" on page 177). Second, make sure that all of the receipts for paid *tenencias* are together in addition to the current *tarjeta de circulacion*. If you couldn't prove that they had all been paid you would have to pay for any missing payments. The proof is on you. The officials will not go back into their records to look for any payments.

This is also true for emissions. Look for the **current** receipt for the *verificacion*. All emissions payments have to have been made on the car, if not you will pay all back emissions charges.

The PGR (*la procuraduría general de la Republica*), in whichever state you are, has a data base of cars stolen in Mexico. As is true with licensing and emissions checks, the process is quickly becoming streamlined on computers and is improving rapidly. You should go to check to be sure that the car you are purchasing hasn't been stolen. You must bring the actual car in to the PGR. In fact, the PGR recommends that in addition to the car, you bring the current owner. Obviously, someone who is trying to sell a stolen car won't come with you to the PGR, so if the owner refuses your request to accompany you to the PGR, *don't* take the car in by yourself. This protects you against getting caught with a stolen car. The officials will check the VIN number on the motor and other places on the car and check for any records on the car in their computerized database.

Why You Must Insure Your Car—There Is No Truth

A car accident would rattle anyone's nerves, but car accidents in Mexico can really wind you up. The reality that Mexico is dramatically different from back home really hits you after being in an accident in Mexico. It's quite a shock when you are in the middle of a traffic "situation" involving the police and you realize that they are making the situation worse and potentially more dangerous for you. I had never really understood "shifting sand" analogies before being in one of these situations myself.

The police in Mexico have no commitment to the truth, but they do have power to define it. One minute you can be standing firmly on what you think is wet, solid sand—your innocence in a collision. Suddenly, in the next moment the sand is shifting under your feet and you are in danger of falling—you are being declared at fault. When it comes to car accidents in Mexico, responsibility for a collision is determined by a number of factors, none of which have anything to do with the sequence of events that actually created the collision, and all of which have to do with the sequence of events that progress afterwards. In Mexico, insurance adjusters are there to get things straight.

As a foreigner it's important that you have insurance so that you can call an adjuster as soon as you find yourself in a car accident. Say nothing to the people involved in the accident, just call your insurance agent. You must call the agent as soon as possible because if they don't arrive before the police are ready to leave you may be leaving with the police. They may detain people until all of the details are worked out. When the adjuster arrives they will do the talking.

I experienced the shifting sands of responsibility when my husband was hit by a taxi driver while riding his bicycle. A friend called me to the scene and by the time I got there, my husband had been taken to a medical facility. I found his bicycle lying in the street near a taxi, badly bent in the fender. I quickly scanned for blood on the pavement, but didn't see any. A gaggle of police officers was standing around.

I walked up and introduced myself. I was obviously scared and I expected one of the officers to talk to me and tell me something about where and how my husband was. I also expected that they might have some questions for me concerning insurance or my husband's information. They said nothing and were joking among themselves. No one said anything to me until I bent to pick up his bike to take it home. That's when they ordered me to leave it there. I asked why and they gruffly informed me that they would be impounding it. This is normal procedure, but I didn't know it at the time.

I was trying to take note of certain information, such as the license plate of the taxi and I was shaking so badly that I could barely write on the paper that I had brought with me. I had to try twice to get the numbers legible. The officers were laughing at my nerve-wracked attempts to be clear headed. Finally, a man who was not a police officer was moved by what I thought at the time was his humanity to tell me that my husband was fine. He did this with a little giggle in his voice, but I was at least glad that he had spoken to me. I think this man may have been the insurance adjuster of the taxi driver. He was the one who

Mexico: The Trick is Living Here 3rd edition
available on www.home-sweet-mexico.com
183

told me where my husband was and reminded me to take the health coverage card (he was at IMSS) otherwise they would not treat my husband. Sly dog. If he was the insurance adjuster, he wanted to avoid paying for a private hospital for my husband.

I got the name of the police officer who was standing nearby and at least looking in charge (in other words, he wasn't lounging around the police truck, cracking jokes or looking bored) but he acted insulted that I wanted it and made no move to show me an ID or badge. He basically acted as if it was a bother to tell me his name, but he would do it anyway because I couldn't do anything with his name anyway. I was so distraught at the time I could not tell you if I ever saw him or the possible insurance adjuster again.

Anyway, I left to get to the hospital and now that I'm more experienced with such things, I'm sure the "humane" man slipped some money to the police to make my husband at fault. To make a long story short, because there was an injury and it was a vehicular accident (bicycles are vehicles too) both my husband and the taxi driver were detained. Because my husband was in the hospital he had a police officer in plain clothes watching him at the hospital while the poor taxi driver was detained at the police station. I know because I kept seeing him in the same clothes sitting in police cars, sitting in the "procu," etc. He would give me hateful looks as if I were doing something to him and I had no idea why at the time. Even now, I'm not sure I could have done anything to make his situation any better.

It took over 48 hours and our hiring a lawyer to get the whole situation straightened out. It was not until afterwards that the guard was pulled from my husband and that the taxi driver was released. The whole while, the family of the taxi driver was trying to pick a fight with me and my neighbors who were helping me deal with it all. Thank God for my neighbors. I simply could not have done it without them. In fact, it was my neighbor who saw the insurance adjusters from the "opposing" side coming out of the intensive care ward after a visit with my husband smiling as if they'd just gone to the circus and won a free car. She said, "Julia, you need a lawyer." I was focused on trying to get the doctors to treat my husband's broken bone and in my naiveté was assuming that the police would make a determination of the fault, that the insurance company would sign the release forms and the whole thing would progress ahead. How wrong I was.

It was worse than being in the Twilight Zone. Even the "Procru" was behaving weirdly. They were saying that they were there to serve us, but getting mad when we asked them to write the truth in the documents. We later realized that they were fishing for bribes. Even the lawyers (They kept switching our lawyer on us, which was disconcerting.) couldn't get them to do what they were supposed to do.

A friend and I went back to the scene of the accident to get witnesses. Lots of people said that they had seen the accident and wanted to know if my husband was OK. They wished him well, but as soon as we asked them to be witnesses they vanished like smoke in the wind.

One lawyer who understood where I was coming from more than the others, pulled me aside at one point and told me that it was customary at that point for one of the two "sides" to pay a bribe to the "Procru," but he thought that the other side would do it in this case. I just stood there with my mouth hanging open. As he was looking at my fillings, the lawyer told me that it was sad, but that's how it is in his country right now.

Anyway, the lawyers did their thing. Who knows how many bribes they paid. Finally, it was all said and done and

Mexico: The Trick is Living Here 3rd edition
available on www.home-sweet-mexico.com   185

my husband was being treated for his broken bone (*days* later!) in a private hospital chosen by the taxi driver's insurance company. At this time I learned that we were actually lucky that the taxi driver didn't just hit and run. He was young and inexperienced. He got out of his taxi and asked Luis if he was alright. I wish I could thank him for staying. It cost him days of stress and discomfort, but it was his insurance that paid for Luis's care and we really needed that support.

In an interest to keep this description short I've left out details. This summary really doesn't do it justice, yet I'm sure that you can tell that you would never want to find yourself in a nightmare like this. If Luis hadn't been injured he would have been in whatever hell-hole the police detain people in. The police have to detain people here otherwise they would disappear and the injured people would never get the care they need (and they couldn't collect their bribes). You don't want to be detained. YOU MUST HAVE INSURANCE IN MEXICO.

Finding insurance in Mexico isn't that different from finding it at home, with one minor exception. When you are shopping around for the best insurance company here you are **shopping for the level of service, not the price**. I recommend that you get a referral from someone who has had cause to call their insurance company. If they say that their adjuster arrived promptly and was helpful, then that company could be for you. Make sure you ask the person what their relationship to the insurance company is. If, for example, they are related to a person who works in the company (i.e. a brother-in-law), then you may not want to consider their recommendation. There is no guarantee that their brother-in-law will treat you the way he treats them.

Rolly Brook has an excellent description on why you need insurance in Mexico on his web site at:

http://rollybrook.com/auto-insurance.htm#why. After reading my story above, you can see that Rolly has hit the nail right on the head. Also, scroll down and read his section on "Some things to consider." He has some tips about avoiding sneaky insurance companies that (luckily) I don't know about. When you are choosing your insurance company, remember that in Mexico there isn't the same level of consumer protection as there is in the U.S. and Canada and that in some companies dishonesty is the way they do business. Rolly Brook advises his readers to **read the insurance policy before signing and paying**. I have to agree with him.

Tips from an Insurance Agent

My insurance agent has given me the following tips:

1. Do not talk to anyone. Call your insurance company immediately and request that an agent meet you right away. Just say, "My agent is on the way." If people try to get you to talk.

2. If anyone is injured—no matter who is at fault—have the person sent to the nearest *private* hospital. *Do not have them sent to IMSS or any public hospital.*

   - She was vague about why, but based on my experience I can surmise that it is for two reasons. One is that all those corrupt officials mentioned in my story about Luis's bicycle accident are at the public institutions and they'd get involved. Two is that if the person is at a private hospital they will be incurring a cost and the insurance companies will benefit from expediting the process. If the person is at a public hospital, they would not be incurring any costs and the insurance companies would be free to let them rot. Meanwhile, you could be detained by the police, waiting for matters to be settled.

3. Have **photo copies** of the following things in your car at all times

- the emergency phone number for your insurance company

- insurance policy

- your driver's license

- your identification

- You want to have photo copies available so that you won't ever have to hand over your originals. A friend saw a family member on vacation hand over their documents to an insurance adjuster who took them away to process the paperwork. It took multiple calls and shouting over the phone to get the adjuster to drop off the original documents at the place they were staying. He showed up at midnight the night before they were heading home on a twelve hour drive.

When *Not* to Use Your Insurance

Even though you have insurance, it's still a smart idea to try to settle any minor matters on the spot with the other driver. If you are at fault, offer some cash on the spot (200 pesos seems to be the standard amount for scratches and bumper dents). Most of the time, the other person will prefer this over involving any authorities. My husband has successfully used this method a couple of times and it works well. If you are not at fault and the other person offers you some money for any damage to your car, take it and thank them.

Insuring Your Car from the United States

All of the above reasons for having insurance are also true if you have brought your car from the United States or Canada.

While you are at the border you can purchase insurance for your car. This is especially important if your insurer in the U.S. does not cover you in Mexico – and even if they do, they must be able to send an agent to the scene of an accident wherever you are in Mexico. Check with them before you leave to find out if they do. If you would like to you can buy a temporary policy at the border that will cover you until you can get to your new home and buy the policy that you will want for long-term use.

You need to choose an insurance company that will insure your foreign car. Not all companies will. Getting a referral from someone you know is a good idea, but make sure you read the policy carefully to be sure that they will insure a foreign car just to be sure. Also double check to be

Mexico: The Trick is Living Here 3rd edition
available on www.home-sweet-mexico.com
189

sure that they will insure your car even if you don't have the license in the U.S. up to date. If for some reason you ever let that lapse, you don't want to be unwittingly forfeiting your insurance. Also, as I state in the section above, make sure that you pick a company that can **send you an agent when and where you need them**. The cost for this insurance is likely to be higher than it would be to insure a car with Mexican license plates.

12 Banking and Bill Paying

With an increasing number of young people using banks for a variety of money management services, they are slowly waking up to the need to offer convenient, affordable services. Yet, I still find the banks to be completely inconvenient. Their customer service almost rivals that of Telmex in complete unresponsiveness. Their interest rates on savings accounts and CDs are either non existent or are discouragingly low. Bank statements arrive in the mail inconsistently so months can go by when you won't know what's going on with your account. You can ask about internet access to your account but also ask how much they charge for it. They charge fees for anything they possibly can -- like internet access to your own account. When I look at my bank statement each transaction is followed by *two* different charges. I wouldn't be surprised if they charged a fee for sneezing while using the cash machine!

Most expatriates in Mexico are smart and maintain a bank account in their home country and then open a second account here in Mexico, accessing the funds in their home account at cash machines in Mexico. [Note: Canadian citizens have to be sure that they are either still residents of

Mexico: The Trick is Living Here 3rd edition
available on www.home-sweet-mexico.com
191

Canada or have fewer than around five "minor ties" to Canada if they wish to hold a bank account in Canada. (See "Giving up or Retaining Residency for Canadian Citizens?" on page 149 for more information.)] Before you move to Mexico you will want to make sure that you have reliable internet banking with your home bank. Here is an important tip: find out what their "swift" number is so that you can use it to transfer money (for international transfers sometimes you have to know both the sending and the receiving bank's number codes) and they won't give you this information over the phone because of security reasons. Ask them about their services for international transfers, etc.

You will probably have to provide them with a secure address in the U.S., Great Britain or wherever you are from so that they can send you new cash cards, PIN numbers and other things. You'll need a quick, secure way to access this mail. It's always difficult when cash and credit cards expire because the bank can never seem to get it to you in the mail – then when you do get it, watch out, because the phone number you have to call to activate it surely won't work from Mexico. You may consider having a trusted friend or relative help you with banking in some way. You can also get your own street address and mail forwarding service see "Mailbox Services" in the Useful Links for more information. Even though it's not a common occurrence, we all do sometimes receive the odd personal check and it's most helpful if someone can just deposit it into the account in the U.S. because, though it is possible to deposit "foreign currency" checks into a Mexican peso bank account, doing so is a pain and costs fees.

I also recommend setting up a Paypal account and getting it connected with your home account before moving to Mexico. If you've never used Paypal, it seems

Mexico: The Trick is Living Here 3rd edition
available on www.home-sweet-mexico.com
192

logical to expect that it'll be a huge pain, but it's really not difficult and can be a real life saver for expats.

I first learned to deposit a foreign currency check into my Mexican bank account when I received my first payment for this e-book from Clickbank! At my bank in Mexico, I have to wait for a turn at the customer service counter and give them my immigration visa and account numbers, then wait for special approval. Next I wait in line to see a teller. For all of this my bank charges me a $10 peso processing fee and I have to wait 20 days for the money to be available—but it can be done.

There is no trick to banking in Mexico that will make it "perfect," but if you know the following details it will make your experience of choosing a bank in Mexico a little smoother. When you go to sign up for a bank account bring a proof of address (see "The Basics" on page 210) and either your passport or your Mexican visa. Once you have an account you will need either the passport or the visa to do any transaction, so always remember to bring one of them with you. If you are planning to do a "major" transaction, such as open a CD and transfer some of your money into it, bring a current proof of address. Even though you are already a customer, they will still want to see the proof of address.

In order to choose your bank you will want to know which service charges they apply and for what. This information may be hard to get. I've asked before and found that the customer service representatives gave me blank looks. Then when I explained what I was asking about, they told me that there weren't any, which is an Untruth if I've ever heard one. (More about Untruths on page 99.) It's hard to figure out exactly how the banks differ, but a friend and I were comparing notes. Between the two of us we have experience with four major banks.

An important difference between them is that some charge a fee to *receive* an international transfer, which means that your bank in the U.S. charges you to send it and your bank in Mexico charges you to receive it. Another bank charges you a fee to withdraw money with a teller if you haven't already maxed out your amount at the cash machine. One of these banks charges 30 pesos per bank statement you request to have printed out (which you often have to do since they don't arrive reliably through the mail). Another bank charges a 10 peso flat fee to cash checks in U.S. dollars and there is a 20 day waiting period before the money becomes available in pesos in your account.

IXE
The Bank that May Make Julia a Liar

A friend writes, "We just switched to IXE which gives the best exchange rates for the dollar, and they are super nice; *it is a customer service orientation* [emphasis mine]. They offer free coffee or slushies while you wait, but the thing is you never really have to wait. When I went to close my Banamex account it took me 4 tries and I got yelled at twice, and my [Mexican] husband once. IXE is the way to go. They even go to your house to pick up deposits and do paperwork like opening an account. We used them at my business and had them come all the time."

Want to try this bank? Here's their web site:
http://www.ixe.com.mx/portal/

A "Short" List to Get Straight Answers About Fees

Probably the best way to get straight answers about fees would be to sit down and make a list of all of the services you expect to use. Make the list as specific as you can because I've noticed a tendency for them to operate on the if-you-don't-ask-I-won't-tell system. I've found that when I ask general questions I don't get good answers, but if I can think of just the right question, then I get more specific answers. After you have the list, go down it detail by detail with a representative from each prospective bank and ask them how much you will be charged for each service. Here is a partial list to get you started:

- Open a bank account
- Close a bank account
- Minimum amount that you must keep in the account before it is closed and they keep your money. (Yes, they do this.)
- Monthly "maintenance" fee
- Receive transfer from foreign bank account (specify country)
- Send money to a foreign bank account (specify country)
- Cash a check in Mexican pesos from same bank
- Cash a check in Mexican pesos from a different Mexican bank
- Cash a check in U.S dollars (or other currency) from a major bank
- Cash a check in foreign currency from a private party
- Interest rates on accounts

- Interest rates on CDs (called *inversiones a plazo*).
- Internet banking
- To replace lost cash cards
- For over-drawl
- Cash machine: withdrawal fee
- Cash machine: fee to check balance
- Cash machine: at special location, such as the grocery store

The If-You-Don't-Ask-I-Won't-Tell System

To give you an example of the if-you-don't-ask-I-won't-tell system, I'll explain an experience that I had while putting my money away in a CD. (This is a good idea because it makes it so that your money is not available through the cash machine and you are thus less susceptible to loosing all of your money through a "mini-kidnapping/express kidnapping.")

The first time I had put my money in a six-month CD (that's "American" for "term deposit" for you Canadians), the customer service representative drew up the papers and explained to me that on the date that the CD matured the money would be rolled over into my bank account, complete with the minuscule amount of earnings accrued. On a second occasion I was again putting my money into a six-month CD. The customer service representative drew up the papers in a similar fashion without asking me any questions about my preferences. I was assuming that the CD would roll over into my bank account automatically—just as it had the first time. Well, I didn't know it, but he had set the CD up in such a way that it would roll back into another six-month CD! Of course, if I had wanted my money put away for twelve months I would have chosen a twelve-month CD with the slightly higher interest rate that it offers. Not to mention that a year was too long for me to be without access to my money because I would have run out!

Thank goodness this "minor" detail was clarified when I asked on what day the money would be available. He told me, and I restated back to him in my own words what I had understood. This has become my habit to be sure that I'm communicating correctly in my second language. Based on my reiteration he corrected me, telling me that I had to come on that day and only on that exact day if I wanted to prevent the money from rolling back into a second six-month CD. I very nicely explained to him that that was not acceptable. He gave me a look like, "Come on, do I have to redo the paperwork?" If I hadn't had the CD that released into my bank account the first time, something that had happened by "accident." I would have believed that the one day window option was the only one available. Imagine how that would have worked. On that arbitrary day I would have had to have a big note on my calendar and gone running to the bank no matter what, in order to get my money!

Bank accounts in Mexico generally don't pay any interest. Putting your money in a six or twelve-month CD might only earn three percent interest. These low interest rates mean that you shouldn't leave you money sitting in a Mexican bank because you will loose it due to inflation and all of the service charges that they apply to your account. You can use your home country bank for long term savings and money markets (that's American for high interest savings accounts), etc. You can then use internet banking to make movements and a cash card or wire transfer to spend your money in Mexico.

Mexico: The Trick is Living Here 3rd edition
available on www.home-sweet-mexico.com
197

Some electronic payment services are available through some banks in Mexico. For example, you can have your phone bill paid automatically. If you are interested in using such a service, wait until you have a year or two in Mexico under your belt, then go set the service up with your bank. Ask if you can place an upper limit on the amount of payment. It works something like this. As long as the bill is lower than X amount, the bank pays it. If the bill is over X amount the bank doesn't pay it and you must go to pay it in person. The problem with this is that since bank statements arrive only sporadically there is a risk of either the bank not paying the bill or the bank charging you some cooked up service fee and you not finding out about it until months later when you have accrued penalty fees. This is a big risk and I don't recommend trusting the bank to make payments for you until you are completely sure that you can trust them. Another potential difficulty, particularly when dealing with Telmex is that when it comes time to cancel the automatic payment you might either be double charged or end up paying some kind of late fee. If you can't understand how this could possibly happen you haven't been in Mexico long enough. Trust me.

When I go to the bank it is always an exercise in Zen patience. A quick trip to the bank takes thirty minutes, a normal trip forty-five, and a long one an hour or more. Since I often walk to the bank to make it a positive exercise experience, the whole trip can take an hour and a half. I usually use the time standing in line to exercise two parts of myself. The first and most important is my patience. For the second I work on my posture. Once I worked on my humor writing. You can read the results on my web site at http://www.home-sweet-mexico.com/retire-in-Mexico-bank1.html.

Mexico: The Trick is Living Here 3rd edition
available on www.home-sweet-mexico.com
198

Good luck and remember to practice your patience. It's a virtue after all.

Paying Bills

It is usually necessary to pay bills in person with cash. You can go to the office from which the service is provided and can also go to any local bank. Look on the back of your bill for a listing of the banks (and other places such as grocery stores) that accept payments for that particular bill. Be ready for surprises. I once stood in line for 30 minutes only to be brusquely told that unless I had an account at that particular bank, I could only make payments until 2:00 p.m.! Oh, of course! How obvious. Silly me.

The grocery store is a nice option for paying things such as your telephone bill because, unlike your bank, they won't charge you a service fee. The only rule is that you must pay the bill before the due date, otherwise you have to go to the office of the service provider.

Mexico: The Trick is Living Here 3rd edition
available on www.home-sweet-mexico.com
199

13 Financial Matters for U.S.

Citizens

Receiving your Social Security Benefits in Mexico

Below are some of the important points from the Social Security Online web page. You can check out the page at http://www.ssa.gov/pubs/10137.html for more information.

1. "If you are a U.S. citizen, you may receive your Social Security payments outside the U.S. as long as you are eligible for them."

2. "If you receive benefits as a dependent or survivor of the worker, special requirements may affect your right to receive Social Security payments while you are outside the U.S." Find out more at http://www.ssa.gov/pubs/10137.html#additional.

Mexico: The Trick is Living Here 3rd edition
available on *www.home-sweet-mexico.com*
200

3. "You may want your Social Security payment to be directly deposited into your account at either a financial institution in the country where you live or a U.S. financial institution. Even if you use the direct deposit service, you must keep us informed of any change in your current residence address.

   "Direct deposit has several advantages. You never have to worry about your check being delayed in the mail, lost or stolen. With direct deposit you receive your payment much faster than if you are paid by check (usually one to three weeks faster than check deliveries). You also avoid check cashing and currency conversion fees." Mexico is one of the countries in which you can receive direct deposit of you S.S. check. Find out more at http://www.ssa.gov/pubs/10137.html#direct.

4. "Since Medicare benefits are available only in the U.S., it may not be to your advantage to sign up and pay the premium for medical insurance if you will be out of the U.S. for a long period of time. But you should be aware that your premium, when you do sign up, will be 10 percent higher for each 12-month period you could have been enrolled but were not." Find out more at http://www.ssa.gov/pubs/10137.html#whatyouneed.

5. "If you are living outside the U.S., periodically we will send you a questionnaire. This lets us figure out if you still are eligible for benefits. Return the questionnaire to the office that sent it as soon as possible; if you do not, your payments will stop.

In addition to responding to the questionnaire, notify us promptly about changes that could affect your payments." See http://www.ssa.gov/pubs/10137.html#things to learn what to report (such as working outside the U.S.) and how to report it.

6. Below are the Social Security offices in Mexico:

Federal Benefits Unit
American Consulate General
Avenue Lopez Mateos 924 Nte
32000 Ciudad Juarez, Chihuahua
Mexico
Phone: 526-5661-31512
Fax: 526-5661-34698
Email: FBU.Ciudad.Juarez@ssa.gov

Federal Benefits Unit
American Consulate General
Progreso 175
44100 Guadalajara, Jalisco
Mexico
Phone: 523-3326-82139
Fax: 523-3382-57942
Email: FBU.Guadalajara@ssa.gov

Federal Benefits Unit
American Embassy
Paseo de la Reforma 305
06500 Mexico D. F.
Mexico
Phone: 052-55-5080-2852
Fax: 052-55-5080-2706
Email: FBU.Mexico.City@ssa.gov

Make sure that you clarify with your benefits provider how you must receive your first disbursement. Some systems that allow electronic deposit require that you receive the first disbursement as a check which you must go to deposit in person. You may need to be sure that you are in your old home to receive this before you move to your new home.

Maintaining a U.S. PO Box

You can get "mailbox service" through the UPS store in the U.S. [information for Canadians on page 159]. This service does what an expat needs, including providing you with a street address, not a P.O. Box number, package acceptance from all shipping carriers, package and mail receipt notification, and probably most importantly, mail holding and forwarding.

> The UPS Store web site:
>
> http://www.theupsstore.com/products-services/mailbox/Pages/index.aspx

Mexico: The Trick is Living Here 3rd edition
available on www.home-sweet-mexico.com
203

14 Cultural Information:

Important Etiquette & What

Not to Do

Culture Shock

Culture shock is a sneaky thing to experience. Often while it's affecting you, you just can't put your finger on what it is that's on your nerves. You can't pinpoint any problem but you're still darn sure something's wrong – with everybody else. At other times, you know exactly what's wrong. Maybe you latch onto the unreliable mail service or maybe it's the fact that the veggie store closes at random times, leaving you without avocados. The line of thinking in this mood goes something like the following: It's just inconceivable that a store expect to have customers

Mexico: The Trick is Living Here 3rd edition
available on www.home-sweet-mexico.com
204

and stay in business if the service is so unreliable. Half the time when you go by, the doors are closed and it makes it impossible to plan your errands, let alone your meals and back home grocery stores are always open all day long and.... on and on and on. We've all heard others complaining about something **they** find completely obnoxious about their host country until they are the obnoxious ones.

Of course, you don't plan to move to Mexico and act like an "ugly American," but I don't think I've met a person yet who is immune to culture shock. Some things will bother you. Sometimes you'll feel overly tired or out of sorts or like you are a weirdo because it's hard work figuring out how to act right, speak right, and what to expect from others. Still, if you use patience, stay flexible, be a good listener, and keep your mouth shut (feet stay out better when our mouths are shut) as much as possible you'll make it through and come out the other side a better person. You'll become more practiced at being flexible in your own daily activities and plans. You'll come to more easily perceive details such as, that the vegetable shop owner is a mom and is probably off attending a school event for her children or accompanying a family

> Read more tips about culture shock and how to handle it on my web site:
>
> http://home-sweet-mexico.com/cultural-differences.html/

member to the doctor. You'll be able to value such balance between work and family. Your perspective will shift to a new logic – one based on Mexican priorities.

Greetings and Leave Takings

Hellos and goodbyes are very important in Mexico. People (neighbors, acquaintances, and coworkers) actually get their feelings hurt if you don't greet them properly. If they don't go so far as getting their feelings hurt, they are guaranteed to notice and will tease you about it. Jokes about how it is obvious that someone doesn't like them because they didn't greet them are common among coworkers and neighbors. In fact, you're lucky if they're teasing you. In Mexico, it is common to be quiet about genuinely hurt feelings. I've lived in all three North American countries, and I know that we Americans often ignore each other unless we need something from another person and Canadians, being quite reserved, tend to leave each other alone as well. Regularly, if I do greet someone, it is with a loud, "Hey, so-and-so" from across the room. This does not fly among Mexicans.

Greetings vary by region and social status, but they all involve two basic aspects. It will not take you longer than a day among people who expect to see you on a regular basis for you to observe the basic greeting pattern in your region. Make note of nuances such as body language, gestures, phrases, and timing as they apply to the various settings in which you find yourself. First, in many settings, you must actually walk up to the person you are greeting regardless of what they or you are doing or carrying. Second you must look them in the eye and speak to them. Do not worry about interrupting them, even if they are deep in conversation with another person. Just greet both people. If you do these two basic aspects, the people around you will initiate the finer nuances that they use in their region/social group.

In general, educated people "air kiss" your right cheek. If they move toward you, expect to move left or hold still and let them do the moving. Personal styles develop regarding the amount of noise you should make. Obviously, a loud smack that could hurt someone's eardrums is too much noise, but it is ok to make a slight "pecking" noise. The mistake foreigners often make is actually contacting the person's cheeks with their lips. I used to do this—still do occasionally. I know this is a foreigner thing to do because the only person who has ever (and in fact consistently) gets my cheek wet is an Australian. Yucky. Make sure the person knows you are going to kiss them by touching their shoulder and if they are seated facing away from you, give them time to turn their head to face you. Otherwise, your lips end up lined up facing the same direction and you could end up planting a good one right on their lips. Double yucky. I'm sure you guessed that I learned this the hard way too, but luckily it was with a friend who doesn't worry about such little mistakes. No, I didn't actually get her lips, but it was much too close for comfort. Remember, you are not bothering them by interrupting what they are doing for a kiss. You are doing what they like: greeting them. If you didn't do this, you would really be bothering them, because not to greet is to snub.

I've observed that country folk shake hands and greetings are recorded by day. Each new day, your greeting slate is blank and the first time you see someone other than your housemates or nuclear family, you walk up to them, extend your hand and say good morning, good afternoon (knowing what time it is helps, but is not critical), good evening, or good night. If you see that person later in the same day, you don't need to shake hands again, but if they are with others whom you haven't seen, you must shake

Mexico: The Trick is Living Here 3rd edition
available on www.home-sweet-mexico.com
207

the hands of the others. When you pass the person whose hand you have already shaken, you should mention that you have already greeted them earlier in the day or others may think you are deliberately snubbing that person.

If children are present, they will be nudged and told, "*Saluda,*" which means "greet." Some kids will pucker up and you will have to lean over so they can reach your towering cheek. You can also extend a hand and they will reach out and let you shake it. If you have children, I would advise that you encourage them to greet the adults. If they are shy you can talk to them about it ahead of time, so they are prepared. Mexicans are very flexible about children's greetings. They know that children get tired, hungry, or out-of-sorts and sometimes can't act like mini adults. In these instances, any gentle, but earnest attempt on the part of the family to instill good manners is considered appropriate. If your child can't pull off a greeting, just smile and say "*esta cansado*" (he or she is tired) – but *don't* say this before encouraging your child to greet the person. As an American I was impressed with the way my son -- supported by his community -- learned before he could even talk how to greet and break the ice with others. His social skills are stellar. I'm now embarrassed to say that I was surprised by this, previously believing that children didn't talk to non-family members. Up north, we've taken the "don't talk to strangers" message so far that our children live in terrifying isolation in their communities. Later, we wonder why our teens are so isolated!

Leave taking is also important in any setting with people with whom you are in regular contact or who are friends of friends. Search people out to say goodbye to them. If it is not appropriate, tell someone to say goodbye to them for you. If you are saying goodbye to a roomful of people, for example the extended family of a friend, you can go around the room to each person or just look at each in turn and say goodbye – and don't act like an American and leave out the children. Another option is to raise your voice and say goodbye to the whole room. If the people are strangers, don't do this, or they will think you are strange, of course. Seriously, the best option is to make the round around the room. Touch each person on the shoulder, lean over and air kiss their cheek or shake their hand and say "goodbye" (*hasta luego*) or "nice to meet you" (*gusto de conocerlo/la*), depending on which is appropriate. Don't worry about interrupting their individual conversations. They expect to be interrupted to say hello or goodbye to others and smoothly break off their conversations to do the greeting or leave-taking routine with you then return to their conversations.

If you are walking past a neighbor at some distance, you can just wave and say hello. If the person is someone you know, and is obviously working, for example, doing laundry outside their house, you can ask, "*¿Ya mero?*" which means "almost done?"

Getting Help at Stores

One major difference between our two countries is the way people get attention at the counter in a store. In Mexico, it is the *customer* who must *ask* for things. The clerk will continue working and completely ignore you when you walk up to the counter until you ask for something – *especially* if you have forgotten to greet them upon entering the store or approaching the counter. When I first got here, I would stand there for whole minutes, waiting, knowing the person knew I was there and feeling

Mexico: The Trick is Living Here 3rd edition
available on *www.home-sweet-mexico.com*
209

like it would be rude to say something, then getting mad because it was rude of the person to ignore me so blatantly.

To top it off the customers were upsetting me as well because each individual customer is only responsible for him or herself. You don't have to concern yourself with whether there is someone before you; you just walk up to the counter and request what you want. So, there I would be, patiently waiting, and a bunch of school kids would elbow into the counter next to me and start calling out their orders and the attendant would serve *them*! I felt so insulted. Attendants never ask people, "Who's first?" the way they do back home. They just serve whoever is ready, whoever is closest to them, whoever already has the exact change, whoever is loudest, or whoever has the smallest purchase. Your goal as the customer is to be one of the people described above. While I haven't achieved the middle-schooler's level of self-centeredness when ordering, I do call out my requests (*¿me da _____, porfavor?*) without worrying about the attendants' feelings or "busyness." It takes some getting used to because it requires us North Americans to do something that in our own culture is inconsiderate, but once you've waited long enough, you'll get the hang of it. You'll also learn to greet as you enter the store, thus opening the communication lines for when it comes time to make your purchase.

Lies that Protect Someone's Ego

While I'm on the topic of Mexican customs that seem inconsiderate to people from the U.S., I think I will have to describe the "lie." In Mexico, sometimes things that we consider lies, aren't lies. Since, in Mexico, not all lies are lies, let's call the lies that aren't lies untruths. You have to learn to recognize untruths so that you don't believe them and aren't led astray. The major red-flag that usually tips me off to untruths is whether the person I'm talking to might have to go to some effort to give me the truth. If the effort level to reach truth-hood is too high, a Mexican person might opt for a common untruth, which would save them a lot of energy or embarrassment. It seems that "I don't know" is a taboo phrase. It can be frustrating because often people who opt for the untruth are those whose job it is to assist us in some way. If you are confused, please stick with me here. Those who follow this concept quickly have already lived in Mexico for some time! Trust me.

I think a simple illustrative anecdote will clear up your confusion (and if not, you will just have to come down here and experience the shock and frustration of realizing that you are being lied to and are expected to accept the lie as if it were truth. To the credit of the people of my dear adopted country, this type of experience is greatly exacerbated by one's unfamiliarity with the language.) I was recently doing some paperwork to renew my immigration papers. I found one form confusing and called the immigration office to ask them how to fill it out. The phone call produced a confusing untruth and went something like the following, except that it was conducted in Spanish. (I'm permitting myself to remove some of the stammering and false starts produced on my part due to my less than perfect Spanish. See? It was my difficulty with the language that caused this.)

> **Me:** Hello. Excuse me. I have a question about how to fill out my "marriage link" form. [Yes, it really is "link"]

Immigration Official 1: ...Uh... I'll transfer you.

Immigration Official 2: Hello.

Me: Excuse me. I have a question about how to fill out my "marriage link" form.

Immigration Official 2: One moment please.

Immigration Official 3: Hello?

Me: Excuse me. I have a question about how to fill out my "marriage link" form.

Immigration Official 3: Yes?

Me: Uh... Well it says, [and here I start reading from the form] "He or She who signs blank of the nationality blank promises...." Whose name goes in the blank?

Immigration Official 3: ... [Here I wonder what word to use besides "blank" because the person doesn't seem to know how to respond to me.]

Me: Should I put my name here or my husband's?

Immigration Official 3: ... Yours.

Me: Mine? Really? Because that's what I thought at first, but then my neighbor told me she thought it was wrong.

Immigration Official 3: ... Well, hold on, let me get the form. [Here I think that we must be getting somewhere because we'll both have the same form and my using the word "blank" will make more sense to the person—even if that's not the way you say it in Spanish, because the person will see the long lines where I'm supposed to write my name or my husband's name, in some particular order.] ... Ok. Yes. It's yours.

Me: Good, then on the second line, I put his?

Immigration Official 3: The second line?

Me: Yes, where it says, "give all my support..."

Immigration Official 3: No, it says... [Here the official reads something that is not on the form I have.]

Me: Mine says something different. Mine says... [I read mine again, hoping that it will help the person to get the correct form.]

But, the untruth is coming. Are you ready for it?

Immigration Official 3: You have the wrong form.

Me: Really? I just got it two weeks ago from an official at your office. [I don't say it, but I'm thinking that guy was pretty professional and seemed to know what he was doing. I'm thinking back now, and yes, he had given me lots of forms that had changed from the previous year, but he had clarified many of the differences and really seemed to know his stuff. At this point in our conversation, I'm thinking like an American and assume that the person will go try to find the form I have. I don't realize it, but the effort level has just gotten too high for this official. It's not that they don't want to help me, it's that they might have to use the taboo phrase: "I don't know." Besides, if I go in to pick up a different form, someone else will help me to fill out whichever form ends up being the correct one, thus getting this person off the hook.]

Immigration Official 3: Yes, it's the wrong form. You'll have to come in to get the correct one.

Me: Oh… I was just there two weeks ago. [I'm thinking, "shit." This is at least a two hour undertaking] …Can I get it off of the internet or something?

Immigration Official 3: We don't have forms on the internet.[‡‡‡‡] You'll have to come in to get it.

Me: Oh… Thanks… Bye….

Immigration Official 3: …

So after the conversation, the untruth telling official almost had me convinced. I mulled it over a bit and used my experience with untruths to see that it was quite possible that I had been delivered an untruth and that I should call the office a second time before dragging myself in. I decided that if I called the next afternoon it would be likely that I would get a different person—one who knew about the form I had. In fact, Luis called the office later and got someone who knew how to fill out the form I had. The untruth was confirmed; as was the correlation with limited Spanish language abilities. Learn Spanish as quickly as possible and get rid of that accent!

This is not the first untruth I've been delivered, and it certainly won't be the last. Whenever someone wants to conveniently get out of figuring something out, explaining something, or just saying, "I don't know," they turn it around and put the ball back in your court with a little untruth. Let's face it, dealing with foreigners who don't speak your language well can be challenging. Have you ever had to help someone with an accent over the phone? In this case, the verbal stumbler is me… and you….

There is no need to get mad about untruths. In fact, that would just hurt you more than the other person because it would increase their motivation for creating even more untruths. The trick to dealing with untruths is to recognize them for what they are and to find a way quietly

---

[‡‡‡‡] This has now changed. Yay!

around them at a later time with other people. Doing this creates a win-win situation. You get to try for what you need and that person gets to avoid doing something they don't think they can do.

Never Say No, Just Tell an Untruth

While it may or may not be ok to "say never," you should never say "no" to someone in Mexico. Let me explain. Refusing an offer is an insult. In order to avoid insulting someone it is important that you say "yes" when you mean "no." In other words, you must use positive untruths. If someone invites you over to their house, you have to say that you will go—even if you know for sure that you are not going. While you are saying "no" you can try to work in something that might work as an excuse, just to keep your lying conscience clear. On the flip side, know that people will always say "yes" to you, even when they mean "no." Just like the common untruth, once you learn to recognize a yes-no, you will not be confused. I can pretty much always tell when someone is saying "yes" but means "no."

This difference between my culture and Mexican culture can be stressful in maintaining close friendships. Sometimes I worry that someone did me a favor, such as giving me a ride somewhere because they didn't want to say "no," when they really were too tired or too busy. It can be hard to be sure that your friends aren't "just being nice." Additionally, you have to be more careful about what you ask for from your friends. Since they probably won't feel comfortable saying "no" to you, it's better to just wait for them to offer. If they offer, it's because they wanted to do you a favor, if they don't it's either because they didn't think of it or because they didn't want to do you a favor. Sometimes I miss just being able to trust that my friends would just tell me to "buzz off" if I'm being a pain. That's how I used to know that I wasn't being a pain.

An expatriate friend of mine from the U.S. had a similar problem involving an invitation. A Mexican friend of hers invited her to a birthday party but promised to give details in the future. As the date of the party approached, the Mexican friend didn't say anything about the party. My friend wondered if the party had been cancelled or if she wasn't invited after all. She didn't want to ask because she thought that her friend may have been deliberately not saying anything because she couldn't invite her after all (for whatever reason, such as that the cost would have been too high to invite many people, the location was too small, another family member was hosting the party, etc.). She didn't want to make her friend uncomfortable and "force" her to invite her. At the same time, she didn't want to insult her friend by "forgetting" such an important event. She opted not to say anything and the issue was resolved about a month later when her friend contacted her about the party—which was just on a later date than she had remembered. Ah for the old days back in the U.S. when she could have just asked, "Hey, what's going on about the birthday party?" and trusted that her friend would either tell her where and when it was or say, "I'm so sorry, but my Aunt Bertha is going to host it and she has a tiny house, so it's only going to be for family."

It's a growth experience maintaining cross cultural friendships. You learn a lot of useful social skills—especially those related to diplomacy, when you live in Mexico.

"Yes-Saying" Techniques

It's wonderful to let your experiences in Mexico give you opportunities to become increasingly polite and considerate of other's feelings. This is an especially interesting challenge when you are learning to do it in a new language. Being a really good listener will help you with this. Observe both what and how people say when they are accepting and/or "rejecting" invitations. Here's a tip: listen for what they say when they are *not being specific*. How do they indicate acceptance and appreciation without actually committing? If you can, you might even consider writing down the phrases that people use. It's also helpful to have a trusted Mexican friend who you can ask questions of about how to say things in certain situations.

Two blog entries on my web site relate to this topic:

http://home-sweet-mexico.com/cultural-differences-friendsfirst.html/

and http://home-sweet-mexico.com/cultural-differences-friendships.html/

Gestures

Some of the basic gestures are different here than in the U.S. and Canada. If someone is occupied and cannot talk with you—for example, they are on the phone—they won't hold up their index finger like we do at home. They will hold up their hand in a "pinching" gesture as if they were holding something small between their thumb and index finger. The little thing they are holding is something like a short amount of time and means, "Give me a moment, I'll be right with you." The gesture for "no" is an index finger held aloft and slowly waggled from side to side. Our son makes ample use of this one. The gesture for "yes" seemed a little weird to me for quite a few months. For this one, you hold your index finger up and move the tip of your finger up and down, as if it were a tiny head nodding "yes." I know I've been here long enough to adjust because I now do this gesture when eating with friends. If my mouth is full and I want to show someone that I agree with them, I do the finger wiggle and nod.

Talk Softly

In general, Mexicans talk softly. If you have ever worked in an office building with cubicles, then you may have already learned to do this. In most Mexican houses and office buildings there are open windows or gaps between the ceiling and the roof that allow sound to travel quite easily to other rooms. Others can easily overhear what you are saying and it is wise to always assume you have a defenseless audience. I find that I often notice my voice is louder than the person to whom I'm talking. Then I start to wonder who could have

One time I was on the bus and heard an American tourist coughing so loudly it startled me.

That was the day I learned to take Luis seriously when he tells me not to cough in front of other people! You can read that story on my blog at http://home-sweet-mexico.com/am-i-that-loud-dont-cough-in-public-when-you-retire-in-mexico.html/

Mexico: The Trick is Living Here 3rd edition
available on www.home-sweet-mexico.com
219

heard what I was saying and if it had all been completely benign. It is not a good feeling and consistently using a low voice is by far preferable.

Most city buses are silent except for the music the bus driver has selected. Luis and I can be talking nicely before we get onto the bus and no matter how good the conversation is he clams right up. Some people still talk, but generally they do it quietly while sitting next to each other.

If you need to get the attention of someone who is far away, don't shout out their name – even in an outdoor setting. Stand up and walk over to them. There is so much noise in Mexico it's often lost on me that the noise is from vehicles and sometimes music, but not people communicating with each other. I was at the fair yesterday and saw someone I know. I shouted their name out then realized that I was the only one in the crowd of people in the food tent who had shouted during the entire hour that I had been there. Once, a friend in our neighborhood saw us walking down the hill to catch the bus. He wanted to tell us some important information about an emergency that was taking place downtown (he could tell that was where we were headed). He walked as fast as he could to catch up with us. It took him about 3 blocks, but he never shouted out to us.

Being Alone and Culture Shock

Culture shock is a strange thing that I still haven't been able to understand but it does affect everyone in its own way. I used to have to spend a few hours during the day lying on my bed, reading novels in English. I had no desire to go out, nor to see anyone except Luis (and some

Mexico: The Trick is Living Here 3rd edition
available on *www.home-sweet-mexico.com*
220

people back home, who were 2,000 miles away). Some of the best advice I got just before I left for Mexico was from a friend who had been in Veracruz for a few months counting hawks on their southerly migration. She said, "Give yourself time." I thought she meant time to get to like it, but when I asked her to clarify she explained that she meant time everyday for myself and time to do only one thing a day.

Often during the first six months or so, you **really** need to be alone. The problem arises because, in general, Mexicans don't like to be alone, especially the women. They misinterpret your desire to hole up for a while. All of the women neighbors that I have had notice when Luis is gone at work and I'm around the house, cleaning, doing laundry, or working on my class preparation. They often ask me if I'm alone. The message I get from their tone of voice and facial expression is that they wonder if I'm doing ok. I already knew from experience with my in-laws that people worry about you when you are alone. The hard part is that they often want to help you out and include you. They call you in to be with them. "Come watch TV." "Here take little Emilio to the store with you. He'll accompany you." "Come on over to have dinner with me." This is only a problem if you really aren't in the mood, and sometimes when culture shock hits, you aren't. You just have to be as appreciative and gentle in refusing as you can. Just give yourself time—and bring a couple good novels and a fully loaded music player. You can also watch movies in English on the internet. At the same time be careful not to establish a pattern with those who will be around you in your new life. As a newcomer it can be hard to feel that you are connecting with others and you don't want them to give up on you.

Later, you will grow to love this attention. This is part of what will make you want to stay in Mexico and makes you feel sad when you return to your old home. The "bother" of people including you is much better than the isolation and loneliness that can happen to people up north.

Hey Ladies, Tummies are Allowed

I'm one of those "real" women (that's how we refer to ourselves as we munch our chocolate bars) who fluctuates between size 10 and 14, with most of my time spent at good, ol', not big, not small, size 12 and I am happy to report that tummies are allowed here in Mexico. Here in opulent Cuernavaca plenty of women have gym memberships and clomp around town in their lovely heels and size 3 pants, cute belly buttons peeking out from under their spaghetti strapped tank tops. But just as many regular women—women, who if they were in the States would never let anyone see the part of their body where their waist once was during high school, proudly wear their shirts tucked into their jeans, a dress belt extending beyond the forward reach of their breasts completing their ensemble. I'm a conservative dresser, but if you want, you can show cleavage—in fact cleavage is more acceptable than too much leg. You can even wear sheer blouses and show your bra to the whole world, if so inclined (this may just be the large cities; somehow I just don't think this would fly in smaller towns). Don't worry about drawing the attention of men—they'll whistle at any youngish person with breasts, so you might as well wear what you want.

Clothes are worn much tighter here than in the U.S. I was recently shopping for slacks to wear to work. It was a delicate thing because I wanted to find something that would look well pressed even during a long hot day, but due to the heat I didn't want too much polyester. There I was with my I-haven't-exercised-since-the-heat-wave-started stomach, trying on pants being marketed to a show-all-your-curves culture. The sales lady and Luis were helping me to find sizes and to evaluate fit. I tried on one pair of pants that I would have been ashamed to wear in the U.S. because it was so tight and ill-fitting that you could see stress folds leading away from the bulge of my tummy and extra material pushed up under the pant waist by the ampleness of my buns. Why I even came out of the dressing room to model this one is beyond me, but anyway the sales lady commented, "Oh, that looks nice."

"Isn't it too small?" I asked.

"No," she said, "because if it were too small you would see the seams straining."

Talk about no extra room for dessert!

When you move here, bring some slacks with you, to give yourself some time to scope out the clothing stores in your city, but by all means, tuck in that shirt and enjoy being you. Eventually, you will probably enjoy shopping here, where some sizes are even in centimeters and you can find something that fits you exactly. Honestly, though, even after eight years, the majority of my clothes are purchased on visits home.

Chinelos

One of the special things about the state of Morelos are the *Chinelos*. *Chinelos* ("chee-ney-los") are dancers, always accompanied by a band that perform for special events, particularly Catholic church festivals and graduations. They are dressed in ankle-length velvet robes decorated with large beads and plastic sequins. They wear slightly tapered canisters on their heads covered with velvet, decorated with fringe and more plastic sequins. The really cool thing about *Chinelos*, besides their sneakers peeking out from under their velvet robes, are their masks. *Chinelos* are a spoof on some European soldiers—Belgian according to the museum placards in the *Palacio de Cortez*. The masks are made from wire mesh, formed into a face with a short, pointy beard. The skin tones are almost white with pink cheeks painted on them. The beards, and eyes painted black.

Chinelos come in all sizes and shapes. Some *Chinelos* are tall, some short, some have large, bouncy breasts, others are lanky under their robes, but my favorite *Chinelos* are only knee-high and bounce along in time to the music holding hands with a bigger Chinelo. The vertical motion of these tiny *Chinelos* is always proportionately greater than their horizontal motion.

Here is the scene from our second story window one fall:

Here go the Chinelos, preceded by exploding bottle rockets, passing below our window. They are leading a band with drums, trumpets, clarinets, and one tuba-like thing right down the middle of the road. Holding red rags, three men and one woman flag the traffic by, one direction at a time. One man observing from the other side of the street, helps to wave the line of traffic by, a one-year-old sound asleep, snuggled against his chest. As the band changes roughly to a more energetic song, the Chinelos bounce more vigorously, the plastic decorations on their long velvet suits bouncing more wildly.

The real excitement of the *Chinelos* is dancing with them. They dance their way up and down the street, collecting residents of the neighborhood, who come out and dance with them. You throw confetti on each other and enjoy yourselves. Don't always stand outside and watch Mexicans being Mexican. It creates a gulf and keeps you as an outsider; whether or not you mean it to, it takes you into the realm of being judgmental. If you want to be accepted, you must participate.

Neighborhood Parties

The neighborhood parties are usually centered around a church's patron saint. Each saint has his day, as it were, and each day its party. Keep your ears peeled for events that happen in your area as they are one of the very best ways to enjoy the fun of Mexico. Some churches have *kermeses* (ker-**may**-ses), which are fund raisers a lot like the carnivals I remember having at our elementary schools, but without the cake walks and dunk tanks. At *kermeses* you buy tickets from some old ladies, sitting at the ticket table, and you use the tickets to purchase food, and—if the kermes is large enough -- carnival rides. Generally, prices are a little high, but the proceeds go directly to the church. *Kermes* food usually includes things like tacos, *tamales* (Photo Essay: Making Tamales), *atole*, (a thick, sweet, hot drink made from corn dough), *buñelos* (elephant ears), *elotes* (corn on the cob), and ice-cream. Sometimes churches sponsor fairs (*ferias*), which are about the same, but without the special tickets sold at a table.

Many churches erect huge flower-covered lattices, which cover the entire front of the church, with carefully designed cut-outs around the doorway. Some have *palo encebado* (pah-lo en-seb-ado) activities during the day. The *palo encebado* is a tall, smooth tree trunk erected in an open area and thickly coated in lard or other industrial strength lubricant. Way up at the top of the pole is a rack holding bags of prizes. The goal is to climb the pole and collect the prizes. This can take an hour or more to achieve and requires the cooperation of many men. Women don't participate because of the amount of physical contact required during the climbing. It would be socially unacceptable to have a "co-ed" *palo*. The participants remove their shoes and build a pyramid of bodies. Up they climb, stepping on each other's knees, hips, shoulders, heads, and faces, until somewhere the pyramid will start to collapse and they all slide back down to earth. So far *palo encebado* has been a spectator sport for Luis and me. He says:

I like to see people climbing the *palo*

encebado. I haven't participated in one yet

but I would like to. Watching is fun. You

can see when the ones at the bottom are too

tired and their body is twisting as they try to

continue resisting. Their legs are shaking

and you can see that they are soon going to

let go. The people's feet on top of them are

slipping from their shoulders while they

desperately try to grab on to the slippery

palo. Some of them can't stand the weight

of the people on top and try to do all kinds

of things like grabbing each other or getting

their chests closer to the *palo* while their

legs are moving away from it. You know

that soon it's going to be over and they are

going to go down.

After they go down, there are often pauses in the action as the men regroup and recruit friends and family

Mexico: The Trick is Living Here 3rd edition
available on *www.home-sweet-mexico.com*
228

from the crowd to help out. Commentaries from the crowd include suggestions about strategy, and from Luis and I, quiet comments on how hard it will be for mothers, sisters, and wives to get all of that grease out of their clothes. Sometimes people try cleaning the grease off of the pole with their shirts. Occasionally someone else will create some kind of compression-based loop of rope around the pole and try to use that to help him keep his grip. In the end, it is cooperation that allows one skinny, bare-chested teenager to reach the top and pull himself up.

As you wander the street and church yard, keep your eyes peeled for a rickety-looking tower of lashed-together bamboo sticks, because this will form the best part of the party. No, no one will climb this unstable piece of architecture. Look closely and you will see that the tower is actually covered with fireworks. After dark, the crowd will gather close under this pyrotechnic delight to risk singed hair and trampling. This is the *castillo* (KA-stee-o). When the moment is right, 15 foot long fuses leading up to the *castillo* are lit. The flame shoots up and sets off the first tier of colorful, sprays of flame.

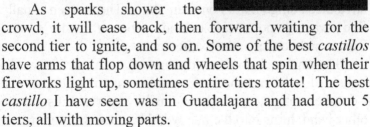

As sparks shower the crowd, it will ease back, then forward, waiting for the second tier to ignite, and so on. Some of the best *castillos* have arms that flop down and wheels that spin when their fireworks light up, sometimes entire tiers rotate! The best *castillo* I have seen was in Guadalajara and had about 5 tiers, all with moving parts.

After the *castillo* comes the preferred male activity: *los toros*. The bulls are smaller versions of the *castillo* with a papier-mâché bull as the base. The bull's feet narrow down into four sticks—the handles. Above the bull is a lattice of sticks, fireworks, and strips of crepe paper. If this contraption sounds dangerous, then you've got the idea. One man will hold the bull on his back, while a second ignites his interconnected fireworks. Meanwhile, the children and  young men of the neighborhood gather close on light feet. As soon as the hissing of the shooting sparks is heard, the bull operator takes off full tilt into the crowd. He chases people with his flaming toy, and they run from him, smiling with delight. If the bull temporarily fizzles out, they come closer, until suddenly another series of fireworks explodes into light. Suddenly, the crowd runs for cover behind parked cars and street-side trees as the bull showers them with sparks. If he can, the bull operator will swing the bull at the head of someone who hasn't quite gotten out if reach to see if he can singe his hair and eyebrows right off. Bull after bull will come out of the church yard, until the crowd is tired and a few teenagers have black singe marks on their shirts. The women usually find a vantage point, safe behind a fence or vendor's stand from which to watch the excitement.

Personally, I don't enjoy running from the fireworks bulls. I'd rather not be in a crowd of running people, and I'd rather not get my clothes ruined by sparks. Luis, on the other hand, turns into the happy kid he once was and insists that I enjoy the bull experience with him. He says the following about this colorful tradition:

> It's good to see that people here in Mexico haven't lost their customs. When I see people running away from the *toros* it gives me such happiness. I remember those days when my heart was pumping from all the excitement of running for me not to be caught in the middle of all the fire crackers. From time to time I would go to my mother with a big smile on my face and she would tell me, "Be careful *niño*! Look at you! You are all sweaty!" It's a joy to be running; doing something you aren't really supposed to be doing with the OK of your parents.

In order to drag me into the joy of this experience, he finds a relatively safe spot that will require only a little running for cover and holds my hand tightly so that I can't escape him before the bull gets close enough to be at least a little fun. One of my favorite toro experiences was watching a girl and her grandfather stand together in the street waiting for the bull to approach, then running, hand in hand for cover behind a tree. Huge grins covered their faces as they ducked into the safety of the branches.

As at any good fair, you can also eat, go on rides, and buy house wares. There are clay cooking pots, plastic stools and laundry tubs, clothing, and even pirated music on CDs. One of the best smelling foods available at *ferias* and *kermeses* here in Cuernavaca is sweet bread. Bakers bring their ovens out into the street and sell hot, fresh breads. If you have kids, let them jump on the mesh-surrounded trampolines and buy them potatoes cut on an apple corer, mounted on a stick in a stretched out spiral, and deep fried. *Ferias* and *kermeses* are great for just tooling around and people watching.

Festivals and Celebrations

JANUARY

JANUARY 1ST: NEW YEARS DAY

Celebrations throughout Mexico.

JANUARY 6TH: *DÍA DE LOS SANTOS REYES*

The table is set to cut the *rosca*.

Day of the Holy Kings.
In Mexico this is the day that children receive their Christmas gifts. All over Mexico, children can be seen zooming around on new tricycles, bicycles, roller skates.... On this day people buy *roscas* or braided sweetbreads in the shape of a wreath. Inside of each *rosca* is at least one tiny plastic doll representing the baby Jesus. People get together to cut the bread. If your piece contains a doll it is good luck, but also gives you the responsibility of "making" (everyone buys them) tamales on February 2nd for everyone present.

Mexico: The Trick is Living Here 3rd edition
available on www.home-sweet-mexico.com
233

FEBRUARY

FEBRUARY 2ND: *DÍA DE LA CANDELARIA*

"Candle man's Day." People get together to eat the tamales provided by the lucky/unlucky people who found a plastic doll in their bread on January 6th. There is a running of the bulls in the state of Veracruz. Other places hold parades and bullfights.

FEBRUARY 5TH: CONSTITUTION DAY

A national holiday. Banks, schools, and government offices close.

FEBRUARY 24TH: FLAG DAY

This day is celebrated mainly in schools where a flag ceremony (*honores a la bandera*) is held in which participants sing the national anthem and pledge allegiance to the flag.

FEBRUARY-MARCH: *CARNAVAL*

The date depends on the ecclesiastic calendar. Celebrated throughout Mexico. Parades are held in Mazatlán and Veracruz.

MARCH

MARCH 21ST: BENITO JUÁREZ'S BIRTHDAY

Benito Juárez, born in Oaxaca, was the only aboriginal person to be president of Mexico. Observed everywhere, and celebrated most in Oaxaca, his home state.

MARCH 21ST: *FERIA DE LA PRIMAVERA*

The start of Cuernavaca's "Fair of the Spring." Sometimes the start date is adjusted so that the fair coincides with the school vacations of *semana santa*.

MARCH-APRIL: *SEMANA SANTA*

The date depends on the ecclesiastic calendar which determines Holy Week. Banks and government offices close Thursday through Sunday of this week. Schools are closed for one or two week vacations.

APRIL

MARCH-APRIL: *SABADO DE GLORIA*

A day in which people throw water on eachother, although throwing water has been outlawed in Mexico City.

APRIL 30TH: *DÍA DEL NIÑO*

Children's Day. Mostly a marketing ploy.

Celebrated in schools.

May

MAY 1ST: LABOR DAY

Workers hold parades in the streets.

MAY 5TH: *CINCO DE MAYO*

The celebration of the defeat of the French army in Puebla in 1862. This holiday is not celbrated in Mexico as much as it is in the United States. It's mainly a day off from work.

MAY 10TH: MOTHER'S DAY

This is a very important day in Mexico. In cities, many mothers don't work on this day and their families give them flowers and gifts, take them out

to dinner and serenade them with *las mañanitas.*
Las mañanitas is the same song that is sung to
people on their birthdays. It talks about how the
world became a better place when the honored
recipient of the song was born. Some families hire
mariachis to come sing or young people get
together with their friends, traveling to each other's
houses, playing the guitar and singing to their
mothers.

MAY 15TH: TEACHER'S DAY

Teachers don't work on this day. Students bring
them presents and schools give a meal or gift to the
teachers.

JUNE

JUNE 1ST: NAVY DAY

Celebrated in Mexican ports such as Acapulco,
Mazatlán, and Veracruz.

JUNE 24TH: SAINT JOHN THE BAPTIST DAY

Celebrated in some places. People toss water on
anyone they can.

JUNE 20^{ISH}: FATHER'S DAY

Next to Mother's Day, this day slips by in
comparative silence. It always falls on a Sunday in
June.

JULY

AUGUST

AUGUST 15TH: THE ASSUMPTION OF THE BLESSED VIRGIN
MARY

Celebrated with religious processions, *kermeses* and *castillos*.

SEPTEMBER

SEPTEMBER 8TH: *VIRGIN LA MILAGROSA*

Celebrated with a fair and *castillo* that spans two weekends in Tlaltenango Cuernavaca, Morelos.

SEPTEMBER 15TH: INDEPENDENCE DAY

Celebrated with parades, music, festivals, and fireworks in *zocalos* large and small throughout Mexico. People gather at 11:00 p.m. for the "*grito*," literally, "the shout" in which people are lead in a cheer for their country and the people who make it great by shouting "*Viva México!*" These celebrations are wonderful, but we had to stop attending due to lack of crowd control and the tradition some people have of shooting their pistols up into the sky. A huge celebration is held in Mexico City, which includes a remarkable parade and the appearance of the president and military in the *zocalo*. Schools, banks, and government offices close on September 16th.

OCTOBER

OCTOBER 12TH: *VIRGIN DE ZAPOPAN*

Celebrated with religious processions.

NOVEMBER

NOVEMBER 1ST: DAY OF THE LITTLE ANGLES

Celebrated with religious processions. Light candles for children the night of October 31st.

NOVEMBER 2ND: DAY OF THE DEAD

Celebrated throughout Mexico to varying degrees. Light candles at dusk on November 1st and stay up until the wee hours of the morning. There are wonderful festivals in Oaxaca, and reportedly in Michoacán. Cuernavaca, has two lovely festivals. One, in Ocotepec, where people are invited into the homes of families who have lost a member during the year. There guests from the street present candles, sugar, or coffee as gifts and sip hot punch or coffee as they admire the room-sized altars. Another is held in a park and includes music and dancers on stilts dressed as "the dead."

Note: See appendix for a gallery of photos taken on the day of the dead.

NOVEMBER 20TH: REVOLUTION DAY

The anniversary of the Mexican Revolution is celebrated throughout Mexico. Schools, banks, and government offices close. Many cities and schools hold parades.

DECEMBER

DECEMBER 12TH: VIRGIN OF GUADALUPE DAY

Celebrated with religious processions. Processions and folk dances at her shrine in Mexico City. Fairs are also held by churches whose virgin is Guadalupe.

DECEMBER 16TH: *POSADAS*

Posadas begin on December 16th and Continue nightly until Christmas Eve. Generally, *posadas* are processions held after dark, sometimes by candlelight. Sometimes they include people dressed up as Mary and Joseph who sing a song at a series of doorsteps in the neighborhood, representing their journey in search of a place to stay (literally, "*posada*"). Often they end at parties with piñatas and gifts of food and candies and hot punch made with real fruit and cinnamon.

Schools generally close for two weeks including Christmas and New Years.

> Our family has had some magical experiences at *posadas*. You can read about them and see some pictures at:
>
> http://home-sweet-mexico.com/Christmas-Mexico.html/

DECEMBER 25TH: CHRISTMAS DAY

Banks and government offices are closed.

DECEMBER 31ST: NEW YEAR'S EVE

Banks and government offices are closed. Celebrations are held in *zocalos* throughout Mexico.

A note about virgins: Each church has a virgin, and each virgin has her day, as it were. Some churches throw big parties for their virgins. Since the dates vary they can't all be included in this calendar but you can find out when the biggest and best parties happen in your area and join the fun. Ask your new neighbors when the celebrations are.

Quantity Schmantity

Mexicans don't tend to quantify things. I grew up with maps that told the distance between road junctions and parents who could recite the elevation at timberline on the mountains near our house. We all know exactly how hot it is when we are sweating it out on a hot summer day or exactly how cold when we are shrinking down into our scarves on those bitingly cold winter days. Mothers check thermometers mounted outside kitchen windows before recommending a coat ensemble for their sons and daughters.

When we travel we love to read facts that tell us about the places we visit. When was it founded? How many people live there? How many thousands of years did it take for that stalactite to form? The complete absence of quantifiable data is a continuous frustration to my father, who never fails to ask me for this all important information. How can he really know anything about my experience here if all I can tell him is, "It's hot Dad." "How hot it is?" he repeats. "Um, hot enough that I'm sweating."

As a teacher, I have learned that other things are also not quantified, including learning disabilities. I've met people who don't know the name of the disease they have—even if they've had it for years. Mexico forces you to experience moments on a day by day basis. If you really need to know quantitative information, look in an American tour guide. Otherwise relax and go with the flow.

Sounds that Communicate

Sounds here are continually surprising to me. Information is always being communicated through sounds in Mexico and each town has its own sound-vocabulary. Every itinerate service has its own sound to let you know when they are in your area and ready to sell. In Cuernavaca, the gas trucks all have continuous sirens that produce an ear-splitting sound as they roll through the neighborhoods. In other areas I've heard them signal their passing with rhythmic honking. The idea is that if you are out of gas, you can hear them coming and get out onto the street to hail them down when they go by. A second option is to call their dispatcher and have a truck sent to your house. This works well if you live on a quiet side street where the trucks come by less often. You will still be glad for the siren when they come because the dispatcher gives them the street and house number, but house numbers are so confusing here they still only have a general idea of which house they are supposed to stop at. When you hear them coming you can go out and wave to them so that they can find you.

The garbage collectors also have a sound. In Cuernavaca they used to send a guy walking up ahead of the truck with a section of metal pipe on a short rope and a metal bar to use as a hammer. He clanged the pipe as he walked, letting people know that the garbage truck was on its way. When they switched to honking the new truck's horn, I went nuts. Without the forewarning of the walking bell ringer, I couldn't get our son installed in a safe place and get out the gate and down the street with the garbage fast enough. There was no way I'd have time to load him into his stroller and get both the stroller and the garbage out the gate. More than once, I was left standing at the end

Mexico: The Trick is Living Here 3rd edition
available on *www.home-sweet-mexico.com*
241

of our street, watching the garbage truck recede up the main road. Our son was alone and I wasn't willing to try to run up the street to catch the truck. I mentioned it to the retired neighbors, hoping they would help me by either yelling at me when they heard the honking or by asking the garbage men to wait because I was just coming out of my gate with the garbage. The did help, plus I got faster.

Other services that have their own sounds include guys who buy scrap metal, guys who sell roasted sweet potatoes, guys who sell ice cream, guys who sell tamales, guys who deliver bottled water, and guys who sharpen knives, just to name a few. Each city will have different sounds for their services, so you have to spend some time observing the street to learn what all of the sounds mean. You can also ask your neighbors about the sounds for specific services, and when they hear those services coming they will call you outside.

My neighbor clued me in to the itinerate "chicken guy," as I refer to him. He stops on every block, holds a bike horn in his hand and squeezes the black rubber bulb repeatedly. Honka-honka-honka-honka means grab your change and head out the door because he sells cold, clean chicken and will remove the skin and fat and slice your pieces any way you want.

15 Housing

Housing and Climate

Cuernavaca, elevation 5,118 ft (1,560 m), is located in the state of Morelos, a little more than an hour's drive south of Mexico City. As you read information in books and on the internet about Cuernavaca you are sure to read about its wonderful climate which has earned it the title of "the city of eternal spring." I beg to differ. I'm from Washington, and temperatures in the 90's (that's in the mid 30's for you Canadians) just don't constitute spring weather, no matter how euphemistically you want to think of them. It is April as I am writing this chapter, and it makes it to the mid-nineties every day (although people tell me that this year is an exceptionally hot one and that records are being set). I feel like a giant swollen slug by the afternoon and all I can do is hang out on the tile floor and read.

Excuse me, but I can hear the ice-cream sales man shouting outside the house. I think I will go down and buy myself a lime *nieve*, which is like a smoothie that you eat with a spoon. I love their bright, sharp flavor. This is one of Mexico's many pleasures.

When you select your housing here you can do a lot to give yourself relief during the hottest months of the year. Upstairs apartments are hotter than downstairs and some areas are cooler than others such as the areas that border Cuernavaca to the north, which are nestled into the foothills of the surrounding mountains, are much cooler than downtown areas. Other than that, it all boils down to direct sun rays. The less the walls and roof of your dwelling are exposed to direct sunlight, the more comfortable you will be. If there is a shade tree over your house you will be quite comfortable. If there is no shade over your house, the roof should be painted white to reflect the sun's radiation. This is important. Luis painted our roof and there was a noticeable (but un-quantified) difference afterwards.

Luis's solution to the lack of screens on our rental.

Mexican house construction is different from what I have seen in the States. Here houses are built of cement blocks or bricks, with flat cement roofs. They absorb the sun's rays during the day and re-radiate the heat back out during the night. There is no insulation in the walls to prevent this process from happening and during the hot season, some places are like ovens inside by the early afternoon. Cuernavaca's blessing is that nights are cool and often breezy—even during the hottest months of the year. If you can throw open your windows and let in the cool night breeze, it will help you to sleep and to cool your place down before the start of the next hot day.

There are mosquitoes, especially during the rainy season, and the average rental place doesn't have window or door screens, so a fan is also very important. The fan will not ony cool you down, but will blow the little pests away before they can bite you. If you have the luxury of purchasing or building your own house, plan ceiling fans in the bedrooms (depending on the region in which you live, air conditioning may not be needed). You may even want to consider

> Mosquito nets are wonderful. See my blog post on the topic:
>
> http://home-sweet-mexico.com/retire-in-mexico-mosquitoes.html/

putting them in the dining and living rooms if you are from a cooler state like me or if mosquitoes are plentiful where you live. Take cold showers in the afternoons and remember to wash your underarms three times.

Living with the Weather

During the rainy season you will be pleased with the way it generally rains at night, although due to climate changes (I suspect deforestation as the city grows) it now rains in the afternoons sometimes. Still, this is nothing like the long overcast months of alternating drizzle and downpours that we have in the state of Washington, nor like the endless, dark, freezing, drab months of winters in most of Canada. The rains keep it green here. They come up suddenly and end suddenly. When you are here during the rainy season and you see the wind pick up, expect rain within a few minutes. Look toward the horizon for heavy, black clouds. Take any wash off of the line and close your windows because those clouds will be overhead a lot sooner than you think.

When Luis and I first moved here, I learned about the power of these sudden, furious rain showers the hard way. We were just settling into our first apartment in mid May and I happily set all of my books out along the wall. We went downtown to enjoy the atmosphere of the *Zocalo* and while we were there, it suddenly got really windy. We looked north and could see huge, dark clouds coming toward us. Momentarily, the image of our books came into my mind. They were not just any books, they were my favorite ones—the ones worth dragging all of the way down to Mexico in my limited luggage space. Nor were they along just any wall, but directly under the window. I had left it open—I didn't want to come home to a stifling oven. I kept picturing their lovely, smooth pages puckered by rainwater, their covers all warped and rough. Luis remembered our most precious possession of all, the computer, also dangerously near the window. By the time we could hail a taxi it was pelting rain so hard we were thoroughly soaked. It was hard to find an available taxi (hard even to see the drivers through the fogged up windows of their Nissans). Finally, a driver stopped for a boy and his sister manning the same corner we were. The kid didn't seem to like the price and stepped away from the window to discuss it with his sister, who wasn't listening. Luis, normally polite to a fault, stepped up, asked the price, and said, "OK. Get in." We climbed in and sat perched, trying not to completely soak the driver's seats. We plowed through the streets, which were by that time 4 inches deep with running water. Throughout the whole ride I tried not to whimper and cry. Finally, the driver stopped in front of our new apartment building. Luis paid, I unlocked the street door, we ran up the stairs, unlocked the door to our apartment, and gingerly peeked into the room where the vulnerable books were. I was overjoyed to find that only one book—and luckily, not one of my most treasured, had gotten wet. The computer was completely safe and dry in its protective neoprene case. Thank God for small miracles.

There are hotter and cooler places in Mexico than Cuernavaca. For example, the Yucatan peninsula is hot and humid year round. Cooler places tend to be at higher elevations, like the areas surrounding Mexico City which is at 7,350 ft (2,240 m) and Toluca at 8,800 ft (2,680 m). For a comparison that might be familiar, Denver, Colorado is at 5,280 feet (1,609 m) and Calgary, Canada is at 3,440 ft (1,048 m).

In the mountains north of Cuernavaca, Lake *Zempoala* at first light.

Cuernavaca's general climate pattern will give you an idea of what the weather is like and you can figure out how the place you wish to live in might differ:

MONTH	Max °F	Min °F	How it Feels
JANUARY	70 TO 80	50 TO 60	Days are warm; wear a light sweater for evenings out.
FEBRUARY	80 TO 85	55 TO 65	Days are warm; at night you can curl up in your cozy bed.
MARCH	80 TO 90	55 TO 70	Nights are still cool, but you can feel the days heating up.
APRIL	85 TO 95	65 TO 75	Hot and dry. People start to complain about the heat.
MAY	80 TO 95	65 TO 75	Hot and people are sick of it.
JUNE	80 TO 85	60 TO 70	Hot; relieved by occasional rains.
JULY	80 TO 90	55 TO 70	Short torrential rains evenings or nights. Cool at night.
AUGUST	75 TO 85	55 TO 70	Short torrential rains evenings or nights. Cool at night.
SEPTEMBER	75 TO 85	55 TO 65	Short torrential rains evenings or nights. Cool at night.
OCTOBER	70 TO 80	45 TO 60	You can get out your extra blanket.
NOVEMBER	65 TO 75	30 TO 50	You may need a sweater in the morning and evening.
DECEMBER	65 TO 75	30 TO 50	On some nights you can see your breath.

Finding a Place to Rent

Many people feel that they need to have arrangements made prior to coming to Mexico, yet this is not necessarily the best way to plan the big move. In Mexico it's best to be on site before deciding on your accommodation – especially if you are looking to reduce costs. Even though it can feel uncomfortable arriving without having a home waiting, you have the greatest chances of finding just the right fit at a comfortable cost if you put off long term decisions and look in person. Housing is less standardized in Mexico than we are used to. One house may be perfect for small-sized people, another for those who don't do a lot of laundry (You'll get what I mean when you see a few quaint bungalows.) Unless you have family here you can start with a hotel room and spend the first few days looking at apartments and rooms for rent. In larger cities, you can find rental information listed in the newspaper, just like at home—except that it will be in Spanish. In larger cities, it's worth it to ask if there is an online classified (think "Craigslist"), but these haven't yet reached the same level of popularity as up north.

For some ideas on how to make your new Mexican house or apartment a home see Enjoy a More Outdoors Lifestyle [http://www.home-sweet-mexico.com/lifestyle-retire-in-Mexico-outdoors.html/] and Neighborliness [http://home-sweet-mexico.com/lifestyle-retire-in-mexico-neighborliness.html/] on my web site.

Older people, who own land, haven't adopted computers to the same degree as their counterparts up north. Even once you find a place to rent it might be a good idea not to get yourself into a long-term commitment because as you

Mexico: The Trick is Living Here 3rd edition
available on www.home-sweet-mexico.com
249

make acquaintances and get to know your city you may find your preferences have changed, for example, a particular neighborhood may stand out to you or you may be ready to reduce your costs by reducing creature comforts. The best places with low prices can only be found through someone you know and that can't happen until you know some people.

Picking your neighborhood is especially important. Neighborhoods allow you access to important services ranging from staple foods to dentists and lawyers. The contacts that you make in your neighborhood will allow you to function in Mexican society and are especially

This photo is the best I could do of a lovely starlit night.

helpful in emergencies. When one of us got into a car accident, it was through relationships with our neighbors that we quickly got into contact with a lawyer. Since we didn't know the lawyer before that, the fact that we had

Mexico: The Trick is Living Here 3rd edition
available on www.home-sweet-mexico.com
250

met him through personal referral really helped us to relax and trust him. In the land of the famous "*mordida*" (literally "little bite") and corruption, personal referrals really help you to know that the person is trustworthy and professional. Still, you have to take it all with a grain of salt because I found my dentist, who has a small office in our neighborhood, through a referral by a neighbor and was at first very happy with his work, but over time I changed my mind.

Here in Cuernavaca the housing costs are unbelievably high compared to other places in Mexico. Most single people I know pay about 1,500 pesos a month for their housing—even if it is just a room in a house. By getting to know people in a neighborhood it is possible to pay less. Housing in most other cities – especially, in the smaller ones you've never heard of before – costs considerably less. A Mexican friend in Guanajuato pays 700 for a small, complete apartment, although places such as Cancun are pretty pricey as well.Some landlords will let you rent from month to month and others will ask you to sign a paper saying you will rent for 6 months or for a full year. There is so much variety that you will just have to ask about places you are interested in and see what the landlords require.

It is incredibly difficult to put Mexican housing in a nut-shell, partly because of the differences between their houses and ours and partly because of the wide range in the level of opulence among houses. Some Mexicans live in unpainted concrete boxes with tiny open-air flush bathrooms annexed out back (or worse, but that's beyond the scope of this book). Others live in mansions surrounded by moats of clipped grass and impenetrable fifteen-foot high walls topped with spirals of razor wire. Where you choose to live will obviously depend on your funding and your tolerance for "rustic-ness."

Even though it is scary arriving in a new country without a place to call home, I strongly recommend against renting sight-unseen. Price does not necessarily indicate quality, nor does it indicate how easy or difficult your landlord will be. There are so many little differences between renting in the U.S. and Mexico that any assumptions you make—and you probably won't even know you are making them – could cause you serious problems later. Meeting people face to face is very important in Mexico. It lets both parties get a feel for each other in order to establish a good working relationship.

Typical Rentals

Probably the greatest surprise to Americans and Canadians first looking at apartments will be the complete lack of appliances and storage space in rentals targeted for locals to rent. When you walk in the front door of a prospective apartment you will see a floor (hopefully tiled), metal doors between most of the rooms, the walls (hopefully freshly painted a cheery color), the windows, a small flat cement sink attached to the wall... and that's it folks. There are no closets, no kitchen cupboards, no little vanity in the bathroom for your

Our *boiler* (hot water heater).

toothbrush, no curtain rod for the shower. Do look for the *boiler*, a small on-demand gas hot water heater, which may

Mexico: The Trick is Living Here 3rd edition

available on *www.home-sweet-mexico.com*

252

be mounted in a corner either inside or outside of your apartment. This is your ticket to hot showers. Also confirm that your apartment is equipped with its own *tinaco* (large water tank or *rotoplas*, a common brand of water storage tank). This way when the municipal water is distributed to your neighborhood, usually for a few hours every day, you will have a reserve tank that will fill up and allow you to shower and wash dishes or clothes at any time of the day or night.

The author's *tinaco*. You don't want this one. It's asbestos!

Your place may or may not have an underground cistern for storage of emergency water, but this is important to have, if you can. Another thing your apartment won't have is a telephone (unless you are truly a lucky person). See the section on telephones for the complete story on getting your own phone.

When choosing your place, I recommend that you use the following checklist:

Landlord

☐ Does the landlord seem patient and responsive enough to work with you?

☐ Will you be able to get hold of him when you need him? Don't ask this question. The answer is too obvious. Ask him/her where he/she lives and if they live there year around. Listen between the lines when they answer you.

☐ Many renters are expected to pay for repairs! Confirm with you potential landlord.

Location

☐ Will you be close enough to a bus to come and go easily?

☐ Are there services within walking distance of your new home?

  ○ a neighborhood store—especially to buy water in *garrafones*.

  ○ a *tortilleria*

  ○ a laundromat

  ○ a store that sells veggies (*fruteria*)

  ○ a small restaurant that sells lunches (*comida corrida*)

  ○ other services that are important to you such, as a gym

☐ How close are you to your work or school?

☐ What is the average travel time to places you will visit often, such as a grocery store?

Noise (Mexicans accept a lot more noise pollution than we do north of the border.)

☐ Do large trucks and busses drive down the road your house is on?

- [ ] Are there barking dogs next door or on the roof?
- [ ] Are there neighbors who will play their stereo at full blast all day?
- [ ] Are there neighbors who will play there stereo at full blast at night?

Cost

- [ ] Can you afford the place comfortably enough that if something changes (and it always does) you can still pay?
- [ ] What costs are associated with living there, such as transportation?

Safety

- [ ] Do the doors and windows lock?
- [ ] Is there an outside door or fence that you can lock?
- [ ] Are there a limited number of neighbors who will go in and out?
- [ ] Are there large crowds of young men hanging out on the street outside your door?
- [ ] Are there people moving around your neighborhood throughout the day and early night? (You want the answer to this to be yes).

Services

- [ ] Is there a *lavadero*? (a *lavadero* is a flat, wide sink with a washboard bottom. You use it to wash clothes, and sometimes dishes. They work a lot better than the supposed "laundry tubs" we have at home and even if you have your own washing machine or take your clothes to a laundry service they are still really important to have. See the section on laundry below for more information.)
- [ ] Is there a place to hang your clothes to dry outside?
- [ ] Is there a *tinaco*? (a *tinaco* is a tank on the roof that holds the water for the house. They are necessary because the municipal water supply is only turned on

for part of the day. They are usually at least 100 gallons and the best ones are black and say "*rotoplas*" on the side.)

- ☐ Is there a hot water heater (*boiler*)?
- ☐ Can you get a phone line installed?
- ☐ Is there an electrical outlet in every room?

Little Extras that Make Your Place Nice

- ☐ Is there shade on or near your house?
- ☐ Do you have a small outdoor patio or rooftop to get outside and sit for a while, maybe to have a small container garden?
- ☐ Does it look nice enough to show your family and friends back home a picture of it or will they take up a collection to fly you home immediately upon seeing it?
- ☐ If you buy a car is there a safe place where you can park it off of the street?
- ☐ If it is a second story room, will it become too hot during April, May and June? If the roof is painted white, this helps a lot.
- ☐ If you open the windows will you get a cross breeze?
- ☐ Are there screens on the windows and doors?
- ☐ Is there a working cistern and pump you can use to get access to water in times of shortage? (Believe it, there will be.)

Furnishing Your Place

At this point, I have to say that as with any "rule" in Mexico there are plenty of exceptions. Here in Cuernavaca there are places advertised as furnished and these do have stoves, fridges, and other kitchen amenities, even closets— but you have to pay for these amenities in your monthly rent. In our case, we found it more worthwhile to purchase our own appliances and amenities. At the local appliance and furniture store, Elektra, you can find appliances that simply don't exist north of the border. There are two and four-burner gas stove tops that can go on your kitchen table, small, free-standing stoves, with and without ovens, even high-end gas ranges with high quality burners and electric lighters. Some of the high-end stoves look large enough to cook for a family of ten. There are medium sized fridges that provide plenty of room for 2 or 3 people. If you are going to be here for a while, I recommend that you plan about $500 U.S. dollars to set up a kitchen that you can feel at home with. Ours consists of a small, by American standards, low-end gas stove that does include an oven (Luis has to have his pumpkin pie and I my chocolate chip cookies, when I can get my aunt to mail me the chocolate chips), but no electric lighters; a short, chest-high electric fridge (it is bigger than those mini-fridges many of us used in our college dorm rooms at 7.7 cubic feet, fridge and freezer combined); a wooden kitchen table and smaller prep table; four chairs; and some metal garage storage style shelving, covered with contact paper which act as cupboards. You will also have to buy a *garrafón* of drinking water. There is a deposit for the returnable 20 liter bottle, so your first one will cost you 8 U.S. dollars. Other necessary purchases include a set of plates, silverware, cups, etc. For six people, this will cost about another $30 USD. Your first portable propane tank will cost you 20 USD empty, plus another 13 USD to fill it; after that refills will be about 13 USD. Our propane bottles last more than a month for the two of us. You can stretch the gas by not leaving your hot water "boiler" on all of the time. After you purchase your first tank you can get refills at will from one of the many roving gas trucks. You can't miss them;

they drive up and down the main streets with overly loud sirens on them causing hearing loss to all around and sometimes shouting "Gas." Leering men ride in back with the tanks, ready to hop down, carry, and hook up a full tank, then take away your empty. Have exact change for their convenience—and to avoid their assuming that you just wanted to tip them. Or tip them, if you want. You can learn the price by reading it on the back of any truck before you purchase. The company spray paints the current cost on a sign on the back, updating it as the price increases—which it has been doing rather consistently for years now. There will be two prices listed. The higher one is for the larger tanks and the lower one for the smaller tanks. The size difference is

Typical propane tank for stove and hot water heater.

substantial, so you will know which you have just by looking at your tank.

If you are the independent, tight-budget type, you can go for a mini-fridge and two burner table top stove. This would only cost you a couple of hundred dollars. On the other hand, if money is no object, make yourself comfy in a furnished place.

Another difference between furnishing an apartment in Mexico and furnishing an apartment north of here is that Craigslist is barely taking off in some larger urban areas and there really aren't any garage sales to speak of. Some people do sell used items and you can find these by looking

Mexico: The Trick is Living Here 3rd edition
available on www.home-sweet-mexico.com
258

for signs posted on people's outer gates to their houses. They will say *Vendo* or *Se Venden* followed by a list of the items for sale. Also, some people have things called *Bazares.* These are not the Christmas bazaars from back home with little crocheted Santa Clauses and tea cozies, but sales of used items, more like a cross between the Salvation Army Outlet store and a garage sale.

Close up of the valve on a propane tank.

Coming from the U.S. where you can pick up an old lawn mower for ten bucks, we were disappointed by the price of used items. I guess people figure that if they are going to bother to sell something, they might as well get some money for their trouble. Many items offered for re-sale would be in the "free" box back home, so plan to buy new.

In the neighborhoods of cities in central Mexico, traveling salesmen often come by with simple pine tables and chairs on hand trucks. You may find some of these things useful for your kitchen and bedside table. If you are flush, there are many local carpenter shops that will make you made-to order entertainment centers, kitchen tables, bed frames, whatever you want. I really recommend this route as a long as you have the communication skills and experience at screening for undercharging that would indicate forthcoming poor quality products. As our furniture needs evolved, we had items made to our specifications, such as the water bottle cabinet pictured in the chapter on eating and a mouse-proof clothing storage. For mattresses there is a chain store, called *Dormi-Mundo*

Mexico: The Trick is Living Here 3rd edition
available on www.home-sweet-mexico.com
259

(sleep world) that sells Sears Posturepedic and other mattress brands with which we are familiar from back home, offering five and ten year guarantees. They deliver.

If your place doesn't have screens on the windows, don't worry, you aren't alone. Millions of Mexicans sleep every night with mosquitoes singing in their ears. One trick to a good night's sleep is to aim a portable fan at your bed and blow the little buggers away. I also recommend mosquito

> For more ideas see the article Make your Bed a Mosquito Free Zone [http://home-sweet-mexico.com/retire-in-mexico-mosquitoes.html/] on my web site.

nets. I have very fond attachments to our mosquito nets. Another requires a little more effort on your part, but provides a long term solution. Go to the nearest *tlaperaria*, which is a store that sells tools, and buy a tube of silicon caulking and a length of plastic screening. It comes on a roll and they will sell it to you by the meter. Back at home, measure your window and cut the screen to fit. Use the silicon to "glue" the

This plastic screen is attached with silicone caulking.

screen to whichever side of the window frame won't prevent you from opening and closing the window. If you have a window with a sliding bar or some kind of handle that gets in the way you can easily cut a slit into it to allow latches and handles to pass through it. This is easy to do since the screen is plastic. Don't cut out the shape of the window handle; just cut a slit and the screen will remain virtually closed when the handle isn't pressing on it, but will flex enough to allow the handle to move.

Renting a Room

Many people who are only going to be here a year or two and have come down on their own prefer to rent a room in someone's house. This is a good alternative as all of the appliances will be provided and you will have the security of another person or family. Here in Cuernavaca, I have been shocked to hear that people who choose that option are paying the same as we are for our bare-bones apartments with 2 rooms, a kitchen, and private bathroom! If you can go it alone, it may not cost you extra money. In other cities, rooms will cost you much less.

Cost of Living

The cost of living in Mexico depends on two factors. The first factor is your lifestyle "level" and the second factor is the area in which you live. We all know that it costs less to live in Virginia than it does to live in San Francisco. In the same way, it costs less to live in Morelia, Michoacán than it does to live in Mexico City or Cuernavaca.

Below I present to you three levels of lifestyle (low, medium, and high) at Cuernavaca prices. They provide a snapshot that will allow you to imagine how you would like to live in Mexico.

Mexico: The Trick is Living Here 3rd edition
available on www.home-sweet-mexico.com
261

The prices are estimates that will give you ballpark ideas. Keep in mind that really touristy areas, such as Los Cabos and Cancun, cost much more. Also keep in mind that if you don't need to work and can handle a less "modern" city, you can find lovely places in Mexico with much lower prices. If you do need to work, you must consider the amount of industry or tourism in the area.

Once you get serious about living in a particular area, you can use the ideas in this section to investigate the actual prices and cost of living in your area of choice.

Low:

This lifestyle is rustic in many ways compared to life in the US, but covers the basic needs (you have to actively define your basic needs).

Click here to find out the value of Mexican pesos in your own currency.
[http://www.xe.com/ucc/]

This lifestyle costs a total ballpark figure (in Cuernavaca) of about 10,000 to 12,000 pesos per month for two people.

At this lifestyle level, eating out consists of tacos and *comida corrida*, with a very occasional trip to a more expensive restaurant. It involves eating very few packaged foods and shopping for fresh meats and vegetables at the market, rather than in a supermarket. It does not include many movies, nor many trips in a taxi. It might include having one economical car per family and may include one or two extras such as

See Letting go of Materialism for a Simple Lifestyle to
[http://www.home-sweet-mexico.com/lifestylesimple-retire-in-mexico.html/]
read about peeling your lifestyle-onion.

exercise or language classes, but the extras have to be prioritized. For example, "Do we want cable TV or to ride in taxis regularly?"

Housing at this level costs between 1500 and 3000 pesos per month, with 2,500 being most common. You'd have to get lucky to find something for less than 2,000/month, though we did by accepting a roof that leaked in heavy rainstorms, an asbestos water tank, and a sink that was hazardous to scrub. At this lifestyle level, features of the housing are considered separately. It is possible to find several of the ones that are most important to you, but probably not all of them together (that would jump you up to the medium level).

Features to consider are the following:

- There may be asbestos in the roofing or water tank

- A separate sink in the kitchen and bathroom

- Hot water to the kitchen

- An outside area to put a washing machine (covered vs. not covered)

- Private area to hang clothes to dry

- A private vs. shared patio area

- Space for plants in a patio area

- Closets

- Convenience of the hot water heater

- Cupboards/shelves in the kitchen (if these don't exist, they can be purchased separately or made by the resident)

- Number of rooms (kitchen divided from living area)

- Size and layout of the bathroom (often the shower head is very close to the toilet)

- Size of kitchen and other rooms

- Electrical outlets in all rooms

- A phone line or cable access to the house vs. having to get one (or both) installed.

- Windows in all or most rooms

- Screens on windows

- Mildew in walls or ceiling

- Noise level from traffic and/or neighbors (consider stereos, children, dogs, and roosters)

- Other kinds of pollution, such as smells from food stands

- Safety of neighborhood

- Frequency of bus service (I recommend that it come by at least every 15 minutes because this lets you get by without a car)

- Protected off-street parking for a car (room for two may be too much to ask for)

- Stores within walking distance

Note: at this level of lifestyle you have to buy ALL of your own appliances—even your shelves and cupboards. Small, less expensive stoves and refrigerators are available. You will have a wider range of appliance options than are available up north. If you can purchase these, then it represents a one-time purchase rather than a cost that would otherwise be included in the monthly rent.

To see some of the variety in appliances available go to www.elektra.com.mx. Use the search tool where it says "buscar" to type in the words "*Estufas*" and "*Refrigeradores.*" It's not really easy to see, but some stoves don't have an oven under them, and many of the fridges are actually slightly bigger than our mini-fridges (you know the ones college students have in their dorm rooms).

Medium:

This lifestyle is simpler in many ways compared to life in the US, but doesn't force you to peel your lifestyle-onion down very much.

This lifestyle costs a total ballpark figure (in Cuernavaca) of about 13000 to 15000 pesos per month for two people.

Conveniences at this lifestyle level often include having a cleaning lady come to the house a couple times a week. This person could do more than clean, if you would like, such as do laundry or iron, even cook a meal. You can expect to have all the appliances you're used to having back in the states, even a window-mount air conditioner. While you will still have to prioritize your expenditures, your lifestyle would more closely resemble the lifestyle of someone in "middle class" America. Prioritization of expenditures is nothing new in life, after all. Very few people in the world actually feel as if they have more money than they need.

Mexico: The Trick is Living Here 3rd edition
available on www.home-sweet-mexico.com
265

Housing at this level costs between 4000 and 6000 pesos per month. At this lifestyle level, the features of the housing which were considered separately above (in the "low" lifestyle level) are mostly taken for granted, though the house may be quite small by U.S. standards.

Note: at this level of lifestyle you probably have to buy your own appliances, but your house will include some cupboards and closets. The monthly rent covers the costs of having an actual kitchen with cupboards, and a shower stall with a door and drain inside the stall. The house will seem more like an actual house, with bedrooms with homey-looking wooden doors, a separate living room and kitchen, finished light fixtures, etc.

In the "medium" lifestyle level you have two major choices in types of neighborhoods you choose. You can get a place inside a community, surrounded by a garden and with a nearby parking lot, or you can choose an individual house with its own entrance and gate.

Features to consider are the following:

- Is there a store within walking distance?

- Will you be able to meet neighbors and build a sense of community?

- A community vs. an individual house

- Security such as a huge gate with razor wire on top and an automatic opener

- For some communities, there is a "rent-a-cop" in a guard house at the entrance

- Parking (In communities, how many spaces do you get? In an individual house, how large is the area?)

- Frequency of bus service

- In communities, there may be a shared swimming pool. (Some are quite nice and you don't have to take care of it.)

- In communities, what are the grounds like? (Often there are green, mowed grass and shade trees, taken care of by a gardener. In an individual house, you would hire the gardener)

High:

This lifestyle can actually be more luxurious than life in the U.S. With the average day-laborer in Mexico getting 100-200 pesos a day, once you hit a certain critical mass in potential budget expenditures, low labor costs can make it possible to do almost anything.

This lifestyle costs a total ballpark figure (in Cuernavaca) of about 30000 to 35000 pesos per month for two people.

Housing at this level costs between 8000 and 12000 pesos per month. At this lifestyle level, the housing can be quite posh. The house is big, with many rooms and surrounded by a green, shady yard with private swimming pool and ample parking space. It often includes a guest house, which can be rented to others at "medium" rent.

The interior of the house has all the conveniences of cupboards, closets, and shelves, cable TV piped into more than one room, and beautiful Mexican tile and finished woodwork. There are "extra" rooms, such as dining rooms, or an office. There might even be a downstairs bathroom and upstairs bathroom. (There might even be a downstairs and upstairs.) If you build the house yourself you could have a large kitchen with an island and room for a dishwasher.

Features to consider are the following:

Mexico: The Trick is Living Here 3rd edition
available on www.home-sweet-mexico.com
267

- Jacuzzi or just a swimming pool?

- artistic value of the tile and other finish work

- bathtub

- view

- location, traffic on access roads

- live-in care taker or day labor

- body-guard (if you are reeeaaaally rich)

Conveniences at this lifestyle level often include having one or two full-time maids (I'm not kidding). These people cook meals or do prep work for you to cook, do laundry, and obviously clean. You can expect to have all the appliances you're used to having back in the states, even a dishwasher and nice oven. You can have a gardener and a driver. Someone else can do your errands, such as grocery shopping and going to the dry cleaners. You will have someone come to take care of the swimming pool regularly.

If you are at this lifestyle level, you might want to build your own house, since Mexicans have different ideas about how to lay out a house. If you do decide to build, I recommend that you be present during the construction and hire a good architect who can make sure that your specifications are met.

Another advantage to building your own house would be huge savings in housing costs. As the owner of your own house, there would just be a nominal charge for property tax—which is extremely low by U.S. standards.

16 Laundry: No, You Don't Get

to Operate the Machine

Yourself

Coming from the Pacific Northwest, I have been engendered with an unbendable self-reliability, which is certainly useful when living an expatriate lifestyle. But here in Mexico, there isn't the big trend toward the do-it-yourself; instead the focus is on earning money by providing customers with services. Back in Washington all of our gas stations are self-serve; we pack our own groceries at the grocery store, we fit our own shoes from stacked boxes in warehouse style shoe stores, we look up basic auto parts and accessories in counter-mounted manuals that match products with makes, models, and years of cars, we wash our own cars in quarter operated car washes. Here in Mexico there are people to do every small task, even people who guide you as you back out of your

Mexico: The Trick is Living Here 3rd edition
available on www.home-sweet-mexico.com
269

parking space in a parking lot. Gone are the days of making your own photocopies, of packing your own groceries. Also gone are the hours of sitting in stiff plastic chairs, dividing your attention between soap operas on wall-mounted big screens and the gray slop flopping around and around in a Laundromat washing machine. Until you get yourself tucked into your own place with your own washing machine, here you must take your clothes to someone else to do it.

You must advise them on what can and can't be dried, what can have bleach and what can't, what bleeds and what doesn't. Then, you have to walk away, leaving your wardrobe in the hands of another person. You should find a Laundromat (*lavandería*) somewhere close to your house and get to know the people who run it. They will charge you by the kilo, weighing your dirty clothes upon arrival in a laundry basket hanging below a scale. Hopefully you will like your neighborhood service, since the other option is washing by hand.

Hand washing in Mexico isn't as impossible as it is in the States. Here it is much more common and therefore, there is an infrastructure that makes it much more convenient – at least as convenient as the backbreaking job of hand laundry can be. Each residence has a concrete *lavadero* (wash board/tub) mounted nearby. Once they were no longer stream-side, the original *lavaderos* were set up next to a large, square, above-ground concrete cistern, called a *pila*. The *pila* was the answer to keeping water at the house so that the women didn't have to trek to the nearest river to wash clothes and dishes. Each house had a *pila* from which the women dip water to do the household washing. In places where household water is stored on the roof of the house in a *tinaco* (water tank), the *lavadero* has two parts, one with a washboard pattern on the bottom of it and the other a miniature tub-shaped *pila*. Water is plumbed into the *pila* side of the *lavadero*, then dipped from the *pila* with a scoop and poured over the clothes on the washboard as needed. The scoop is a light plastic bowl.

My mother-in-law patiently trained me in the practiced art of *pila-lavadero* household cleaning. You don't hold clothing in both hands and rub it together in order to clean it. You lay it flat on the washboard pattern of the tub, pour water over it, and sprinkle powdered detergent or rub "cake" soap on it. You pick up one part of the cloth in your dominant hand and work this briskly across the rest of the material, while stabilizing it with your other hand. You pick up and relay the material, grab another section of material and again rub it against the material below it on the washboard. If you are really skilled you will be able to take the material in both hands and put the weight of your entire upper body on it as you rub and rub. Soon brown suds will lift out of the material and glide down the drain. Pour more water and scrub. Lift and re-lay. Scrub and pour more water. Rinse with copious dips of water, wring, then hang.

It didn't take me long to see that socks and underwear washed in this way came off the line stretched out and basically de-elasticized. Also, I was disappointed to find that sometimes the armpits of shirts didn't quite lose their formerly unwashed odor. Coming from the land of automatic, spin-cycle washing machines, I soon began to develop my own laundry systems. Now I presoak my clothing in laundry tubs with handfuls of detergent in them. After about an hour of soaking in the sun, the bluish soap color of the water has changed to a dingy brown. This means that the detergent has had time for its chemical reaction with the dirt in my clothes to take place and that I can give them a quick rinse and second scrub with fresh soap. The presoak guarantees that the soap has time to do its work and you don't have to scrub and scrub on stubborn stains. It also eliminates the wear and tear on socks, undies, and delicate blouses. After perfecting my personal hand washing system, I find that my clothes are cleaner than they ever were in the States. My laundry belief system has been permanently altered.

Another wonderful system which utilizes the laundry tubs was one a friend of a friend discovered while traveling in Turkey. Word has it that over there women take their clothes to in-ground community washing tubs where they put their clothes into the tubs with soap, climb in in their bare feet and work the dirt out by stomping their clothes. This method worked well in my test-runs, but I found that the difficulty comes in when it is time to change the water from the first wash to the second and from the second to the rinse. You end up having to hurk the heavy tubful of water up to the *lavadero* to pour out the water then contrive to refill the tub. Now, with an in-ground drain and a specially installed faucet... oh yea, the neighbors would talk.

What is the advantage of washing my own clothes, you might ask. Well, there are two. One is that your clothes end up cleaner than if washed in a washing machine. You will find that you can eliminate virtually all of the stains that, in the States, you would have considered permanent. The other is that it saves you money.

Once you have a place to live and the money to do it, you can buy yourself a washing machine. Available washing machines range from agitating tubs that you fill with water by hand to the same multi-cycle machines we have up north. Most people just put them in an outside courtyard near the *lavadero*, covered with a small shed-type roof to prevent rust. If your machine is outside or in a

Mexico: The Trick is Living Here 3rd edition
available on *www.home-sweet-mexico.com*
272

visible location, you can buy a pre-made cover for it, called a *forro*.

Now that we have one of these washers, I use my new soaking knowledge to help approximate the level of cleanliness achieved by hand washing. I let the washer agitate for a few minutes, then lift the lid and leave the load soaking for a while before I drop the lid back down and let it continue. This trick, combined with the natural bleaching action of the sun keeps our clothes stunning.

The washing machine, under a shed-type roof, is the centre of a multipurpose outdoor living space.

I have a fondness for my *lavedero* now that I don't have to spend so much time beside her washing all our clothes. It lets me work on troublesome spots and save my favorite garments from the trash bin. I don't even want to imagine handling diapers without an outdoor *lavadero* and the bleaching sun.

17 Communication

Chapter Forward

Before you begin reading this chapter, you will be glad to know that nowadays there are many more options than having a "land-line" phone through TelMex. When I got our first phone in Mexico, we didn't have another option. Now cell phone companies and cable and internet providers have elbowed TelMex to the side and created a much better world for the consumer. I am keeping this chapter, with its detailed instructions, because they are useful for handling any type of bureaucratic situation in Mexico. Hopefully, this chapter will only serve as a guide for your decision-making process, but if you find that you actually have to use some of the tips in here, send me an email and I'll reply that I'm not surprised.

Cell phones have become the preferred option in Mexico in most settings. See "Telephones: Cell Phones" <u>on page 282.</u> If you want the convenience of having a home phone, you should also consider a company that provides

Mexico: The Trick is Living Here 3rd edition
available on *www.home-sweet-mexico.com*
274

cable and/or internet services. See "Cable, Phone, Internet Packages" on page 284.

Telephones: The TelMex Torture

Some buildings which have many apartments in them have a "*Ladafón*" phone in the entryway; not to be confused with the *Ladatel* phones found on the street and in public buildings. It is the responsibility of anyone who is home to answer the phone when it rings and to try to track down the recipient of the call. This works fine for most people, but if you want internet, you will have to get one kind of line or another installed in your place. If you are planning on living in a building with multiple apartments inside, you should ask around about the possibility of getting a private phone installed; it may not be possible under all circumstances. I have always lived in apartments or houses with an outside wall facing the street, through which the telephone line can be passed. The first installation of your phone will cost you $170 and more than you can imagine in patience.

Once you have chosen your place, you should make what is called a *croquis* (pronounced kro-kees), which is a map of your neighborhood depicting the location of your house. *Croquis*es are required for most official interactions so that people can actually find your house. In a country where there are at least five *Avenida Emiliano Zapatas* in each city and where the houses are numbered chronologically by date of construction, they are quite necessary. A telephone *croquis* must include the locations of the nearest telephone poles as well as your residence. Telephone poles are usually painted green up to eye level, but use your deductive skills to figure out which poles are the telephone poles, just in case they aren't. Put the identification numbers found on each pole onto your map. The pole outside my house was missing some of the numbers, reading "XAR 4? B?." I deduced from the other poles near here, "XAR 32 A2," and "XAR 22 C2", that I should put XAR 42 B2 on my map. You can also include the location of the chest-high stainless-steel box that apparently distributes the lines. Ours has "XAR" painted in black letters on it and is a block away on the main street.

With your *croquis* and an hour's worth of interesting reading material in hand, go to the TelMex office. Find the customer-lack-of-service desks and wait your turn. You can keep a positive attitude by enjoying your reading material. When it is your turn, you can go up to the desk and ask nicely to have a telephone installed. Be patient while the TelMex employee flips through the screens on her DOS-based computer program and talks to her coworkers for thirty minutes. She may try to tell you that it is impossible to install a phone in your house, your neighborhood, your city, planet earth…. Remain calm and explain that you must have a phone. Bring up your family back in the States or your impending internet account, if you want. She may go talk to someone behind an "employees only" door. When she stalks away from her desk, you can say a prayer—I firmly believe in the power of prayer at TelMex—and continue reading your novel while you wait. You must pay the cost of the installation, and show her the receipt when she gives you the go ahead. Do not be surprised if you cannot get all of this worked out on the first visit. Other steps may be requested from you and you may have to return to complete them. After getting the final go-ahead from customer-lack-of-service you will go home to wait for the installation repairman to come and bless you with 21st century technology. He will come within one and 30 days of your request for a phone. If you are not home, too bad. I write that sarcastically, but somehow, these things have a way of working out.

Once your phone is installed you will find that all is normal. I was happy with our dial-up internet service (back in the day), as well as the professional and polite tech support, available with a toll-free call. In fact, the person at tech support who helped me to set up my connection and email account even knew all of the commands and dialog boxes in English, since my computer is in English.

Beware, phone service is expensive here. On some plans, TelMex only gives you 100 local calls included each month after which you will be charged for each outgoing call. National and international rates are more expensive than those in the States, and if you are earning in pesos, they can be prohibitively expensive. Ask when the "Reduced" rates are in effect. For me, they are Saturday and Sunday, excluding Sunday night. Finally, ask if there is a charge to call cell phones, even if they are in the area.

When you move from one place to another in your new town, you can have your service moved with you. In order to do this, you must pay a re-connection fee of about ½ the original connection price and go through the same processes you went through to get your first phone. Get out your interesting reading material; customer-lack-of-service here you come. If you do not wish to have your service moved, don't count on TelMex to stop your phone service. To avoid another person making calls on your account either cancel the service well in advance so you *know* it's done or cut the lines outside your old residence the day you move out. Even TelMex employees advise people to cut the lines, so don't feel weird. It beats the you-know-what out of paying for someone's call to their uncle in Chicago.

And to round this section off, guess what? It's harder to cancel your service than to get it set up. When I switched from Telmex's dialup internet service to a privately owned high-speed cable internet service it took me about 10 phone calls and more patience than I knew I had to get the Telmex service canceled. The toll free service was hanging up on me. (How can a telephone company have their customer service number so out of order that it's dropping calls?). The customer-lack-of-service people were transferring me from one to the other and never canceling the service. They were trying to charge me for a month of service because I called to cancel after some arbitrary dead-line for monthly cancellations. I was nice to everyone. I asked nicely for help. I explained my problem so they could help me. I called on different days and at different times. I spent 35 minutes waiting to be transferred, but actually in some kind of cyberspace netherland. I spend *hours* each time I called. Guess what? I didn't get the service canceled until the day I lost it and screamed (in Spanish, of course), "Please help me! I just want to cancel my service!" I wailed, "No! NO! DON'T TRANSFER ME! I've already been transferred 5 times!" Later I had to say in a very severe voice, "You can't *charge* me for a service I never *used*!"

My experience is normal. My friend and I were having a two-person group therapy session to heal ourselves of the emotional scars created by dealing with Telmex. In her case, Telmex switched her internet service to a more expensive service without informing her. When she went in to get it switched back a customer-lack-of-service person forced a modem that she didn't want on her. She took it and went home because she has two kids under 3 years old and they were getting squirrelly. Later no one would receive the modem back and they wouldn't cancel the

Mexico: The Trick is Living Here 3rd edition
available on *www.home-sweet-mexico.com*
278

service... until she yelled at them on the phone. Now her phone service is temporarily canceled. She can receive calls but she can't make any.

Now I know what you are thinking. Those silly women. *I'm* not going to be Telmex's victim. *I'm* going to use another service. This is a good idea, but don't think you'll get off scot-free. My cable internet company also switched my service to a more expensive one then played dumb about why my bill came back with a higher monthly charge. Granted, it wasn't as bad as the Telmex thing because it took only one call to straighten it out and required no yelling.

Telephones: Pay Phones

If you need to use a pay phone on the street, you will need to buy a *Ladatel* card. These are for sale in 30, 50, and 100 peso amounts at pharmacies and very occasionally at local neighborhood stores (*abarrotes*). The card comes wrapped in cellophane with the amount printed on it. You insert the card into the slot at the bottom of the pay phone and dial the number. International calls start with 00, then 1, then the area code to the U.S. and Canada. National long distance calls start with 01. The trick is to find a *Ladatel* phone on a street quiet enough to hear the person that you call. *Ladatel* phones are widely available and many schools and other public buildings have a small, indoor *Ladatel* phone in the foyer.

Warning, many people are sucked into buying the wrong pre-paid international phone cards. You *don't* want the kinds that have the pin number on the back that you rub the gray sticky stuff to reveal the number. The *Ladatel* cards have little brass computer chips visible at one end of the card. The telephone will read that chip and allow you to make the call.

While there appears to be a backwards trend towards pay phones in some areas, I recommend carrying a *Ladatel* card in your wallet for any unexpected need to use a pay phone, especially if you are traveling within Mexico.

Telephones: International Calling

After living in Cuernavaca for a while I was overjoyed to discovered a pre-paid phone card that offers 7 U.S. cents per minute anytime to the U.S. and Canada. The name of the company, if it doesn't break e-book protocol to give the name, is InterRom and I am overjoyed with their service. It has been such a blessing to be free of the ridiculously high TelMex rates. I am no longer forced to abstain from communication with my family until some emotional crisis point develops in my life at which time I would dial their number and say really fast into the receiver, "Canyoucallmebackrightnow?...Thanksbye." It is such a blessing to be able to call my family and friends when I'm in the mood and to be able to pay for my fair share of calls.

Often you can find good international rates available at places where a lot of U.S. and Canadian citizens are found, such as Spanish language schools. Equally as often you can find overrated phone cards that don't offer good deals.

If you have a phone card from a large U.S. company call them and ask them the rate that you will be charged to use it to call Mexico or to call within Mexico. Often the rates are so high it'll make your eyes water. Take a moment to call them before leaving the U.S. because they usually don't have toll free numbers that work internationally—and they'll tell you they will. I can't count

Mexico: The Trick is Living Here 3rd edition
available on www.home-sweet-mexico.com
280

the number of customer service reps who have given me a toll free number expecting it to work from Mexico. Even if I ask them if they are sure it will work because I've had many experiences where it doesn't they still insist that they are sure it will work—and of course it doesn't. It's eternally amazing to me how few people in the U.S. know one iota of information about Mexico. Sometimes I feel like I'm trying to call from the Black Hole rather than the U.S.'s next-door neighbor! Anyway, I am diverging. At a time when you have a few minutes call your phone company and find out what their international rates are. Sometimes the first customer service rep you get won't know international information so you may have to wait until they can direct you to someone who does. Have your "B.S." radar up and be sure that they aren't guessing at the info they give you. Often their training programs don't include information about Mexico.

Back in the day, family and friends back home used to shop around for a long distance deal that included good international rates, now they can use the internet to call us (see more on page 285).

If you want to use phone cards to call from the U.S., to Mexico, the ones that are sold to the average person won't do, though. Fred Meyer, WalMart, all those type of cards aren't a deal at all. You need to find a so-called "Mexican store." If you have a neighborhood in your city that has a lot of Latino residents, look there for a small store that caters to Latinos. Those stores stock phone cards with excellent rates. Ask the attendant there to recommend the best card. The deals and card types change on a regular basis and they know which ones offer the best option at any given time. I prefer cards with no connection fee, even though they have higher per minute charges than those that charge more for the first minute. Some of the cards are just out to charge you for that first minute then disconnect you so they can charge you again. Also, buy cards in small dollar amounts because once you use your card you generally have only a month to spend all of the money before the phone card company deactivates your card. All these little details will be printed on the back of the card so you can ask the store clerk to let you read the best cards before you make your final choice. Some cards tend to give a busy signal every time you dial into the card's toll free number, of course, this information is not printed on the back of the card, so ask the store attendant which cards don't give a busy signal. Generally the no-connection fee cards offer about five U.S. cents per minute. Teach your sister where the Mexican store is so she can call you for less money.

Telephones: Cell Phones

Cell phones are now generally the best way to get phone service in Mexico. In urban areas, Mexican cell phone companies beat the pants off of Canadian cell phone service for affordability and flexibility of plan types, while beating the pants off of American cell phone services for flexibility and affordability of types of phones used, making use of phones with SIM cards in them.

Cell phone companies are regional, so once you move to Mexico, ask around about what companies offer services in your area. You will then easily find the kiosks and storefronts operated by these service providers. You can walk in and ask them the details of the plans they offer. For example, I've heard of one plan that offers unlimited talk time back to the U.S. for $400 pesos a month.

Texting is quite poplar in Mexico, so even if you aren't a fan of texting, I recommend that you at least learn the basics of how it works for your particular phone. If you travel back and forth from Mexico and your home country you can use a SIM-type phone, simply changing the card as needed. Of course, this will change your phone number and contacts lists, but cost-effective phone services which work in Mexico as well as the U.S. and Canada aren't really available yet. Finally, cell phones in Mexico are so affordable you really can have a phone that you buy and use only in Mexico.

If you are snowbirds (especially from the U.S. where cell phone companies offer inexpensive packages. Canadians…. *sigh* …it might be worth a try) you can contact your cell phone provider and see what kind of a deal they might be able to offer you so that you can use your own cell phone while you are in Mexico.

E-mail: Staying in Touch

Since the phone is so expensive, and can be inconvenient for the folks back home to reach you, often internet is the best option. Before you get yourself set-up in an apartment or house with internet, you can use one of Mexico's nicest services. There are many internet cafés throughout Mexico. If you intend to use Skype, ask them if they provide that service. You must pay an hourly rate to enjoy their services and will be charged the entire hourly amount for any portion of the hour. The cafés have printers. Sometimes smoking is allowed, but each café is individual and you can find one that you like.

Generally, the prices are determined by location and do not indicate computer speed or quality. In fact, in

Cuernavaca, the slowest computers are often the ones in cafés in neighborhoods that, because of their locations, also charge more. Hourly rates in neighborhoods range from 7 to 11 pesos per hour while rates downtown, where the computers are better, go as low as 4 pesos per hour. Tourist areas defy this price trend, by increasing internet café rates. Los Cabos, for example has higher prices downtown (20 pesos per hour or portion) and lower rates in the neighborhoods (15 pesos per hour or portion).

Occasionally, you will end up with a computer that is experiencing problems and may not be able to complete your transaction. Yes, you will still be charged—regardless of computer quality. Each café differs in quality of computers and amount of assistance from the attendant so, shop around and find your favorite café.

E-mail: The @ Key

The Spanish keyboard is slightly different from those back home. You may have trouble typing the "at" key. Sometimes it is shift and the letter Q, other times it's not. Often computers side by side in the same café will have been set up differently. You can ask the attendant how to type the "@" symbol. Another quick trick is to navigate to some screen that has one, highlight, copy, and paste it. The question mark, and commas are also in different places, but hey, you have an "enyay" (ñ).

Cable, Phone, Internet Packages

Consider getting a cable service that includes phone and internet (even without the cable television bit). Similar to cell phones, different providers operate in different regions, so once you move to Mexico, ask around about what companies offer services in your areas. You can walk in and ask them the details of the plans they offer. Shopping around can pay off. As an example, anfriend has a package that costs her $450 pesos a month and includes 100 local phone calls, cable, and wireless internet. She then uses Skype for her long distance calls to the U.S.

Phone Calls via Internet

If you don't already know how to use Skype, it's time to learn. Most laptops and tablets now days have web cameras built right into them. If yours doesn't, you can buy a camera that plugs into your computer as an attachment. All you need to call friends and family on Skype is high speed internet and the free Skype program downloaded onto your computer. Start at www.skype.com and start in the "Get Skype" section of the menu. If for some reason Skype is not right for you, other programs exist.

Now Skype (or other) is the best choice. Make sure the people you want to talk to the most know how to use it, though you can use Skype to call any phone number for a reasonable cost, paid directly to Skype over the internet. Just have a back up plan for the first short while before you get set up in Mexico.

Mail: Receiving it at Your House

There are no rules for mail. It is a surprisingly individual service and different at every house. In the cities the mail may be delivered to your house by a mailperson (*cartero*) on a motorcycle with saddlebags. Get to know this person's name and face. Greet him warmly; ask him from where he hails. Tell him where you are from. You don't need to invite him in for tea, but spend a minute in a basic Mexican greeting ritual. This is the person who will leave your mail at your door or with a neighbor. He will learn whether or not you have an untrustworthy neighbor and avoid giving it to that person. He will wait at your door for you to run back to your house for your ID when he delivers official documents that require a signature. His feeling that he is appreciated will go a long way toward you receiving excellent mail service. Don't think you'll ever receive any? This is expatriate life. You probably will. You can give him a nice big tip in an envelope whenever you would like, especially at Christmas time, which is traditionally the time for *aguinaldos* (Christmas bonuses). Be on the look out for *Día del Cartero*. One of our mail carriers took this seriously and put little official envelopes into our mail boxes for us to give him extra money.

Generally houses in Mexico are closed off from the street and often mail people have to ring bells and wait for someone to open the door. Moreover, in some residences, there are no mail boxes so mail is delivered to neighbors to protect it from the rain and theft. I lost one box to an untrustworthy neighbor when the *cartero* set the box inside the shared doorway to our apartment building. Maintaining open communication with your *cartero* creates a network of people who know who last had a piece of mail and therefore can't claim that they have never seen it. I would never have known that the box was stolen right at our house if he hadn't remembered to ask me if I had received it. I told him no and we decided that he should leave my mail with the lady who sold tortillas next door to my house.

When you are not home, mail networks develop of their own accord, thanks to the efforts of your *cartero* and neighbors. Generally you won't have to assign a person as I did at the apartment. Usually people who find themselves home during the day offer to give you your mail when they see you, and *voila* a mail network has been formed! So, be nice to your neighbors too. Don't forget to say *Buenos dias* and *Buenos tardes* when you see them. When you move to a new house you could go into the branch office of the postal service that serves your neighborhood and fill out a change of address card, but you and my husband would be the only two people that year who do (just kidding, it actually did work and I received something at a new house that had been sent to the old address).

If you receive a notification that you have a box at a branch office of the Mexican postal service, look on the sheet for a phone number and/or address. The office that serves your neighborhood will not necessarily be the one closest to your house. You can call and find out how to get there, what hours they are open, etc. Get there as soon as you can because there is usually a delay of a number of days between the arrival of your package and your receipt of the notification slip. The postal service will return unclaimed boxes (once one made it back the sender even) after a set number of days and they don't take into account how long it may take you to receive the notification.

Mail: Sending International Mail

Your international mail is inspected. Occasionally you will receive a box that has been cut open and re-taped. If it makes you and the sender feel better, they can put an itemized contents list on the underside of the lid. Ninety percent of my mail makes it all of the way to my hands, but I always tell my family and friends not to send anything they would be heartbroken if it didn't make it. Novels in English always make it. Chocolate makes it—un-melted. A walkman made it, but it was an outdated technology when it was mailed. A box of used professional clothing from my aunt didn't nor did a personal-sized reading light.

Never mail clothing from the U.S. to Mexico – even if it's your own used items. They are not permitted due to the huge market for used clothing from the U.S. (Many a tianguis has used clothing stands full of gently used items.) You many send 1 or 2 items via courier, if needed.

For official documents, I have used Federal Express (from the U.S.) and Estafeta (from Cuernavaca). UPS is also active in Cuernavaca. I learned about Estafeta from a friend in the neighborhood. She even recommended the branch office which always offers the best customer service. If you aren't in Cuernavaca, ask around and someone will be able to recommend a good service.

For standard mail items, tell your family and friends to stand in line at the USPS office and fill out a customs form—but NOT to declare a value because you will have to pay a 50% tax on any declared value. In some cases a value is required and the value can be **one** U.S. cent. Once I practically had to buy a pair of shirts that my mother sent because she declared their actual value. Looking back on it, though I probably shouldn't have been so surly, considering that they were the only clothing item that has made it down to me (sorry, Mamma). The sender should put "Air Mail" on all boxes and envelopes to avoid their automatic alternative routing by "slug."

18 Safety

Since the first edition of this book was written, kidnapping and threats of other violence have become a real and present danger. It's something we barely thought about when we moved to Mexico, but you don't have that luxury. Do not take your personal safety lightly. I'm sorry I have to write it, but I don't recommend moving to Mexico right now – especially not with children.

I can easily spend 30 minutes telling real-life horror stories that I have heard and a number of them end in death. In my case, these stories are thankfully second hand – but some were quite close to home. My family moved from Mexico to Canada a few years ago and I'm glad we did. When I talk to our friends on Skype, I see how their facial expressions change when they talk about it. This is slow, painful terror.

I almost stopped selling this book because the violence and lack of security in Mexico make it a bad idea to voluntarily re-locate there. In the end, I decided to be brave and publish this third edition because I know that some readers won't have a choice about whether or not they move to Mexico, as I didn't. Other readers may read this section, decide not to go, and be glad of it.

Protecting Your Home

Luckily, I don't have any firsthand experience with how important it is to protect the safety of your home in Mexico. Judging by the way Mexicans construct their homes, there must be a real need for security. Mexican homes tend to look like Fort Knox. When I first came here, I felt threatened and reduced next to the 20-foot-high walls people build around their houses.

An architect from UNAM (*Universidad Autonoma de Mexico*) told me how the cultural history has influenced Mexican home design. The Spaniards brought with them an ancient Arabic tradition where external windows were small, permitting people to shoot arrows out through them, while the interior courtyards were private family spaces. He stressed the macro-cultural factors influencing this, such as tribal warfare. I noticed the micro-cultural factors surrounding women's roles in private and public life.

Anyway, when these Spaniards came to Mexico to rape, plunder, steal, and control, they had good reason to reproduce architectural features that kept them safe from upset native people. Sadly, the modern situation STILL reinforces these same home safety features (not that the features themselves are bad). Once someone breaks into your house, your stuff—and possibly you and your family are toast. The police don't or can't keep you safe.

Prevention is the key to the safety of your home. Below are some tips to prevent breaches in safety in your new home.

Physical precautions:

Choose a home in a neighborhood where people are out and about. This would be a not-so-rich, not-so-poor

Mexico: The Trick is Living Here 3ʳᵈ edition
available on www.home-sweet-mexico.com
290

neighborhood. Some rich neighborhoods are terrifyingly lonely, with nothing but blocks and blocks of 20-foot-high-walls topped with razor wire. Who will hear you if you get into trouble? If you don't want to be with other people, why not just stay in the U.S. where the police are professional?

Mexican houses and housing complexes generally have a wall surrounding them, with a huge metal door. Only people with keys can get in through the giant door, called the "*portón*." You have two good choices. You can choose a home with a private entrance. Or, if you want to live in a complex, choose one with a limited number of people who have access from the street.

Keep your street door (*portón*) locked, even when you are inside.

Ground-floor windows need to lock and have bars protecting them.

If your house doesn't happen to have a wall around it, lock all windows when you leave. People will know your schedule.

Make sure there is no place where people could climb up, around, or into to reach unprotected windows and doors.

When you take a quick walk to the neighborhood store (doesn't that sound great?!) don't leave your door unlocked. There are always many people around. Most will protect you, but someone just might decide to steal something.

Community precautions:

Form networks with your neighbors by saying hello when you see them and trading little favors. This is actually our TOP safety precaution. I admit I don't always

Mexico: The Trick is Living Here 3ʳᵈ edition
available on *www.home-sweet-mexico.com*
291

follow the physical ones listed above but Luis has helped us to get our community protection firmly in place.

Don't let people know what you have inside, such as stereo system, computers, etc. – not even most of your neighbors until you really know them.

Generally, you must take care not to "stand out" in any way. As a foreigner, this is basically impossible to do and the main reason I don't recommend moving to Mexico right now. How can you meld in with the crowd when you just got there?

Keep jewelry to a minimum

Only display miniscule amounts of cash

Drive an old car

Leave your house looking partially constructed. If you have to do home repairs, do only a little bit at a time so no one sees you spending large amounts of money.

Don't let go of children's hands when you are out on the street, in the grocery store, in a parking lot, in a park – basically anywhere but home. Walk or drive school-aged children to and from school.

If you donate to a charity, do it anonymously.

Consider discreetly borrowing money from neighbors, coworkers, and acquaintances occasionally so that no one thinks you are rich. Be without any money and borrow some, "Would you loan me 10 pesos for lunch? I'm out." Don't set a time when you will pay the person back and take 2 to 4 weeks to do it. Only do this if you feel that you can carry it off in a socially unobtrusive way. The idea is to give the impression that money is tight for you NOT to draw attention to yourself and money matters. Drawing attention would be more dangerous than not ever talking about it.

If someone asks to borrow more than a few pesos, don't just hand it to them, like there's more where that came from. Maybe offer half of what they ask, explaining that you need your money for groceries.

Remember that most kidnappings and other attacks on people are perpetrated by people who are known by the victim. This includes acquaintances, friends, and extended family. If the perpetrator isn't known to the victim, then they are likely to have gotten inside information from someone who is. Keep all evidence of finances strictly confidential.

19 Planning/Scouting Visit

Checklist

You Must see for Yourself on a Scouting Visit

One of the best things about Mexico is the uniqueness of each town, neighborhood, business, school… basically everything. This of course means that you can't plan to move to Mexico over the phone and internet. **You simply must go and see it in person**. Do **not** make any **assumptions** about how things will be. Once there, in order to avoid being distracted only by what you love about it (Don't let the euphoric effect of sunshine fog your decision-making abilities.) make sure you visit the following places before making your final decision about if and where to live in Mexico.

The checklist is on the next page so you can use it to take with you.

Scouting Checklist

Housing

How to: Look for signs posted on gates and fences that say "*se renta*" and knock on the door. Even if you plan to buy or build your own home, please take my advice and look at what's "normal" in your area. It will help you to have reasonable expectations.

☐ See a **furnished** apartment/house

Notes:

☐ See an **unfurnished** apartment/house

Notes:

☐ Check prices of **furnishings** by window shopping at a furnishing store, such as *Electra*.
  o Stove(s) [note the size/if it has an oven]:

  o Fridge (s) [note the sizes]:

  o Microwave:

  o Bed:

  o Table and chairs:

  o Couch:

o   Other appliances/furnishings:

Insurance

How to: Look in the phone book for *agencias de asuguranzas* or *seguros*.

☐   See an **insurance agent**
     Note the quotes they give you and your observations:
     o   *Menores*:

     o   *Mayores*:

     o   Vehicle:

Hospitals

How to: Ask people how many hospitals there are in town and visit all of them. This may seem like a drag, but if you want to feel safe in your new home, you've got to be comfortable with what's available and if you're not, you'll need to know that before you make solid plans.

☐   See all of the **hospitals** and other important health care centers
     Note your observations:
     o   IMSS:

     o   *Seguro Popular*:

     o   Private (note the name):

     o   Private (note the name):

o   Military Hospital:

o   Red Cross:

o   Other:

Food

How to: Ask anyone for a nearby *"supermercado/tienda de abarrotes," "mercado,"* and *"tianguis"* and take a typical grocery list with you.

☐   See where you would **shop for food**
    Note costs of items, ease of access, parking, etc.:
    o   Supermarket (*supermercado/tienda de abarrotes*):

    o   Market:

    o   *Tianguis:*

    o   Local neighborhood stores, such as *fruterías, tiendas de abarrotes, carnicerías* etc.:

Water

How to: Ask a few residents about the municipal water supply. If they say there is "no problem" ask another person until you hear the "…except sometimes" story. Trust me, there will be one of these stories. It's just a matter of how bad it is.

Mexico: The Trick is Living Here 3rd edition
available on www.home-sweet-mexico.com
297

Notes about the **municipal water**:

 o Is it daily?

 o Does it ever come out dirty?

 o Are there any changes during the rainy or dry seasons?

 o Are there neighborhoods that have issues?

 o Do people ever get sick from it?

Expatriate Community

How to: Keep your eyes peeled for non-Mexican-looking people and your ears peeled for English being spoken and stop and talk to people. Go sit with expats meeting somewhere and see if you like the mood of the group. Sometimes they can be quite negative and focused on complaining.

Notes about the **expat community**:

 o Café where people meet?

 o Neighborhood "they" tend to live in?

 o Newcomer's club?

 o Golf club?

 o Rotary club?

20 Parting Advice

Where's Waldo-Like Street Scenes

Hopefully you will enjoy the hustle and bustle of Mexican life. I often feel as if I'm inside one of those *Where's Waldo* street scenes where you look for the little guy in the red and white striped shirt in a busy scene. Someone is always doing something. You see people carrying heavy items down the street, or salesmen pushing towering loads on their hand trucks (you can buy inexpensive furniture from some of

Image from: http://veryaware.com/2011/11/yes-a-wheres-waldo-movie-is-in-the-works/

these guys). There is a tiny old lady, who must be in her 70s, who pushes a Popsicle cart up the mile-long hill through our neighborhood every afternoon. Once I saw a hugely fat woman waddling along the sidewalk hugging a watermelon against her stomach as she went. There is the four and a half foot tall parking attendant at a restaurant on one busy corner near my neighborhood who wears a long-sleeved blue dress shirt as his uniform. The sun faded his shirt over a period of a couple months and tanned his face mocha brown, darkening it as much as it had lightened his shirt. Then one day, there was a new dark blue shirt and the process began again with the sun working oppositely on his face and the cloth. There are the children who ride standing up in the back seats of their parents' cars, or resting in their mothers' laps, their tiny heads within inches of deadly dashboards. Luis stood in an upstairs window once and counted how many children traveling along the street below had been buckled into the proper safety equipment. He only needed one hand to keep track.

Mexico is a lively and energetic place. You can always enjoy yourself just watching people out the bus window, or sitting on a bench in the *zocalo*. Try to look for less morbid things than safety hazards, though, or you'll get depressed.

Advice: Dr. Julia is in

I'm sure that Mexico will offer you boundless joys and enough frustrations, infinite opportunities to grow and learn, and a healthy appreciation of the wealth and luxury that we enjoy back home, as well as a perspective on what that wealth costs our neighbors to the south. When you come here, for whatever length of stay, let Mexico reveal itself to you through interaction with the people. Mexicans love to share. Enjoy their generosity, humor, and flexibility—even let it rub off onto you. One lady in our neighborhood had a little walk-in restaurant where she served hot, quick meals. She became our friend and we could stop by for a chat about movies, or history, or whatever topic came up. When my dad visited, he could go over there and get first class service with a mixture of Spanish and English. She would often prepare us traditional dishes just so that we could learn about them. She would explain the recipes to us so we all learned a lot about the special regional dishes.

Don't judge people for being different from you; ask yourself how you can fit in. Mexicans' world makes perfect sense to them, so watch and listen to the people around you. Do more watching and listening than speaking. Remember that most people in neighborhoods know each other; some of them have known each other for years, like the ones that have grown up together in my neighborhood. They have old grudges and old friendships that don't show on the surface. Step lightly at first. Accept hospitality with a quiet grace. Give back in simple ways. Keep your eyes peeled for who is related to whom and who talks to whom. Never say anything negative. This bears repeating: <u>Never</u> say anything negative. Mexicans won't show you whether or not they appreciate your negative attitude, but your complaint may just relate to their brother-in-law's business, and you wouldn't even know it. Compared to the US, even large cities are like small towns, and everyone knows everyone's business.

A Mexican friend of mine, for example, moved into a brand new housing development. She brought me over to her new house for the first time and we were parking in front. Across the street, two ladies were holding the curtains aside, openly watching us. She commented about them. They were already making it their business to watch her and had criticized her parking on her own grass just the day before. This is an extreme example, but as a rule, Mexicans watch each other. Usually they are just more subtle about it. They know when you came home and in what car you arrived. Make friends with your neighbors and this watching becomes a mutual security system; make enemies, and it becomes a form of cruel entertainment. This same advice works in your professional life. I expect to see the same English teachers and administrators over and over throughout my teaching career. It would be unwise for me to make enemies.

One of the first American traits that should be let go when coming to Mexico, is the belief that one can control things. Many Americans manage to spend years under the stressful delusion that they are controlling the events in their daily lives. Mexico has done me the favor of curing me of that belief. Here you control nothing. The sooner you let go of the desire to control, the sooner day-to-day life will stop controlling you. You have no control over how things are done, nor how long things take, nor whether or not they make sense to you. My new improved belief system came out clearly when I was talking to a couple of American women about paying taxes here. One woman, who is spending the summer here perfecting her Spanish,

Mexico: The Trick is Living Here 3rd edition
available on www.home-sweet-mexico.com
302

asked why something worked the way it did. Without thinking I said, "I don't ask why, I just ask how—and that is hard enough to figure out." The other woman, who lives here permanently, said, "That is so true." With patience, things always work out fine.

Learn to do only one thing at a time. Unless you are in Mexico City, you don't need to multi-task. If something can't happen when you planned it, well, there is always tomorrow. Take deep breaths often and stop to look around you. There is a lovely lady in her forties who came to my neighborhood this summer. I'm pretty sure she's from the U.S. by the way she dresses and walks. The thing is she doesn't even know I'm here at the end of her block, because she never looks around and I can't catch her eye. She zooms out of our street and heads down the main road with her backpack on—I guess she's going to a Spanish class. I understand her; she probably feels kind of like a sore thumb with her short, wavy blond hair among all of the Mexicans. She might be wary of the extra attention that foreigners get, and maybe she's from a big city where you never see anyone you know on the street anyway. Hopefully over time, she will slow down a little; look around more. When you slow down and look around, you start to see so much. You notice the little details like what things are sold and advertised, what people are doing, how people are interacting, and you get a chance to say hello sometimes. Maybe you'll even run into an expat living two doors down the street from you (she never did).

Live in the moment. Be flexible and learn to let go. Being flexible creates opportunities for exciting bursts of creativity. The same American friend mentioned above was telling me that her oven has pictures of a pie and a turkey on the temperature dial. The question was; how would she set her oven to the 350°F required to bake her cake? "I have it half way between the pie and the turkey," she told me. After my burst of laughter subsided I told her that I had asked for an oven thermometer for Christmas last year since my oven has only the pie and an unmarked line surrounding the temperature dial, and I offered it to her for future baking projects. Then we got creative. She could just use it once, mark the temperatures onto her stove and return it. I had already tried that and found that I always washed them off of the polished face of the stove right away. So then we got *really* creative. She could make a special template, marked with the temperatures on it that she places over the dial when she is baking, then removes to clean the stove. There is always a way to do what you want to here—and often the results are pleasantly surprising. When you're flexible you end up with days full of tailor-fit moments.

One of the best things about living in Mexico is the amount of face to face interaction that goes on. People are rarely too busy to stop and talk to you for a moment or to help you out with something. They enjoy networking and interacting. Mexicans are so generous with their time, money, and food that I am often surprised and touched. It stretches me in a positive way to share back. Recently, Luis suffered an accident that put him in the hospital. Our closest neighbors were with us for two days straight, dealing with legal and health issues for 12 hour stints, missing meals and spending money on transportation to and from the hospital. We were touched and really couldn't have done it without them. After Luis was released from the hospital and I returned to work, our neighbor would pass us plates of food when she saw that I didn't have time to cook.

The connection between our families is an invaluable mutual support. The other day I dragged home from an unusually long and stressful day at work, stopped at the store and bought myself some potato chips, which were to be my solace and dinner (I was assuming Luis had already eaten). I was planning on climbing into bed and munching my chips while I forgot about the world with a good book. Just as I was opening the door, my heavy bag hanging over my shoulder, my neighbor popped out of her door and invited herself over. Since in Mexico you can never say "no," I knew I was trapped (see "Never Say No, Just Tell an Untruth" on page 216). I put on my game face and told her *Pásele* ("Come on over") with as much gusto as I could muster.

Sharpening some scissors.

Being the dear she is, she didn't mind that I didn't offer her anything. By Mexican standards I should have given her some dinner and something to drink. I had only bought a small bag of chips and didn't have enough to share, so I had to leave it hidden away in my bag. She just chatted and chatted and let me just listen as I helped her make some Christmas ornaments (I like handicrafts). She told me all about Christmases and New

Ready to move on to the next customer.

Years past and about Christmas and New Years future. By the time she left I was relaxed and looking forward to the upcoming holidays.

The Joy of Discovery

It is amazing how much you will discover on your own during your time here. After two years I was still having little "ah-ha moments" in which I discovered some useful piece of information, like what that little whistling sound is every Wednesday afternoon: an itinerant knife sharpener announcing his passage through our neighborhood. Be patient with yourself. You don't have to like everything all at once, though, the longer you live here, the more you'll like it. I promise. Mexico will go revealing itself to you thousands of little wonderful moments at a time.

21 The Back-story: How I Came to Mexico

When I wrote the bulk of this book I was 29 years old and had no children. This was a good thing because otherwise I never would have gotten it done. I have both a bachelor of science and a bachelor of art degrees from a state university in Washington. I used to work doing population studies on endangered salmon species in Washington. In the U.S., my husband, Luis, and I lived in a cute duplex within walking distance of my parents. We cultivated flowers in our yard and had barbecues outside our back door. I had already paid off my college loans, started saving for retirement and taken all of the money management seminars available through my credit union.

I'm not the adventurous type, and change tends to be hard on me. So what in the Higher Power's name could have dragged me into a change as huge as a move to a new country and new career? The answer is: my—our (yes, readers from the U.S.) – government. My husband is Mexican and could not receive a permanent residence visa

Mexico: The Trick is Living Here 3rd edition
available on *www.home-sweet-mexico.com*
307

to live with me in the U.S. After the denial, I suddenly had to choose between my country, my career, and my family and friends, and my husband. I chose Luis and moved to Mexico, Luis' country, and started over.

When we moved here, we were literally at square one. It happened like this: nine months after Luis had left the U.S. for Mexico, I followed him on a round trip ticket—the second half of which has long since expired—with two huge suit cases and a snazzy climber's backpack. I had packed carefully selected Goodwill outfits suited to being a teacher in a hot climate; some pairs of shoes; a cast iron skillet (Luis complained about its weight until he saw for himself how no other kitchen appliance can do so much); an iron; some novels in English; the laptop computer, which has enabled this book to exist, given to us by a truly marvelous person; a couple of kitchen towels; an antique family heirloom crocheted hot pad; two sets of sheets; ironically, a woven wool Mexican blanket; three bath towels; a blender; and my great aunt's sewing box full of tatting supplies (my quilt frame wouldn't fit in my duffle).

My sketchy plan was carefully designed to get Luis out of the countryside, where I knew I couldn't live. Luis had been investing in a guava orchard for years by saving and sending money from the U.S. to his father in Michoacan. He spent those first nine months in Mexico working on the orchard he had sacrificed so much for, but he understood that I couldn't live happily in the Michoacan countryside. I had paid an online service to find me a job teaching English in Cuernavaca, Mexico. Neither of us had ever been to Cuernavaca before in our lives, but all the tour books say it's wonderful. Luis, God bless him, let me choose this place and left the guava orchard, spending all of the money he had getting us set up here.

Mexico: The Trick is Living Here 3rd edition
available on www.home-sweet-mexico.com
308

Previous to this move I had traveled with my husband for two months throughout the southern half of Mexico in 2001. As tourists, we visited Puebla and liked it so much we took my parents back there when they came to visit. We were overjoyed to find that we had chosen to come during Puebla's international music festival. We visited Mexico D.F. and spent so long in the museum in Chapultapec that I didn't get to go to the zoo as I had hoped to. We happily discovered that we had chosen to come during the large November 20th Revolution Day parade held yearly in the nation's capital. We were astounded to watch people creating human pyramids on the backs of galloping horses, others doing gymnastics on floats, and many other sights that you will have to come see for yourself.

In Oaxaca, we got so lost in the streets that change name every block we became disgusted and bought bus tickets to leave town the next day, then were treated to the best classical guitar concert we have ever heard in our lives. The concert, like the one in Puebla, and many others, was held for free in the park, called the *zocalo*. The State of Chiapas was our favorite. We listened to marimba music in the *zocalo* of Palenque while we chatted with a man who reminded us how important it is to go to school. He treated us with the care of an older member of a community who wants to encourage the young people. From there we sojourned in the Lacondon forest, enjoying the hospitality of the Mayan people. We visited Cancun and hated it for its overpriced, over-groomed, American-ness. Its one saving grace was the dessert I bought from the Italian restaurant next to our small hotel in the city center. Later, we were wowed by the beauty of the sunrise over the water in Playa del Carmen and the crystal clear waters of Isla de las Mujeres. We fought with the guy who rented us our mopeds in Cozumel, but were helped out when we elicited the support of a tourist police officer. Chitzen Itza revealed its wonders to us in an entire day of walking everywhere and exploring every possible corner. We left there exhausted and starving but full of memories that will never die.

We also explored out of the way ruins such as Kohunlich and some tiny towns, which Mexicans refer to as "ranchos." In ranchos one needs family with whom to stay because there are no services for travelers, but luckily my husband has no shortage of extended family. It is a little known fact that the real reason Mexicans are so famous for being "family oriented" is that they need places to stay when they travel more than a day's trip away from home. It was from the outdoor sink of one of these family members' houses that I saw the first shooting star in my life. It was brilliant and left a trail of red and white starlight half way down the dark sky, undiminished by the light pollution of cities. I've seen chicken pox on chickens, been so hot I had to sleep, had to plug my nose to keep out the smell of hot urine on a street corner, been nearly suffocated by the smoke of burning garbage…oh yeah, you want to move here. I'll get back to the good stuff.

My family and I have been given a private tour of a renovated government building with lovely Spanish architecture by the night watchmen who saw us admiring the central courtyard through the locked entry gate and wanted to share the treasure which he had the responsibility to protect. My husband and I have waded in the crystal clear water of a *cenote* and admired the tiny, colorful fish gliding around our feet and ankles. I've stood on an upstairs balcony and enjoyed the light of sunset over colonial roofs and a lone church spire. I've watched dolphins jumping in the evening coastal light. I've looked up at monkeys in a tree looking down at me.

Mexico: The Trick is Living Here 3rd edition
available on www.home-sweet-mexico.com
310

22 Acknowledgments

This manuscript could not exist without the help of a few high quality individuals, all of whom included helping me in my writing project as part of their friendship with me. I'll start with those who helped with content. I thank my husband José Luis Soto for maintaining the delicate balance between focusing me on the realities of Mexican culture and letting me be "American" in the way I do it. Not only does he guide me through the daily experiences of living in Mexico and relating to Mexicans, he also reads my writing and gives me pointers on content and perspective. He is truly unique in his ability to understand people and interactions from both my culture and his. I thank Brienne Borrows for being an excellent "brainstormer" of important points and for being generous with her personal experiences and the solutions she has formed while living in Mexico. I also thank her parents, Linda and Dick Borrows, for being my model retired people, giving me hot tips on topics to include. I thank Cheryl Allaby for sharing her anecdotes; both funny and frustrated. Cheryl is also always available to cross check both the Canadian experience and the Mexican reality in places other than Cuernavaca.

Two people helped with writing style and accuracy. I thank Nancy Thompson (http://www.cherry-grove.com/thompson.html), author of *Killing the Buddha*, for making time to read my drafts. Her eye for quality content and correctly placed commas are what will make reading this book smooth and pleasant for you. I'm grateful for her honesty in keeping me away from "ranting" and other negative wastes of energy. I thank Marcia Taylor for her joyous, two-hour turnaround readings in which she checked for extra commas, tangents, language that is too informal, and blatant stereotypes, meanwhile always finding something to compliment me on.

I thank Rolly Brook (www.rollybrook.com) for his excellent web site and email responses on the topic of bringing cars and household items into Mexico. Rolly has his own book out now (http://www.rollybrook.com/book.htm). I thank Rod Burylo, BACFP (www.rodburylo.com, and www.canadiansretiringabroad.ca) for spending over an hour of his time on the phone with me explaining the Canadian experience in Canada. I thank Doug Gray, LL.B. (www.snowbird.ca, www.retirementplanning.ca, www.estateplanning.ca, and www.homebuyer.ca) for the use of an excerpt of one of his excellent educational articles. I thank Demetric Batistte and Douglas Taylor for providing the laptop computers on which the first two editions of this manuscript were written. Neither my manuscript nor the web site *www.home-sweet-mexico.com* could exist without the tool to create them. I thank Jonni Good (www.howtothinkthin.com, and www.easydoesitdiet.com) for her tireless technical support on the "mechanics" of developing a website and electronic products.

23 Disclaimer

As I wrote this book I had to generalize about many circumstances in order to communicate a particular point of view that I believe will be most useful and/or accurate to the person recently arrived in Mexico from the rest of North America. I mean no offense to Mexico as a country or to Mexican people, either personally or in general. I know that not everyone is the same nor are all places or institutions the same as I may have characterized them here. By the same token each of my readers will have his or her own experiences and must make his or her own decisions about how to experience Mexico.

Nothing in this book shall be deemed to constitute the giving of financial or any kind of advice. If you are in any doubt, please consult a qualified financial or other appropriate advisor.

Where there are links from this book to other websites such links are provided for your information only. I have no control over the contents of these sites and accept no responsibility for them or for any losses or damages which may result from your use of them.

I do not warrant or make any representations that this book or www.home-sweet-mexico.com (the website) will operate error-free or uninterrupted, that defects will be corrected, or that this book and the site and/or its servers will be free of viruses and/or other harmful components. It is your sole responsibility to ensure that your system has adequate protection against any such viruses and/or other harmful components.

24 About the Third Edition

For the third edition to *Mexico: The Trick is Living Here* I combed through the entire book. My main focus was to double check prices, update all specific instructions, especially how-to information for paperwork, and to make sure all links were working (though the latter achievement is discouragingly ephemeral).

Interestingly, the third edition was written in the third country of North America I have called home: Canada. We left Mexico when we found that we had reached the "glass ceiling" of opportunity for our young family in Mexico. Canada has proven to be a good choice for our family and, rather than making this third edition less useful, the experience of living in Canada has made it even better. Obviously, I am in a better position to include tips and information that is specifically applicable for Canadians.

Not as obviously, but more importantly, I've been through the process of "reverse culture shock." All of those quirky things I so difficultly adjusted to while living in Mexico... yes, I actually missed many of them. I used to bristle when Mexicans would talk about how "cold" Americans and/or Canadians were when they lived up north. Well, I've actually made the same complaint to my

Mexico: The Trick is Living Here 3rd edition
available on *www.home-sweet-mexico.com*
315

Mexican friends back home in Mexico! (And, yes, it goes for both Canadians and people from the U.S.) I really miss the way people take time out every day to connect with each other.

Now I'm mostly adjusted to the culture in Victoria, Canada, but I still get in a tizzy when I see how people avoid talking to our young son when we are out in public. The fear of being seen as intruding on a family or threatening the child because you are a "stranger" is driving me into fits as I try to maintain our son's excellent social skills he learned in **infancy** in Mexico (a battle I'm destined to lose thanks to the almost complete avoidance of direct contact with other people's children here in Victoria.)

While, I maintained the "culture shock" perspective that gives this book its character and helps the newly adjusting resident in Mexico relate, I added some details that I wouldn't have thought of if I hadn't actually *yearned* for Mexico.

Still, Canada has been the right choice for our family these last few years. Our son has faced a grave medical condition and his father and I have been grateful to be in British Columbia rather than Mexico. His life was undoubtedly saved by his permanent residence here at the time of diagnosis. Finally, the violence in Mexico, which I first hoped was slander propagated through the media, is something I am glad we skipped out on. I am sad I have to write this about such a wonderful, rich, vibrant country, but now is not the best time to move to Mexico. When I speak on Skype with family and friends in Mexico, I can see in their faces that the fear of violence is real and stressful. If you can, stay in the U.S. or Canada. Sadly, I know that there are some of you, like Luis and I, who do not have a choice. For you, I hope this book is useful.

25 Useful Links

Note: The inclusion of links in this section should by no means be considered an endorsement by the author. I have no control over the contents of these sites and accept no responsibility for them or for any losses or damages which may result from your use of them.

Visa Information

Article by Rolly Brook a U.S. Expat. living in Lerdo, Durango.
http://rollybrook.com/inm-form-1.htm
and http://rollybrook.com/how_to_move_to_mexico.htm
and http://rollybrook.com/Page%20Directory.htm
Rolly describes both the logistical and the documentation process that he went through, including preparing his *menaje de casa*. He has thoroughly presented the information on the post-November 2012 procedures.

Mexico's National Institute of Migration: Information in English

Mexico: The Trick is Living Here 3rd edition
available on *www.home-sweet-mexico.com*
317

http://www.inm.gob.mx/index.php/page/pagina_principal/en.html
Translation is still in process. Every few month, there are a few more pages in English. Note: "Formalities" = visas.

Yucatan Expatriate web site summary of the 2011 immigration law and their 2012 regulations
http://www.yucatanexpatriateservices.com/resident-services/new-immigration-laws-2012.html

About the new immigration law, implemented January 2012
http://yucalandia.wordpress.com/living-in-yucatan-mexico/new-immigration-law-published-for-mexico-the-article/

The U.S. Department of State information for travelers (long and short term) to Mexico.
http://travel.state.gov/travel/cis_pa_tw/cis/cis_970.html

A list of all of the Mexican Consulates
http://www.sre.gob.mx/index.php/representaciones/consulados-de-mexico-en-el-exterior Includes the U.S., Canada, and Great Britain. (Note: some information is in Spanish)

A Summary of Visa Options for Foreigners in Mexico
http://www.visasmex.com

Article by Julia C. Taylor which includes a section on working in Mexico
http://www.home-sweet-mexico.com/expatriate-author-Teach-English-in-Mexico-Part1.html
This article gives information on how to be prepared with the correct documents.

Apostilles

State Authentication Authorities in the **United States:**
http://www.nass.org/index.php?option=com_content&view
=article&id=262&Itemid=484
At this site, search for the state in which you got/will get
the document notarized.

Foreign Affairs and International Trade Canada & Mexican
Embassy or Consulates in **Canada**
Step 1: Authentication in Ottawa.
http://international.gc.ca/about-a_propos/authentication-
authentification_documents.aspx?view=d
Step 2: Legalization by the Mexican Embassy (or
Consulate) in Canada.
http://embamex.sre.gob.mx/canada_eng/index.php?option=
com_content&view=article&id=1255&Itemid=41

Foreign and Commonwealth Office in the **United
Kingdom**
http://www.fco.gov.uk/en/about-us/what-we-do/services-
we-deliver/legal-services/Legalisation/
The Foreign and Commonwealth Office calls the process
"Legalization."

Moving Household Items to Mexico

Article by Rolly Brook a U.S. Expat. living in Lerdo,
Durango.
http://rollybrook.com/how_to_move_to_mexico.htm#Movi
ng

This is from the *Secretaría de Relaciones Exteriores* – and in English even!
http://consulmex.sre.gob.mx/calexico/index.php/component/content/article/90
and
http://portal.sre.gob.mx/was_eng/index.php?option=displaypage&Itemid=69&op=page&SubMenu

Excerpt from Living Abroad in Mexico 1st Edition by Ken Luboff
http://www.transitionsabroad.com/listings/living/livingabroadin/living_abroad_in_mexico_moving.shtml#what_to_take

Article by Jennifer J. Rose, dated 2006.
Mexico's a Breeze.
http://www.mexconnect.com/articles/1883-mexico-s-a-breeze

Article by Melville King, dated 2001
Moving Stuff to Mexico
http://www.mexconnect.com/articles/1384-moving-stuff-to-mexico

Other related links:
http://insidemex.com/living-in-mexico/the-fixer/the-international-move

http://www.acerelocation.com/intl/mexico.pdf

Arrival by Land, using a Tourist Visa and Mexican Customs

Mexican customs information, in English!
http://www.aduanas.gob.mx/aduana_mexico/2008/pasajeros/139_10179.html

Bringing Vehicles into Mexico

Rolly Brook's "Page Directory"
When you click on this link, you will have hit the jackpot.
To find the information about cars, scroll down a bit and look on the right.
http://rollybrook.com/Page%20Directory.htm

From the *Secretaría de Relaciones Exteriores* themselves
In English: Temporary Importation of Motor Vehicles
http://portal.sre.gob.mx/was_eng/index.php?option=displaypage&Itemid=62&op=page&SubMenu=

Thanks go to the state of New Mexico. This one is a real gem.
http://www.nmborder.com/vehicle.html

Mexican driver's license test
http://www.jalisco.gob.mx/wps/wcm/connect/263aec804dbe31549eb6ff5160bedb77/Guia.Examen.Licencia.pdf?MOD=AJPERES
These are the 103 questions—with answers at the end—from which 20 questions are chosen for each written test for driver's licenses in Mexico. (Note: you must be able to read in Spanish).

Includes information on when you don't need a permit.
http://www.bajabound.com/before/permits/vehiclepermits.php

http://www.yucatanexpatriateservices.com/resident-services/new-rules-for-bringing-your-car-to-mexico.html

http://www.mexonline.com/drivemex.htm

Bringing Dogs and Cats into Mexico

Website for those traveling in Mexico with a pet
http://gringodog.com/

Canadian International Health Certificate to download.
http://www.inspection.gc.ca/animals/terrestrial-animals/exports/pets/canadian-international-health-certificate/eng/1321285405995/1321285496577

United States
http://www.state.gov/m/fsi/tc/34589.htm
http://www.aphis.usda.gov/regulations/vs/iregs/animals/animal_faq.shtml

Banking in Mexico

Mexico Mike and I agree about banking in Mexico
http://mexicomike.com/money/banking.htm

Health Care in Mexico

Rolly Brook's article on health care options is a must read:
http://rollybrook.com/health.htm

Article by Rick Lewis on the public health system in Mexico. Rick claims he's sure his IMSS will save him, but he anecdotes don't convince me.
http://www.mazinfo.com/infofiles/IMSS.htm

International Living's overview of health care in Mexico. I'm trying to offer some positive reviews of health care in Mexico, but these kind of sound like sales jobs. You decide.
http://internationalliving.com/countries/mexico/health-care-in-mexico/
http://internationalliving.com/2010/12/mexicos-health-care-first-rate-and-at-bargain-prices/
http://internationalliving.com/2010/11/health-care-in-mexico/ Offers a "real" experience, but where are the cancer patients, heart attack survivors, diabetics?...

Here's a positive one that's not selling anything:
http://diogenes.hubpages.com/hub/Mexican-Doctors-May-Sleep-Better-at-Night

Mexico Connect Web site's articles on health care
http://www.mexconnect.com/articles/164-living-healthy-in-mexico-insurance-health-care-and-mexico-s-medical-tourism-a-resource-page

Article on health insurance in Mexico by Tony Hamrick on Mexico Connect Web site http://www.mexconnect.com/articles/688-international-insurance-plans-for-foreigners-in-mexico

"IMSS Denying Expats Chronic Disease Care" an article by Dale Hoyt Palfrey in the Guadalajara Reporter
http://guadalajarareporter.com/news-mainmenu-82/lake-chapala-mainmenu-84/30001-imss-denying-expats-chronic-disease-care.html

Buying Real Estate in Mexico

Article on Buying Property in Mexico by Dennis Peyton
http://www.mexonline.com/propmex.htm

Over 20 articles having to do with houses and real estate in Mexico
http://www.mexconnect.com/mex_/realestatemexicoindex.html

Article by Shawn Haley about his experience buying land in Oaxaca
http://www.evrcanada.com/sab6.html

Contact form for Suzanne Marie Bandick, who has personal experience with buying real estate in Mexico. She's a kind lady and will answer any questions you may have.
http://www.suzannemariebandick.com/contact.html

Everything you want to know about property in Mexico on mexperience.com
http://www.mexperience.com/property/

http://www.mexperience.com/property/buying-selling-real-estate-in-mexico.php

If you click on the links in the web site you will get some little tidbits about becoming an expatatriate
http://www.mexicodream.ca/

Building a House in Mexico

10 articles by the creators of Yucatanliving.com based on their personal experiences building their own home in Merida.
http://www.yucatanliving.com/category/real-estate-yucatan

This one is a gem, concise, an easy read and with photos, even
http://zabpat.com/

This one is certainly unique…
http://www.timporter.com/words/casa_070702.shtml

Mexican home construction:
http://vallartablog.com/mexican-home-construction-explained/
http://altbuildblog.blogspot.com/2011/09/building-brick-house-in-mexico.html

For the die hard reader/dreamer:
http://insidemex.com/real-estate/real-estate/building-your-dream-home-in-mexico
http://www.mexconnect.com/articles/473-to-build-or-buy-a-house-in-mexico

Mexico: The Trick is Living Here 3rd edition
available on www.home-sweet-mexico.com
325

http://www.mexicoguru.com/design/construction.php

Here's one built out of plastic bottles:
http://www.instructables.com/id/House-in-Mexico-built-with-plastic-and-glass-bottl/

The Expatriate Experience in Mexico

A web site written by a Canadian couple. They are parents and include related information.
http://www.movingtomexico.ca/

If you are over 60, you can get a 50% discount card through DIF. Rolly Brook gets the credit for finding this out:
http://rollybrook.com/discount_card.htm

Read blogs written by expats from around the world who share their experience of living in Mexico.
http://www.expat-blog.com/en/directory/north-america/mexico/

A collection of articles by expats in Mexico about their experiences.
http://www.transitionsabroad.com/listings/living/living_abroad/living_in_mexico.shtml

http://marcoyucatan.blogspot.com/

Mike Goll contacted me after purchasing my e-book. Now he's in Mexico and you can take advantage of the experiences he shares in his blog.

http://mikeletioscar.blogspot.com/2006_08_01_archive.html

Is Mexico right for you? By Mexico Mike
http://www.mexicomike.com/livebetter/who_should.html
This guy is right on.

Interviews of expats in Mexico. I learned about this when I was interviewed:
http://www.expatinterviews.com/mexico

Yikes!
http://mexicowoods.typepad.com/mexicowoods/2010/07/a-luncheon-in-zacatecas.html

http://www.countdowntomexico.com/about/

About Moving Children and Schools
http://vidamaz.blogspot.com/2010/01/moving-to-mexico-mazatlan-with-kids.html
The blog is full of interesting posts, but hard to navigate. Use the "archives" on the bottom right to read more:
http://vidamaz.blogspot.com/2010/01/who-is-this-guy-jesus-malverde-patron.html

From the Chapala area:
http://lifestylerefugee.vidalago.com/

From Veracruz:
http://www.vivaveracruz.com/blog/
Check out the "**blogroll**" on that one. You could read blogs about Mexico for weeks from this!

From the Yucatan:
http://yucatanbeachbum.blogspot.ca/

Written by "forced" expats (those whose spouses couldn't live in the U.S.), these blogs are chock full of real life details about living in Mexico:
http://bordersaside.blogspot.com/
http://roblesfamilia.blogspot.com/
http://thevacafamily.blogspot.com/
http://livingsouthofsanity.blogspot.com/
http://therealhousewifeofciudadjuarez.blogspot.com/
http://thedeporteeswife.blogspot.com/
This one is very informal and has some "bad words" in it, but I like the author's honesty:
http://gringa-n-mexico.blogspot.com/

There's even a downloadable "app" for those of us who are still learning Spanish:
http://www.spanishverbchart.com/

http://www.expatcommunities.com/mexico-expatriates.html

Forums on Mexico and the Expatriate Experience

This one has the most people on it, which is important for a good forum:
http://www.mexconnect.com/forums/?t=search_engine

Mexico: The Trick is Living Here 3rd edition
available on *www.home-sweet-mexico.com*
328

Expat Exchange's forum on Mexico
http://www.expatexchange.com/expat/index.cfm?frmid=25
4&dbname=ee&shared=N&forumid=0
This one tends to have a slow turnover of posts, but all of
the information is well thought out and appropriate.

Residents of the Distrito Federal

If you live in Mexico City there are conveniently located
Centros de Servicio de la Tesorería [Treasury Service
Centers] found in grocery stores in almost every part of the
city. These are similar to the Canadian vehicle licensing
and insurance service desks open for extended hours in
grocery stores. You can pay the fees and do the paperwork
for a wide variety of municipal services in less than thirty
minutes, enjoying the personalized assistance of a real
person. Information on the Treasury Service Centers:
http://www.080.df.gob.mx/tramites/importante/centro_serv
icio_01.html scroll down to se the large number of types of
transactions you can complete there.
Location of the Treasury Service Centers:
http://www.finanzas.df.gob.mx/cservicio/directorio.html
You can also call the LOCATEL information Number
(555) 658-1111 and they will give you information about
any transaction you need to complete.

Links for Canadian Citizens

Foreign Affairs and International Trade of Canada's Travel Page on Mexico
http://www.voyage.gc.ca/countries_pays/report_rapport-
eng.asp?id=184000

"Retiring Abroad"
http://www.voyage.gc.ca/publications/retirement_retraite-eng
By Consular Affairs. This is article touches on so many topics you can use it to start planning.

Service Canada gives their tips here:
http://www.servicecanada.gc.ca/eng/subjects/travel/abroad.shtml

Citizenship and Passports

Embassy of Canada in Mexico
http://www.canadainternational.gc.ca/mexico-mexique/index.aspx?view=d

Directory of Embassy and Consulates of Canada in Mexico
http://www.canadainternational.gc.ca/mexico-mexique/offices-bureaux/index.aspx?lang=eng&menu_id=18&view=d

Embassy of Mexico in Canada (English site)
http://embamex.sre.gob.mx/canada_eng/

Directory of Mexican Consulates in Canada
http://embamex.sre.gob.mx/canada_eng/index.php?option=
com_content&view=article&id=55&Itemid=35 (make sure
the "consulates" tab is selected).

Information about the citizenship rules after April 17, 2009
http://www.cic.gc.ca/english/citizenship/rules-
citizenship.asp

Canadian Embassy in Canada: Information if you are living
or traveling in Mexico
http://www.canadainternational.gc.ca/mexico-
mexique/consul/index.aspx?lang=eng&menu_id=23&men
u=L

Information about **passports** from the Embassy of Canada
in Mexico City
http://www.canadainternational.gc.ca/mexico-
mexique/consul/ppt.aspx?view=d

Describes the additional things required for the certificate
of citizenship when you get it through the embassy in
Mexico City.
http://www.canadainternational.gc.ca/mexico-
mexique/consul/citizenship-citoyennete.aspx
For those whose children are born abroad.

Step-by-step guide to getting passports. Click on
"Canadians abroad" to start.
http://www.ppt.gc.ca/cdn/index.aspx

Article in the Calgary Herald on Canadians retiring in Mexico.
http://www.canada.com/calgaryherald/news/travel/story.html?id=ad2aa320-a798-4daa-8002-2ee6a1f27ab1&k=91216

Taxes

Residency
http://www.cra-arc.gc.ca/tx/nnrsdnts/cmmn/rsdncy-eng.html

Non-Residence
http://www.cra-arc.gc.ca/tx/nnrsdnts/ndvdls/nnrs-eng.html

What does it mean to *emigrate* from Canada?
http://www.cra-arc.gc.ca/tx/nnrsdnts/ndvdls/lvng-eng.html

"The Non-resident Canadian Canadian"
http://www.escapeartist.com/efam25/tax.html
Article by Canadian Expat in Guadalajara about tax advantage of becoming a non-resident

CBC News: Tax Rules for Canadians Abroad
http://www.cbc.ca/news/business/taxseason/story/2011/02/24/f-tax-season-deveau-international.html

"Retiring Abroad? Some Pointers"
http://en.50plus.com/display.cfm?documentID=8253&CabinetID=369&LibraryID=112
By Douglas Gray

Here's a posting on a Financial Forum by Norbert Schlenker, who makes some recommendations for Canadians moving abroad.
http://www.financialwebring.com/forum/viewtopic.php?t=17
You have to scroll down a ways until you see his name at the left.

Advisors

TioCorp Inc.
http://www.canadiansinmexico.com/

A tax advisory service for Canadian Expats
http://www.expat.ca/

Continental Tax offers tax advice to Expats
http://www.continentaltax.com/canadians.html

RBC Investments page on retiring abroad
http://www.hsbc.ca/1/2/en/personal/hsbcpremier/worldwide-assistance#7_2_KMK

Health Care Insurance

A directory of International Health Resources
http://www.ih.ualberta.ca/handbook/resources.html

A web site that provides free quotes for health care insurance.
http://www.medibrokerinternational.com/products.html
You could try using this free service to get some ball-park figures of the cost of health care.

A directory of companies that offer international insurance
http://www.expatriates.com/directory/ps/insurance/

Banking

The Royal Bank of Canada offers international banking services for Canadian Expats
http://www.rbcwminternational.com/expatriate-financial-services.html

Here is HSBC's expat web site for those living abroad
http://www.expat.hsbc.com/1/2/hsbc-expat/knowledge-centre?WT.srch=1&WT.mc_id=HBIB_2008_11_2011

Mailbox Services

http://www.theupsstore.ca/mailbox-rental-services.html

Canadian Expatriate Groups

For Canadian Expatriates
http://www.canuckabroad.com/

http://www.canuckabroad.com/forums/canadians-in-mexico-vf18.html

http://thecanadianexpat.com/index.php/en/

http://www.expat-blog.com/en/nationalities/canadian/in/north-america/mexico/

http://www.internations.org/mexico-expats/canadians

Links for United States Citizens

Social Security

Social Security Online: Your Payments While You Are Outside The United States
http://www.ssa.gov/pubs/10137.html

Filing US Taxes as an Expat

http://www.expatnetwork.com/Money/Expat-Tax/Tax-for-American-Expats.cfm

Mailbox Services

http://www.theupsstore.com/products-services/mailbox/Pages/index.aspx

26 Photo Essay: Making Tamales

Step 1: Prepare the *Masa* (not pictured)

Boil dry whole corn kernels with lime (*Nixtamal*). This is
usually done over an open fire because firewood is cheaper
than propane for the stove. Grind the cooked kernels. If
you don't have *nixtamal* you can use pre-made corn flour
for tortillas, called *minsa*. One brand sold in the U.S. and
Canada is *Maseca*.

Step 2: Prepare the ingrediates

On the stove Doña Eva has prepared (clockwise from top), two pans of chili *guajillo*, *tequesquite* water for the *masa* (see below for a description), sweetened pineapple with cinnamon, and green chili (not shown). These are "normal" salsas, made as you would make them to simmer meats in. Of course, the term "normal" here is just a relative term as there is nothing ordinary about Doña Eva's salsas.

Step 3: Mix the *Masa* into *Tamale* dough

Here are 4 liters (actually 8 *cuartillos*, each *cuartillo* equivalent to 500ml) of *masa* fresh from the grinder, in a laundry tub, ready to be mixed.

Add 2 kilos of rendered pork fat and 2 kilos of vegetable shortening. Doña Eva says that the pork fat provides the traditional flavor and the vegetable shortening makes the tamales soft.

Mexico: The Trick is Living Here 3rd edition
available on www.home-sweet-mexico.com
339

Mexico: The Trick is Living Here 3rd edition
available on *www.home-sweet-mexico.com*

340

Chef Doña Eva and her enthusiastic assistant, Doña Alma, stop for a photo op. as Doña Eva is preparing to add the shortening to the mix.

Doña Alma brings out the water (left) in which *tequesquite* (shown below) has been dissolved. The water turns dark (next page), and you just pour off the top, leaving whatever sinks to the bottom at the bottom. Doña Eva explains that you don't stir the water at all.

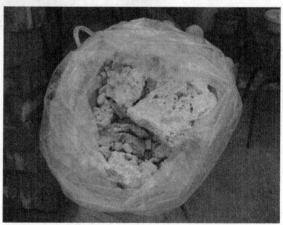

(See http://www.gourmetsleuth.com/equivalents_substitutions.asp?index=T&tid=2546 to learn more about *tequesquite*.)

Adding the *tequesquite* water to the mixture. You add a little at a time so that you don't accidentally get the mixture too wet. For those of us who don't measure when we make them, this is like mixing pancakes.

Mixing is hard work and takes time.

To test to see if the *masa* is ready, you drop a blob into water. If it sinks, you are far from ready. If it first sinks, then floats you are close. If stays on the top of the water the instant you drop it in, you are done mixing.

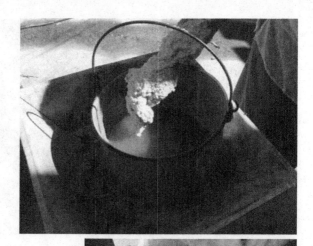

Drop

Mix and drop
again

Done!

Adding the salt. Note that this is done after the float test shows the *masa* to be ready. Add salt until you can barely perceive a salty flavor to the *masa* (It's o.k. to taste it since the corn has already been cooked.)

Tasting the *masa* for a lightly salty flavor. This is Doña Alma's favorite part.

Look how fluffy the *masa* is now.

Step 4: Soak the Corn Husks and Prepare the Steamer

Doña Eva washes her hands and rests while Doña Alma puts the dried corn husks in a pot to soak.

The husks soak in cold water for about 10 minutes before they are ready to use.

Here are the soaking husks and the large steamer into which we will put the finished *tamales*. (There is water under the perforated plate at the bottom of the pot.)

Step 5: Assemble the *Tamales*

Hold the corn husk in the palm of one hand with the round part toward you. Scoop in a spoonful of *masa*.

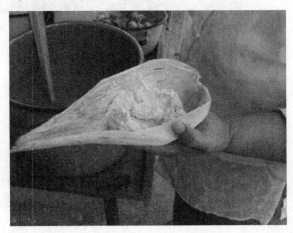

Add a hunk of uncooked meat, usually pork and a spoonful of salsa. Here we started with the green salsa. Doña Eva likes to partially mix the salsa into the *masa* so that each bite will have a little salsa in it.

To close the *tamale*, first wiggle the sides of the "boat" together until they are overlapped. (If your corn husk is small you can add another one over the seam and flip it over.) Then, fold the tip up. It's OK if a little salsa and *masa* are squirted out. Handle the tamale gently and keep the round part up.

Note the wire divider placed in the steamer. This helps you to place the *tamales* all round end up. At this point you are counting how many *tamales* go in because a lot of times there is a certain number that you need to provide for a party or other event.

This is to prove that we did some red *tamales*, too. This salsa was heavenly and we kept dipping our fingers in for a taste!

Doña Alma is in the background getting the fire hot.

Step 5 (Optional): Assemble Sweet *Tamales*

Doña Eva had set aside a small portion of the *masa* before adding the salt for the red and green *tamales*. Here she is adding sugar for a lightly sweetened flavor.

The small steamer for the sweet *tamales*.

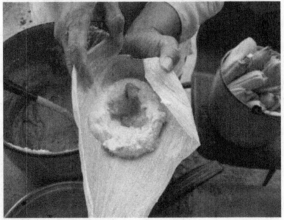

Assemble these tamales just like you do the ones with salsa.

Step 6: Steam the *Tamales*

Doña Alma has the
coals hot.

The old bag on the top
of the steamer trick.
Every great Mexican
chef knows this one.

An improvised lid to cover the bag.

Doña Eva checks to see if they are done. Ouch! Hot! They are done when the dough peels easily away from the corn husk. This takes about 2 hours.

APPENDIX: A Day of the

Dead Photo Gallery

A Small home altar

The night of November 1st 2005 in Ocotopec, Morelos

The dead are welcomed home with big signs over the entryway and a trail of flowers.

In Ocotopec, altars can also be set up in churches.

The man is playing a traditional instrument in the church courtyard.

Children invent their own version of trick-or-treating, though it is discouraged in Ocotopec in order to preserve the Mexican tradition

The market in the days before the Day of the Dead. This is where you can buy your supplies for your altar. See www.home-sweet-mexico.com for an in-depth description of the sights, sounds, and smells.

A Day of the Dead celebration in the Jardin Borda of
Cuernavaca, Morelos 2005

Fireworks shot from
the very edge of the
crowd. The look on the
faces of two white
tourists when the attendant set this contraption up just a
foot from their faces was precious—but only because that's
the kind of face I used to make.

CPSIA information can be obtained
at www.ICGtesting.com
Printed in the USA
BVOW03s1854191117
500842BV00001B/88/P